Human Rights under the African Charter

Allwell Uwazuruike

# Human Rights under the African Charter

palgrave
macmillan

Allwell Uwazuruike
Lancashire Law School
Preston, UK

ISBN 978-3-030-41738-3 ISBN 978-3-030-41739-0 (eBook)
https://doi.org/10.1007/978-3-030-41739-0



This Palgrave Macmillan imprint is published by the registered company Springer Nature Switzerland AG
The registered company address is: Gewerbestrasse 11, 6330 Cham, Switzerland

# Acknowledgements

I thank Dr. Ian Turner and Professor Michael Salter for their guidance in the early days of my research.

My most profound gratitude goes to Professor Rhoda Howard-Hassmann whose belief in this project was a very strong source of motivation for me. Professor Howard-Hassmann graciously read the initial manuscript, offering insightful and invaluable suggestions.

# Contents

# Acronyms

| | |
|---|---|
| APRM | African Peer Review Mechanism |
| AU | African Union |
| AUC | African Union Commission |
| CEDAW | The Convention on the Elimination of All Forms of Discrimination Against Women |
| EACJ | East African Court of Justice |
| ECCJ | ECOWAS Community Court of Justice |
| ECHR | European Convention on Human Rights |
| ECOWAS | Economic Community of West African States |
| ECtHR | European Court of Human Rights |
| EU | European Union |
| HRD | Human Rights Defender |
| ICCPR | International Covenant on Civil and Political Rights |
| ICESCR | International Covenant on Economic, Social and Cultural Rights |
| LGBT | Lesbian, Gay, Bisexual, and Transgender |
| OAU | Organisation of African Unity |
| SADC | Southern African Development Community |
| UDHR | Universal Declaration of Human Rights |

CHAPTER 1

# Introduction

The global monitoring of human rights violations has become the mandate of reputable human rights non-governmental organizations (NGOs) such as Human Rights Watch and Amnesty International. These NGOs monitor and report on human rights violations in countries around the world including in Africa, Asia, Europe and the Middle East. Unsurprisingly, African countries do not fare well in many of these reports owing largely to recurrent instances of large-scale government repressions of civil and political rights. Additionally, the scourge of poverty, often occasioned by war and sectarian violence, means that a vast proportion of inhabitants of a few African countries are bereft of some of the most basic socio-economic necessities.

It is therefore not uncommon for the African continent to be seen as comprising states that either have very little respect for human rights or are simply unable to ensure the enjoyment, by their citizens, of those rights. While such a view may be correct for a few African countries, it may miss some commendable developments, at the regional level, of a near comprehensive human rights model. However, detailed studies of the principles, implementation and challenges of this system are few and far between.

Even more interesting is the fact that, despite the commendable efforts of these African regional human rights institutions, reports of other external bodies on the state of human rights within the African continent are accorded greater media coverage and attention. Of course, there is little wrong with assessments carried out by acclaimed international institutions



A. Uwazuruike, *Human Rights under the African Charter*,
https://doi.org/10.1007/978-3-030-41739-0_1

and states. Indeed, these should be welcome from the perspective of shining more light on human rights violations in Africa and putting pressure on states to abide by human rights norms and standards.

However, the relative lack of attention to the regional human rights system cannot bode well for the development of human rights within the continent. For one, it may promote the narrative that there is no viable regional framework for human rights within Africa. Even worse, it could allow for the misconception that human rights at its core, is alien to Africa and as such has to be policed by Western or other external bodies. Such a false narrative is easily amplified by, for instance, the requirement by Western donors of minimum human rights standards by beneficiary African states. In some cases, African governments or Heads of States have gone as far as ascribing neo-colonialist motives to some of these Western interventions. It is therefore not unusual for an incumbent African government to accuse a Western state or body of meddling or even seeking to impose Western standards on it.

There is no gainsaying the fact that the study of human rights by and for Africans has not received the deserved level of attention. This is notwithstanding laudable human rights developments such as the creation of an African Charter on Human and Peoples' Rights, protocols on a court and women's rights, as well as key human rights institutions such the African Commission and Court. The African continent, therefore, has its own human rights institutions and rarely falls short compared to relevant normative or institutional human rights standards. The aim of this book is to study the normative development of human rights in Africa through the African Charter and its interpretative institutions. It will be shown that Africa has taken strong theoretical and institutional steps towards human rights protections which have been compromised in the area of implementation by a range of factors that will be identified and discussed.

Aside from trying to make up for the lack of analysis of the African regional human rights system, this book, by focussing on the internal African standards, sidesteps persistently recurring allegations of neo-colonialism levelled by some African leaders against perceived Western and external interventions. It also taps into the ever-growing African solutions for African problems approach that has characterised African Union (AU) rhetoric over the past decades. This means that the focus will be on the standards and systems set by 'Africans for Africans' as opposed to perceived external or transcendental standards that may be seen by some as not being autochthonous or emanating from the African people.

Thus, the core question that is examined is whether African states meet their own consensually accepted human rights standards—standards drafted, adopted and labelled 'African'. Another question that necessarily arises from this is whether the institutions for the promotion and protection of human rights in the continent are viable and effective. What are the challenges these institutions face and how can those challenges be resolved? It should not be difficult to see the benefits of this 'in-house' approach in the context of the development of the continent's fledgling human rights system. Such an internal analysis complements broader analyses of human rights and helps in understanding some of the key challenges to the practice and implementation of human rights in the continent.

This book also offers an opportunity to evaluate the content and regional interpretation of the human rights norms contained in the African Charter. It will be recalled that African states, in the early aftermath of independence, and following egregious human rights violations by brutal regimes, drafted and adopted a human rights Chart for the continent in the form of the African Charter on Human and Peoples' Rights which came into force in 1986. In 2003, member states adopted the Protocol to the African Charter on Human and Peoples' Rights on the Rights of Women in Africa—a Protocol that further substantiates the rights provided in the Charter, this time with respect to women. Other similar human rights instruments such as the African Charter on the Rights and Welfare of the Child 1990 and the African Youth Charter 2006 have since been adopted. It is, therefore, necessary to examine just how much the interpretive organs of the African human rights system have borrowed from rulings and interpretations of other regional bodies such as the European Court of Human Rights and other international human rights institutions at the level of the United Nations.

The core idea of this book, therefore, is to critically analyse the African system of human rights developed and enforced by Africa—and the relevance of this idea in the context of the 'African solution for African problems' mentality. Encompassed within this idea is the non-attachment to perceived transcendental standards or examples. In other words, the book does not seek to place other regional human rights systems (such as the Council of Europe, for instance) as models to which the African system should aspire. Rather, the emphasis is on critiquing the practice of human rights in Africa against the internal standards set out for itself by the continent. It also highlights the significance of an effective overarching system of human rights at the regional level. Overall, the book can be split into three parts—the 'African' theory of human rights, the practice and enforcement by states of this theory and the effectiveness of the regional human rights institutions.

## 1.1 The First Part: Analysis of the African Charter

In evaluating the state of human rights in Africa and the performance of the regional enforcement mechanism, the first port of call has to be the African Charter—the document that sets out these rights and standards and establishes the role of the institutions. Even though inarguably the continent's most authoritative human rights document, the decision to analyse the African Charter's content as representing Africa's normative standards is not based solely on its reputation. Thus, Chapter 2 examines the development of human rights in Africa and the role of the African Charter, the aim of this being to establish the status of the African Charter as a true reflection of African standards. Even though it contains what could loosely be termed 'western adaptations', the Charter professes the communal nature and spirit that characterised early African societies. This is shown clearly in its emphasis on peoples' rights and duties. Also, the Charter acts as a perfect tool for analysis based on the nature of its origin and general acceptance as representing the African standard of rights.

## 1.2 Second and Third Parts: State Practice and Institutional Effectiveness

After setting out the norms and standards and how they ought to be applied in principle, the book proceeds to investigate how this system operates in practice. This can be described as examining the relationship between expectation and reality. The chapters accordingly address questions pertaining to the level of compliance with the Charter's provisions and how effective the regional institutions are in ensuring those standards. An examination of how the system is operating in practice necessarily prompts the question of whether such practice reflects a proper implementation of the African Charter. Where this is not the case the appropriate response is to ask what changes must, in practice, be both proposed and then implemented in order to resolve the discrepancy between the normative standards and its implementation.

In keeping with the general theme of the book recourse is generally had to information contained in African sources such as the Activity Reports of the African Commission, Case Law (and statistics) of the African Commission and African Court, state reports of member states, Concluding Observations on state reports by the African Commission, reports of NGOs and Special Rapporteurs, research and data on state compliance with the decisions of the African Commission and Court, and a range of academic articles and commentaries.

CHAPTER 2

# The African Charter as Representing the African Standard of Human Rights in the Twenty-First Century

## 2.1 Introduction

This chapter is an introduction to the notion of regionalism in general and, more specifically, the African concept of human rights. It provides justification for the choice of the African Charter as the basis for analysing and assessing the concept and practice of human rights in the continent. It begins by introducing the concepts of universalism and regionalism and tracing the well-traversed universalism-cultural relativism debate. It then proceeds to examine the origin and foundation of the African Charter with a view to justifying its position as the human rights manual for the continent.

## 2.2 The Case for Regional Conceptions of Rights

In the aftermath of the Second World War, especially the Holocaust which was fuelled by anti-Semitism, there were movements to enshrine universal rights to forestall similar events in the future and a reluctance to allow state and even regional interpretations of rights. Early architects of the post-war institutions favoured a 'universal' over a particularist or regional approach to problems which, in the 1930s, had acquired a bad name.[1] The belief informed by utopian post-war thinking was that only a universal or near-universal collective of states could offer the best guarantee of international order. The 1948 Universal Declaration of Human Rights


A. Uwazuruike, *Human Rights under the African Charter*,
https://doi.org/10.1007/978-3-030-41739-0_2

(UDHR) was a natural outcome of this inclination towards a universal solution.

Arguments for regionalism have however persisted, the debate on the universality of human rights being almost as old as the movement towards universal human rights standards.[2] These arguments have ranged from making a case for regional bodies as the effective machinery for enforcing universal rights to proposing that regions have autonomy in devising their own standards of rights. With regard to the former, it has been argued that neither sovereign states which are autonomous, supranational organisations which depend on voluntary patterns of compliance, nor private organisations which lack resources and enforcement mechanisms, can adequately protect human rights.[3] Thus, the case is made for a protective mechanism which would function at an intermediate level, exercising authority which is broader than the sovereign state yet closer to the affected communities than a global supranational organisation—in other words, a regional human rights organisation.

Initially, the United Nations' (UN) approach was to shun regionalism in favour of the universal approach to human rights. However, given the rise and growth of regional bodies, and in recognition of their role in conducting political and security affairs, the UN eased its stance towards regionalism. After considerable discussions and pressure from parties with an interest in empowering regions, the principle of regionalism was accommodated by the UN Charter though within an institutional and legal hierarchy that clearly favoured universalism.[4] This envisaged that the UN could, for instance acting through the Security Council, use regional arrangements or agencies for enforcement action under its authority. This development, while assigning important roles to regions, did not address, at least satisfactorily, the second issue of regional interpretation and construction of rights.

Non-Western countries were often reluctant to wholly apply some provisions of human rights covenants viewing the supposedly individualistic and capitalistic nature of some of these rights as purely Western ideologies. In the African case, and with the constant emergence of African scholars and critics, there was a strong debate on the actual 'universality' of these rights. Given that Africa had little impact in the drafting of the Universal Declaration,[5] there was the question of whether its provisions, as well as those of subsequent international covenants adequately represented Africa's claimed communitarian disposition and culture. The perceived imposition of Western ideals as universal and the relegation of African norms also prompted allegations of Western imperialism.[6] This led to calls for the formulation of an African concept of human rights based on African history and culture. However, despite the creation of an African Charter, pertinent issues relating to the interpretation of rights such as, for example, the continued clampdown and hostile rhetoric against homosexual activities in African countries continue to rear their heads. Such issues highlight the tension between regional and 'universal' interpretations of rights and pose the question of just how much regional perceptions and cultures have to play in the interpretation and application of universal rights.

This book aims to satisfy proponents of both perspectives of regional human rights. In the first case, it argues for the presence of strong regional structures to promote and protect human rights. As will be demonstrated in later chapters, the often-fledgling political structures in many African states necessitate the presence of extranational bodies to safeguard human rights. However, given Africa's peculiar colonial history, acceptance of such external interventions, especially where they involve Western participation, has been often viewed with suspicion and frequently criticised as interventionist and neo-colonialist. Even perceived 'international' bodies like the United Nations and International Criminal Court are not spared these criticisms. For many Africans, these international bodies are merely tools of Western domination and oppression.

It is not the aim of this book to examine the validity of these perceptions as, regardless of which way the results go, these perceptions will still persist. The effect of this is the existence of systems that, rightfully or not, are not fully accepted by a part of the world. An effective regional system, in this case, a Pan-African institution, perceived as created and owned by Africans, may offer a solution to some of the criticisms that trail these international systems. The case for a regional system is even stronger for human rights given the absence (not least owing to the impracticability) of an effective international system for enforcing human rights.

With regard to the second perspective, that is regionalism from the perspective of substantive internal standards, this book argues that an African conception of rights, as provided in the African Charter and its Protocols, and applied by the African Commission and Court, protects a near-comprehensive gamut of rights. The protection of these rights within the African Charter should also hopefully put to rest arguments against the imposition of perceived Western ideologies of rights on the African people. The creation of the African human rights machinery should give

Africans ownership of the theory of rights propounded within the Charter as well as the institutions created to oversee their implementation. This would also fit into the African solution for African problems rhetoric that has characterised recent African discourse.

The next section examines the concept of universality of rights and how an African concept of rights fits into this discourse.

## 2.3 Universalism, Liberalism and Cultural Relativism

One major point of contention in human rights scholarship is the universality of rights—that is, whether there are universal rules and principles of human rights that supersede other variants and thus constitute universal standards. This universalism-cultural relativism debate proceeds on the assumption that the legitimacy of international human rights law depends on the existence of fundamental principles of justice that transcend culture, society and politics.[7] Universalists argue that the contents of human rights are universal and apply to every person irrespective of culture. Thus, these rights accrue to a person by virtue of his or her existence as a human being. The UDHR is often considered a template of these universal rights. On the converse side are the cultural relativists who mostly argue that the purported universal rights are only products of Western culture bordering mainly on a liberal ideology. They argue that the cultural peculiarities of diverse regions must be respected. This impasse has seen the rise in debates and condemnations of various national laws such as the criminalisation of gay unions in some African and Asian countries.[8]

The Universal Declaration proclaims itself as 'a common standard of achievement for all peoples and nations'.[9] This presupposes that all nations are to be assessed based on how they observe the enshrined provisions. Some commentators have questioned this philosophy which appears to present human rights theory as non-ideological, impartial and the quintessence of human goodness. This idea of an almost divine nature of human rights, it has been argued, ignores the influences of Western history and liberalism. For instance, Mutua argues that human rights and Western liberal democracy are virtually tautological and that the former is, in fact, the universalised version of the latter. In his view, human rights represent the attempted dissemination of Western liberal political tradition. The continued reluctance to identify liberal democracy with human rights, he argues, delays the reformation, reconstruction and 'multiculturalization' of human rights.[10]

The Western origins of human rights, some critics argue, mean that they have limited applicability in Africa. Arguing along this line, Pollis and Schwab assert that Western political philosophy, upon which the Universal Declaration is based, may not be successfully applied or enforced outside the West. This, they argue, is owing to a range of factors such as ideological differences regarding the priority of economic rights over individualistic civil and political rights. They state thus:

> to argue that human rights has a standing which is universal in character is to contradict historical reality. What ought to be admitted by those who argue universality is that human rights as a Western concept based on natural right should become the standard upon which all nations ought to agree, recognising however, that this is only one particular value system.[11]

However, not all Universalists, if any, deny the Western liberal foundation of the human rights corpus. For many, this does not detract from its validity and global applicability. Binder explains that the early attempt to ground human rights as a superior source of authority was in response to the statist or legal positivist model of international law which rooted international law's validity in the will of powerful governments thereby rendering international law of human rights superfluous.[12] It was in the attempt to overcome the 'foundationalist' arguments of defenders of the absolute autonomy of sovereign states that advocates sought a foundation for international human rights law in the natural liberty of individuals. However, Binder does not accept that human rights need a foundation to be legitimate, as the absence of this does not refute its value judgements. He posits that post-colonial states, a description that would fit most African countries, are Western as much as indigenous and are, as such, colonial extensions of a Western-dominated global state system. These developing societies are not 'nations' possessed of 'national' cultures, the idea of national culture being a Western idea closely associated with the institution of the modern state, and the presence of a disconnect between the state sector and other cultural structures. He argues that rather than asking whether human rights standards are authentic to the national cultures of the developing world, the better approach should be to ask how human rights contribute to building decent and democratic societies in a developing world suspended between local and global cultural structures. Thus, the problem, in his view, is not that "human rights standards are too imperialistic but that they are not imperialistic enough."[13]

Binder's argument is very interesting even though it appears to argue only for why human rights, based on Western culture, should be applicable in post-colonial states thus side-stepping other states that may not have been subjects of Western colonialism but remain prone to heavy criticisms of human rights violations. It is not difficult to agree that many post-colonial, especially African, states have been heavily influenced by Western culture such that existing cultural structures have lost most of their traditional flavour. This may partly be demonstrated by the African Charter which makes provisions for a range of civil and political rights even though some, or even all, of those rights were arguably non-existent in several African Communities.[14] Indeed, even though many African authors have tried to draw comparisons between observances in traditional African societies and human rights provisions, they still admit that African societies did not emphasise individual rights in the same way that European societies did for some since the eighteenth century. Also, many African constitutions, rather than adopting the often-touted African traditional communitarian system, are generally modelled after Western constitutions.

Howard and Donnelly have argued that 'a particular type of liberal regime' which must be institutionalised 'within a relatively narrow range of variation'[15] was essential for the practice of human rights globally. Communitarian societies, they argued, were antithetical to the implementation and maintenance of human rights, because they deny the autonomy of the individual, the irreducible moral equality of all individuals, and the possibility of conflict between the community's interests and the legitimate interests of any individual.

Reacting to this seeming proposition on the closed nature of human rights, Mutua argues that the forceful rejection of dialogue leads to the inevitable conclusion that there is a hierarchy of cultures, an assumption that he claims is not only detrimental to the human rights project but is also inconsistent with the human rights corpus' commitment to equality, diversity and difference.[16] The human rights movement, he argues, must not be closed to the idea of change or believe that it is the final answer—'It is not'.

In defence of the charge that the universalists' position is inconsistent with the human rights doctrine on equality, diversity and difference,

Langlois argues against the tendency to translate liberalism's claim to be egalitarian towards individuals to mean that liberalism must be egalitarian towards all conceptions of the good life that are held by these individuals.[17] It is mistaken, he argues, to equate the equality of human beings with the equality of their ideas. Thus, liberalism conceptually separates the individual both from his or her views and from the views of the communities or traditions to which they belong. Every flexibility, he argues, stops at the point where the individual is 'threatened'. However, Langlois fails to set out an adequate test for measuring such 'threat' leaving room for critics to argue that this would be defined according to Western standards. The potential danger of such a perception is that these rights, being alien to the people, or even merely perceived as such, not only run the risk of being undervalued but also could even be despised and rallied against. Thus, there have been calls for a multicultural approach to reform the human rights regime so as to make it more universal.[18] Schwartz sees the necessity of a cross-fertilisation of culture if a universal human rights corpus is to emerge.[19] This way, every culture would have its distinctive ways of formulating and supporting human rights. A similar view is held by Baderin who advocates 'the need for sincere and justificatory cross-cultural evaluations of human dignity' in evolving an international moral value.[20]

Of course, it can be argued that such 'cross-fertilisation' has already taken place in the form of the Universal Declaration. Indeed, Howard-Hassmann argues that even though civil and political rights, which dominate the Universal Declaration, may have emerged in the Western world, 'people from all parts of the world' were engaged in drafting the Universal Declaration as well as other subsequent human rights documents. However, it may be hard to accept this from the African context given that African countries were not effectively represented during the drafting of the declaration. Howard-Hassmann agrees, noting that there was no formal representation for sub-Saharan African countries which were still colonial states at the time. Given their limited participation or representation at the drafting of the declaration, it may not be hard to understand perceived feelings of imposition on the part of African states.

It may of course be argued that such a formal participation by African states may not have resulted in a substantively different document. However, even if this were to be the case, such participation would arguably have created a feeling of co-ownership. It is important to note that some African nationalists and anticolonial groups were present during those deliberations and indeed canvassed for the inclusion of some rights. However, the fact that most African states were still Western colonies at this time cast a shadow on such representation and posed a legitimate question to the "universality" of those provisions.[21] It was essential for a declaration of such global proportions as the UDHR to come into being through a cross-fertilisation of ideas and input from an even representation of countries and social groups across the world. It will be argued that this cross-fertilisation and feeling of ownership is, at least in the African context, evident in the construction of the African Charter.

## 2.4 The Role of Culture in Human Rights Development

Some African scholars have stressed the need for human rights to be built and developed from local culture. This, it is argued, gives legitimacy and acceptability to the 'modern' universal human rights regime.[22] For instance, Ibhawoh argues that a complementarity, if not absolute congruence, of state laws and cultural norms is required if national human rights regimes are to gain grassroots acceptance. Similarly, Cobbah opines that, instead of imposing a Western philosophy of human rights on all cultures, efforts should be directed at developing equivalents in different cultures.[23] On his part, Pityana argues that international norms should not be regarded as an invariable template but as minimum standards or a framework which permits further dynamic developments and expressions. What is required, he asserts, is the legitimisation of all cultures as sources of rights.[24] In a similar vein, Mutua posits that societies at their grassroots have to participate in the construction of principles and structures that enhance the human dignity of all. These norms and structures, he believes, must be home-grown, and must utilise the cultural tools familiar to the people at the grassroots. Also, in his proposed reconceptualisation of human rights in Africa, Shivji states that human rights discourse should be historically situated and socially specific. He argues that any debate conducted on the level of moral absolutes or universal humanity is not only fruitless but also ideologically subversive of the interests of the African masses.[25]

The above arguments reiterate the view that human rights have to be autochthonous—that is, that they have to emanate from the people. This stance or approach is not restricted to Africa but appears to be demonstrated by other regions. It appears that these regions or countries are reluctant to accept standards that are not in tune with their cultural history. For instance, none of the member states of the Council of the Arab League ratified the Arab Charter initially, only adopting a revised Arab Charter in 2004, certain parts of which clearly departed from the general 'universal' standards, for example, with regard to the international human rights for women, children and non-citizens, and in equating Zionism with racism.[26] Furthermore, the discussions in meetings of Asian states in the period prior to the World Conference on Human Rights in 1993 revealed opposition to acceptance of the human rights rules and principles in 'Western-based' UN declarations, conventions and other instruments, as always universally applicable and superior to national and regional norms and principles.[27] This view was captured in the Association of Southeast Asian Nations (ASEAN) preambular statement[28] which described human rights as existing 'in a dynamic and evolving context' and made references to historical experiences and cultural realities. Other regional declarations have expressed similar sentiments. For instance, the 1992 Tunis Declaration[29] adopted by African states affirmed the belief that it was not possible to prescribe a model at the universal level because one could not ignore historical and cultural realities of each particular nation as well as the traditions, norms and values of each people. Also, Paragraph 9 of the 1993 Final Declaration of the Regional Meeting for Asia of the World Conference on Human Rights[30] provides that human rights must be considered in the context of a dynamic and evolving process of international norm-setting, bearing in mind the significance of national and regional particularities, and various historical, cultural and religious backgrounds.

Another example of the fight against perceived Western imposition was at the 1994 United Nations Population Conference in Cairo where the Vatican joined with several Muslim governments to condemn what they viewed as the imposition of Western norms of sexual licence and individual autonomy on the rest of the world.[31] Although most advocates of reproductive control at the Population Conference did not attempt to translate policy claims into the language of international human rights, the issue of cultural relativism was central to the debate over differing visions of the family and the role of women. The Pakistani Prime Minister, while acknowledging substantial problems of overpopulation in Pakistan and other Muslim countries, criticised what she perceived as Western efforts to impose norms of radical individualism on the rest of the world. Several

Muslim countries including Sudan and Saudi Arabia boycotted the talks altogether.

What these examples show is a clear divide on the scope, universality and even interpretation of human rights. By assigning the Western tag to these rights, some regions and states can claim that those rights conflict with their core customs and beliefs and are, therefore, inapplicable. The aim here is not to argue one way or the other. Indeed, the subject of the universality of rights has been thoroughly examined often with clear divides. It has arguably come to the point where it must be acknowledged that, rightfully or otherwise, the acceptability of human rights as developed in international treaties will continue to be questioned. However, as will be demonstrated in this book, regional systems like the one in Africa have created very similar and even more developed bodies of rights. Also, their regional status makes them the closest and perhaps most acceptable bodies to deal with human rights infractions in the event of systematic national abuse. As Beyani points out, regional instruments and bodies are perceived to have more legitimacy than alien institutions and are more able to harness the political will to commit to the protection of human rights. They derive legitimacy through the articulation and implementation of distinctive regional norms and practices. Thus, the Arab League, for example, derives legitimacy through its 'Arabness', drawing on a rich common culture and history while the states of Southeast Asia are known for their articulation of the 'ASEAN way'—a consensus-based approach based upon strict observance of sovereignty.[32]

Perhaps as a pointer to the importance of culture in human rights interpretation, Pityana observes that, although worded in Universalist terms, international human rights norms have begun to espouse a moderate version of relativism. He refers to the Vienna Declaration and Programme of Action of 1993 which he opines sought to address the 'universalism versus relativism' debate by resorting to the principle of margin of appreciation developed within the jurisprudence of the European Convention on Human Rights (European Convention) in order to take account of cultural specificities when applying human rights norms.

This principle of margin of appreciation entails that there would be no interference, in certain cases, with the laws and decisions of a member state where those laws or decisions have a proper legal basis and the domestic authorities have made genuine and reasonable efforts to balance the right in question with other rights or interests.[33] Thus, the European

Court stated in a case[34] that the machinery of the Convention was subsidiary to the national systems protecting human rights and that certain rights, such as the freedom of expression, allowed each state a margin of appreciation to interpret and apply them. That this principle, following Pityana's argument, is now being reflected in international human rights instruments only goes to show the need to recognise region-specific approaches and interpretations based on cultural norms and values. It is on this premise that the subsequent sections of this chapter will examine the African situation and the development of the African regional human rights framework.

## 2.5 Development of Human Rights in Africa

There have been debates about whether human rights existed in pre-colonial Africa. Some writers have pointed to practices in early African societies to show that the inhabitants of these societies had awareness and respect for human rights.[35] For instance, Mutua argues that much of the discussion about whether pre-colonial societies knew of and enforced individual human rights have taken place in the absence of 'considered justice, and reference to, judicial processes in those societies'. His studies, which examined the Akan and Akamba societies of Kenya, sought to show that protection of individual rights was of preeminent importance to those pre-colonial societies.[36] Similarly, Howard shows that many societies in pre-colonial Africa guaranteed economic and political rights through communal structures that recognised obligations to family and kin and ensured practices such as free speech and natural justice.[37] M'Baye states further that pre-colonial Africa had a system of rights and freedoms, although there was neither the recognition nor the clear formulation of such rights and freedoms as they are recognised in contemporary times.[38]

More recently, Metz has made a strong attempt to link the South African principle of *ubuntu* with human rights.[39] By this principle, a person's claim to human rights is predicated on how he or she communes with others or honours communal relationships.[40] This *ubuntu*-based moral theory, Metz claims, serves as a promising foundation for human rights. On the converse side, Howard has argued that there is no specifically African concept of human rights. The argument for such concept, she asserts, is based on a philosophical confusion of human dignity with human rights.[41]

It appears that whether or not human rights can be said to have existed in pre-colonial African societies would very much depend on the definition of human rights adopted by each writer. For instance, some may be of the view that human rights are individual claims or entitlements against the state, and in this sense, there is only one conception of human rights and that is Western. However, others like Asante[42] believe that human rights are concerned with asserting and protecting human dignity and that they are ultimately based on a regard for the intrinsic worth of the individual. Therefore, they are not peculiarly or even essentially bourgeois or Western. This opinion is shared by Metz who makes the presumption that human rights are grounded in human dignity.

However, care must be exercised in the adoption of the word 'Western'. As Howard-Hassmann correctly points out, Western philosophical views include conservatism, communism and fascism the latter two of which clearly deny human rights. Rather than describe human rights as Western, Howard argues that they are liberal or, when examined holistically, "social democratic".[43]

Despite early similarities among societies, it is argued that contemporary (or 'universal') human rights are inarguably steeped in modern Western history. While it may be true that there were semblances of human rights observance in early African societies, those practices are invariably assessed against a certain modern Western standard. To illustrate this position, a parallel may be drawn with similar arguments in the field of anthropology on 'modernity' where the argument was made that it was necessary to rethink understandings of modernity to take account of the many different sorts of 'modern' cultural trajectories that anthropologists were documenting.[44] The object was to develop a more pluralised understanding of modernity—a variety of different ways of being modern or 'alternative modernities'. This expectedly led to questions on the meaning of the term 'modernity' and if, as was argued in one text,[45] Cameroonians practising witchcraft are in fact being 'modern'. Ferguson pointed out that inasmuch as the idea of multiple or alternative tracks through modernity may hold true in East and Southeast Asia where countries like Malaysia, Singapore and Taiwan develop economically like the West without necessarily becoming 'westernized', such may not be the case in Africa where economic convergence with First World living standards 'hardly seems to be in the offing'.[46] Thus, in Africa, the aspiration to modernity has been an aspiration to rise in the world in economic and political terms. Africans see their lack of modernity in the bad roads, poor health care, dilapidated structures and precariously improvised livelihoods. Where anthropologists proclaim Africa 'always already modern' (including in its practice of witchcraft), local discourses on modernity see a continuing lack, not in terms of cultural inferiority, but of political-economic inequality.

In a similar vein, ascribing human rights values to native African practices does not reflect the large-scale inequalities present in those societies. In a largely patriarchal system riddled, at least in the years past, with such mundane practices as the cutting and sewing up of female genitalia, killing of twins[47] and stoning of 'witches' on mere allegations, one can hardly expect an argument for the observance of what are now commonly known as human rights. A couple of similarities of local practices with modern human rights standards do not make up for countless cases of discrepancies. What is important is that there were no clearly established standards in those societies that guaranteed general human rights, as we know them today, to a person on the sole basis of his or her humanity. Buttressing this point, Howard-Hassmann points out that these systems of morality or justice are simply not rights based as they do not articulate alternate or competing conceptions of human rights.[48]

It is not difficult to understand the attempts to establish a human rights culture, no matter how little the basis, in indigenous Africa. By this, African writers seek to paint a different picture from the savagery and brutality that characterise perceptions of primordial Africa—a perception that portrays Africa as being saved from gloom by the West. However, it is contended that this perception need not arise. Even though the modern concept of human rights has its foundation in recent Western history, this does not presuppose that these Western societies had always practised or observed them. Western history is similarly replete with ignominious cases of human rights abuses ranging from slavery and witch-burning to the Holocaust. It was such occurrences that precipitated constant agitations for human rights provisions, culminating in the Universal Declaration. It is the standard of observance as espoused in the Universal Declaration, and subsequent human rights treaties that this book adopts as the definition of 'human right' when used in general parlance—a standard which many pre-colonial African societies, and even their early Western counterparts, did not quite measure up to. Thus, instead of approaching the subject as a debate on cultural superiority, African scholars should confront it as one of cultural development.

### 2.5.1 The African Charter in the Development of African Human Rights

After independence, in the immediate aftermath of colonialism, African countries were more concerned about protecting their territorial sovereignty than the development of a regional human rights system. The Organisation of African Unity (OAU) Charter[49] recognised human rights only within the context of promoting African unity and made no mention of human rights apart from the right of peoples to self-determination.[50] The focal points of interest were political unity, non-interference in the internal affairs of other states and the liberation of African territories still under colonial domination.[51] As Okere notes, the focus on state sovereignty invariably diminished human rights efforts as there was 'apparent antinomy' between promoting the protection of human rights and emphasising the exclusive domain of control of each state.

The implication of these provisions was that the OAU became a guardian of incumbent regimes even when those regimes were oppressive to their own people. Also, the implicit privileging of existing states within their pre-determined borders made it impossible to deal constructively with secessionist struggles within those states.[52]

Okere describes the individuals of these African states as dissolved in the mass of collectivity while despotic regimes, protected by the shield of territorial integrity and non-interference, unleashed barbarous repressions against their subjects. These shortcomings of the OAU agitated African jurists and statesmen who initiated a series of conferences and consultations with a view to creating an African Commission on Human Rights. In 1979, the Assembly of Heads of States and Governments requested the Secretary-General of the OAU to organise a restricted meeting of highly qualified experts to prepare a preliminary draft of an African Charter on Human and Peoples' Rights providing for the establishment of organs to promote and protect human and peoples' rights. A draft charter was prepared and considered by a meeting of government experts before being adopted and signed in June 1981 during an OAU Summit in Nairobi, Kenya.

#### 2.5.1.1 The African Charter: A True Reflection of African Standards?

As has already been highlighted, the African human rights system was created at a time of massive human rights violations and domestic crises in a number of African states. By the adoption of the African Charter on Human and Peoples' Rights ('African Charter' or 'the Charter'), African leaders hoped to establish a common regional standard of rights and accord a semblance of legality to existing governments. By providing for regionally recognised rights and creating institutions for enforcement, the OAU was guaranteeing protection to Africans regardless of the nature of the government in power in their respective countries. This, at the time, could be seen as an ideological improvement on the OAU's initial core principles of non-interference in the affairs of member states even in the face of massive human rights violations. By the creation of the Charter, African states were beginning to accept, albeit tentatively, the necessity of general regional standards and the primacy of human rights even over national sovereignty. The question that however arises, in line with previous analyses on the role of culture, is whether the African Charter is a true reflection of African standards. This question, of course, comes with its own challenges given the size and complexity of the continent.

The African Charter has been described as a product of the ideological cleavages of the Cold War and as reflecting a compromise between the ideological and belief systems represented at its negotiations.[53] These diverse interests have been described as including 'atheists, animists, Christians, Hindus, Jews and Muslims; and … over fifty countries and islands with Marxist-Leninist, capitalist, socialist, military, one-party and democratic regimes'.[54] The presence of a mixed ideology in the Charter can be attributed to the need to appease and win the signatures of member states with varying political and ideological leanings. The infusion of these different ideologies and the need to create a middle ground could partly account for the inclusion and prominence of economic, social and cultural rights in the African Charter—a set of rights often consigned to 'second-rate status'[55] as well as the concept of duties. For instance, Gittleman has pointed out that it was the need to ensure the eventual adoption of the Charter by every state that drove the drafters to provide that if the individual is to have rights recognised by the state, he also must have obligations flowing back to the state.[56]

Human rights as espoused by the African Charter were, therefore, a cross-pollination of different ideas and conceptions of rights. First, there was the intent of the framers to create a charter inspired by African legal philosophy and responsive to African needs. This intent, clearly stated in the Charter's Preamble, was demonstrated by the inclusion of the concepts of duties, socio-economic rights, peoples' rights and even 'family rights'. There was also the Western influence given the existence of the Universal Declaration to which African states had become signatories. This was demonstrated by the inclusion of civil and political rights which bore close semblance to the rights contained in the Universal Declaration and the International Covenant on Civil and Political Rights.

In recognising the need to take into consideration the virtues of African historical tradition and the values of African civilisation in formulating the rights, the Charter underlined the importance of culture in setting out a human rights template while not deviating from general principles of human rights contained in declarations adopted by the OAU and the UN. This approach appears to conform to the moderate form of relativism canvassed by Pityana whereby international norms are regarded as minimum standards or a framework which permits further dynamic development and expressions. Thus, Baderin points out that, while endeavouring to match international human rights norms, the African system appeared 'to be sensitive to African cultural norms, as portrayed by its approach to polygamous relationships under the African Women's Protocol'.[57] Here, Baderin is referring to Article 6 of the Women's Protocol which, rather than prohibiting polygamy as done in most Western countries, provides that the rights of women should be protected in these relationships.

Furthermore, Okere posits that, in formulating guaranteed rights and correlative duties, the African Charter was obviously animated by the Universalist vocation and naturalist principles which underlie human rights. He, however, notes that despite its Universalist leanings, the African Charter has specific characteristics whose inspiration derive solely from Africa's colonial history, philosophy of law and conception of man. He defines this African conception of man as not that of an isolated and abstract individual but an integral member of a group animated by a spirit of solidarity. It may, therefore, be argued that the African Charter adopted both a Universalist and regional perspective—the individual and group, rights and duties.

Another unique quality of the African Charter is its approach to socio-economic rights. Despite precedents such as the International Covenant on Economic, Social and Cultural Rights (ICESCR) that subject these rights to available resources of a state, the African Charter makes no such express concessions. Mbazira opines that this difference reflects a desire by its drafters to produce an 'exclusively' and 'distinctively' African instrument.[58]

The African Charter has often been lauded for its 'originality' vis-à-vis the provision for corresponding duties. Beyani, however, points out that the notion of duties originates from the American and Universal Declaration and is not the novelty of the African Charter that many assume.[59] This can be seen in Article 29 of the UDHR which states that every individual has duties to the community. Beyani argues that through its notions of duties, peoples' rights (derived partly from the principle of self-determination in the UN charter) and issues of progressive culture, the African Charter shows that far from being a threat to universality the document's provisions become concrete expressions of what universality means in specific places. Of course, if the provisions for duties and peoples' rights (and by extension other provisions of the African Charter) are shown not to be particular to the African Charter, then the Charter's 'Africanness' can be called into question. This view may be initially compelling given that the authors of the African Charter recognised that, while sticking to African specificities in dealing with rights, it was nevertheless prudent not to deviate much from the international norms solemnly adopted in various universal instruments by the different member states of the OAU. It thus appears that the drafters of the Charter viewed the Universal Declaration and other international human rights instruments as setting minimum universal standards of human rights which were not to be deviated (or deviated much) from. Thus, the Charter's approach to regionalism is that of moderate relativism whereby regions follow universal standards even though with slight regional adjustments. Accordingly, regional treaties like the African Charter have been referred to as 'supplements to UN treaties' which have mainly been developed to correct the perceived exclusion of the continent from the UN drafting system.[60]

Some experts, like Shivji, have criticised this approach arguing instead for a system suited to Africa's history rather than 'an uncritical acceptance of Western liberal conceptions'.[61] It may, however, not be the best approach to criticise the African Charter for adopting what are arguably Western liberal standards. Despite the imperialist undertones that naturally accompany such approach, it is argued that Africa can choose any set of practices believed to be necessary for the transformation and general well-being of the African populace regardless of whether these beliefs are perceived by some as Western, imperialistic or non-universal. It should be recalled that this adoption was necessary at the time given the oppressive nature of many post-colonial African regimes and the evolving system of governance in many African states. Thus, the argument against the universality of 'universal human rights' does not detract from its adoption by a particular region as valid and applicable in that region. In other words, it is not mandatory for every region to formulate unique principles and norms, and the fact that certain practices originate from a different clime does not mean that they cannot apply to other regions. This is because transnational exchanges of cultural products and ideas are not incompatible with enduring forms of cultural difference. Rather, cultural differences are produced, thrive and take on their significance within social relations of interconnection, not in primordial isolation. For instance, as Ferguson points out, people in Calcutta drinking Coca-Cola would no more spell the end of Indian culture than the colonial adoption of the Indian drink tea by Londoners abolished Englishness. Instead, he argues that 'a host of local studies' show that transnational traffic in meaning led not to a global monoculture, but to complex forms of cultural creativity whose result was not a numbing uniformity but a dynamic 'cut-and-mix' world of surprising borrowings, ironic reinventions, and dazzling resignifications.[62]

Furthermore, it has been correctly argued that the communitarian ideal, which is often touted as the African system on which an African concept of human rights should be built, while adequate for a traditional community would be difficult to attain in a contemporary nation-state in Africa.[63] While traditional African communities functioned within a given set of social and legal relationships particular to each community, the contemporary African state functions through different social and legal systems. Consequently, the checks and balances that were available to traditional communities do not apply to contemporary African States. Therefore, arguments for a system of human rights based on the old 'African' communitarian system, in utter disregard of existing and evolving structures, are necessarily flawed.

It is possible to link this line of thought to Binder's argument above that developing states are extensions of their colonial states and necessarily adopt the latter's cultural heritage. Imperialism, Binder states, is an intractable reality in the global state system and no scheme of human rights norms will be effective unless it is institutionalised within that imperial system.[64] Thus, the adoption of Western principles and ideologies would be a direct consequence and reflection of Western domination. The important task would be to avoid a holistic, uncritical acceptance of these inherited norms but, like Ferguson argues, to cut-and-mix them to suit the African situation—a task that the African Charter clearly attempts.

However, the Charter's origin is not that simple and straightforward. Far from being an adoption of seasoned principles, Shivji believes the African Charter to be almost farcical and built on deceit. Africa's human rights rhetoric at the time of the drafting of the African Charter, he argues, was reminiscent of the American rhetoric led by President Carter which sought to salvage the United States morally and establish the state's legitimacy following the Vietnam debacle and the Watergate scandal. Thus, even while supporting and arming dictators in Africa, such as Idi Amin of Uganda and Nguema of Equatorial Guinea, the United States had to produce a few peripheral actions, such as linking aid to recipient countries' human rights record to show its seriousness.[65] Similarly, in the African case, after the fall of the dictatorships, African Presidents had to salvage their severely battered human rights image before the Western world as well as re-establish their aid-worthiness. This they did by appointing a committee of experts to prepare a draft of an African Charter on Human and People's Rights—a charter which 'bears the birthmarks of essentially a neo-colonialist, statist disposition, and concerns of its founding fathers'.[66]

It is not difficult to accept, as Shivji canvasses, that the emergence of the African Charter may have partly been in response to Western condemnation of alleged brutal African regimes. Whether it was a mere ruse as he suggests may not be easy to determine. The end result was that the continent came up with a set of provisions aimed at protecting Africans both as individuals and as a group.

Of course, Shivji's suggestion of the African Charter as an emergency lifeline to salvage the continent's image as well as qualify for aid, if valid, could weaken the Charter's claim to represent the African conception of human rights. Its emergence would then be best described as playing up to the master in order to earn little favours—a seemingly persuasive analogy given the conscious efforts to stay in line with international covenants. Still, Shivji's position is difficult to accept. It could be the case that African leaders wanted to salvage their image but it did need salvaging. It could also be true that Africa wanted to qualify for aid. These, however, are not the important questions. What is necessary to be established is whether the African Charter was important for Africa at that time, whether it was drafted by Africans, and whether its provisions favoured the masses more than the leaders.

As has been noted, this was a period of oppressive regimes and inter-state wars as well as a pervasive ideology of non-interference in states' domestic affairs. Military juntas—products of often bloody coups—were known to come into power and suspend the constitution. Oppositions were often silenced and the judiciary was in the ruler's palm. Thus, the African Charter, though largely declaratory, was a common stand against national oppression. Even where state agencies failed and national laws were no longer effective, Africans were provided with a regional institutional system to check and address cases of human rights violations. Equally crucial were the provisions for socio-economic rights. Despite being slightly optimistic, they reflected the needs of millions of impoverished Africans. Even though some of these provisions seemed to represent Western ideals and could qualify African countries for aid, principles of human and socio-economic rights quite matched the African situation such that they could be adapted as part of the foundation of African human rights jurisprudence.

Any theory of subservience and if the African Charter may not detract from its validity if it is widely accepted as representing the African conception of rights by the various countries that make up the African Union (AU). In what can be viewed as a demonstration of acceptance of the Charter, all AU member states with the exception of Morocco, which only rejoined the AU in 2017, have signed and ratified the Charter. At least one state, Nigeria, has taken the further step of incorporating the Charter's provisions into its domestic law.[67] Nigeria's Supreme Court has held in a case that the African Charter was superior to domestic legislation even though the Court rejected the argument that the Charter was superior to the Nigerian constitution.[68] The Court based its decision on the fact that the Charter had been enacted into law by the country's legislature. On its superior status to other legislations, the court stated:

> [I]f there is a conflict between it and another statute, its provisions will prevail over those of that other statute for the reason that it is presumed that the legislature does not intend to breach an international obligation.

The court went on to agree with the lower courts' decisions that the Charter possessed 'a greater vigour and strength than any other domestic statute'.

The African Charter has also impacted on countries that have not implemented such domestic translations. For instance, in the case of *New*

*Patriotic Party v. Inspector General of Police*,[69] the Ghanaian Supreme Court partly relied on the Charter to hold as unconstitutional legislation which required a police permit for a demonstration. The court stated that even though Ghana was not, at the time, a signatory to the African Charter, member states of the OAU were expected to recognise the rights, duties and freedoms enshrined therein and to undertake to adopt legislative or other measures to give effect to the rights and duties. The Court further stated that the fact that Ghana had not passed specific legislation to give effect to the Charter did not mean that the Charter could not be relied upon. Also, in their decisions, sub-regional courts of the Economic Community of West African States (ECOWAS), East African Community and South African Development Community, make references to specific provisions of the Charter.[70] The African Charter has thus developed an authoritative status and commands general reference on matters of human rights in the continent.

Even though the position of the African Charter can be further strengthened, its status as the official position on human rights on the continent can hardly be denied. Given that the Charter professes to set out the African standard of right and has been accepted and ratified by a significant number of African states, it is argued that it should necessarily form the basis for any critique on the theory and practice of human rights on the continent especially in the light of arguments on the role of culture and regionalism in the definition and interpretation of human rights.

## 2.6 Conclusion

This chapter set out to explain and establish the role of the African Charter as providing the standard for human rights in Africa and the basis for any such assessment on the subject. It did this by analysing arguments on universalism and cultural relativism and by explaining the role of culture in the development and definition of human rights in different societies. The chapter then traced the history of the African Charter and its underlying *raison d'etre* of charting a human rights path for the continent. It was argued that the Charter, while espousing African communitarian and group standards, also adopts a moderate relativism or 'cut and mix' approach to Western liberal ideas. These have been assimilated into the African system through a process of acculturation and now form part of that system. Thus, while there may have been a few criticisms of the Charter's existence in the past, there should be little doubt that it embodies the African conception of human rights.

Part of the aim of establishing the status of the African Charter as the basis of human rights in the continent was to set the stage for a critique of the system and practice of human rights based on this charter. As has been previously explained, this avoids the difficulties and resistance often associated with the application of perceived external or Western standards. It is by assessing the practice and implementation of the Charter that questions on its suitability and practicability can be resolved. Thus, rather than according the Charter the status of perfection, such assessment permits both theoretical and practical reforms.

Following in a progressive fashion, the next chapter analyses the contents of the Charter with a view to establishing its normative and institutional standards. It is on the basis of these standards that future analyses on implementation and reforms will be done.

## Notes

1. Louise Fawcett, "The History and Concept of Regionalism" (2012) 4 European Society of International Law Conference Paper Series 6.
2. Tracy Higgins, "Anti-essentialism, Relativism, and Human Rights" (1996) 19 *Harvard Women's Law Journal* 89, 92.
3. Carol Tucker, "Regional Human Rights Models in Europe and Africa: A Comparison" (1983) 10 *Syracuse Journal of International Law* 135, 139.
4. Chapter VIII of the UN Charter provides for regional arrangements. Article 53 provides that the Security Council can utilize regional arrangements or agencies for enforcement action under its authority. See Louise Fawcett (n 1).
5. At the time of the drafting and adoption of the Universal Declaration, there were only 4 African member states of the UN: Egypt, Ethiopia, Liberia and apartheid South Africa. See Abdullahi An-Na'im (ed.) *Human Rights Under African Constitutions: Realizing the Promise for Ourselves* (UPP 2013) 9.
6. See, for instance, Makau Mutua, "The Ideology of Human Rights" (1996) 36 *Virginia Journal of International Law* 589.
7. Guyora Binder, "Cultural Relativism and Cultural Imperialism in Human Rights Law" (1999) 5 *Buffalo Human Rights Law Review* 211.
8. See Rodney Muhumuza, ABC News, "Uganda Slapped with Aid Cuts Over Anti-gay Law," accessed March 7, 2014, http://abcnews.go.com/International/wireStory/uganda-slapped-aid-cuts-anti-gay-bill-22693295; Christian Purefoy and Faith Karimi, CNN, "Nigerian Senate

Passes Anti-gay Bill, Defying British Aid Threat," accessed March 7, 2014, http://www.cnn.com/2011/11/30/world/africa/africa-gay-rights/index.html?_s=PM:AFRICA.

9. Preamble, United Declaration of Human Rights.
10. Mutua, "Ideology," 592.
11. Adamantia Pollis, Peter Schwab, and Christine M. Koggel, "Human Rights: A Western Construct with Limited Applicability" (2006) *Moral Issues in Global Perspective*, 1 Moral and Political Theory 60.
12. Binder, "Cultural Relativism," 216.
13. Ibid., 221.
14. See Makau wa Mutua, "The Banjul Charter and the African Cultural Fingerprint: An Evaluation of the Language of Duties" (1994) 35 *Virginia Journal of International Law* 339, 348.
15. See Rhoda Howard and Jack Donnelly, "Human Dignity, Human Rights, and Political Regimes" (1986) 80(3) *American Political Science Review* 801; Rhoda Howard, "Evaluating Human Rights in Africa: Some Problems of Implicit Comparisons" (1984) *Human Rights Quarterly* 160.
16. Mutua, "Ideology," 656.
17. Anthony Langlois, "Human Rights and Cosmopolitan Liberalism" (2007) 10(1) *Critical Review of International Social and Political Philosophy* 29.
18. Mutua, "Ideology," 591.
19. Richard Schwartz, "Human Rights in an Evolving World Culture," in Abdullahi An-Na'im and Francis Deng (eds.) *Human Rights in Africa: Cross-Cultural Perspectives* (BIP 1990) 382, cited in Mutua (n 9) 656.
20. Mashood Baderin, "Modern Muslim States Between Islamic Law and International Human Rights Law" (PhD thesis, University of Nottingham 2001) 20.
21. See Rhoda Howard-Hassmann, In *Defense of Universal Human Rights* (Polity Press UK 2019) 10.
22. Bonny Ibhawoh, "Between Culture and Constitution: Evaluating the Cultural Legitimacy of Human Rights in the African State" (2000) 22(3) *Human Rights Quarterly* 838, 843.
23. Josiah Cobbah, "African Values and the Human Rights Debate: An African Perspective" (1987) *Human Rights Quarterly* 309, 310.
24. Barney Pityana, "The Challenge of Culture for Human Rights in Africa: The African Charter in a Comparative Context" in Malcolm Evans and Rachel Murray (eds.) *The African Charter on Human and People's Rights: The System in Practice, 1986–2000* (Cambridge University Press 2002) 228.
25. Issa Shivji, *The Concept of Human Rights in Africa* (ABC 1989) 69.
26. Chaloka Beyani, "Reconstituting the Universal: Human Rights as a Regional Idea" in Conor Gearty and Costas Douzinas (eds.) *The Cambridge Companion to Human Rights Law* (Cambridge University Press 2012) 177.

27. Gabriel Wilner, "Reflections on Regional Human Rights Law" (1995) 25 *Georgia Journal of International Comparative Law* 40 423.
28. Human Rights Declaration by the ASEAN Inter-Parliamentary Organization (AIPO), 14th AIPO General Assembly.
29. Final Declaration of the Regional Meeting for Africa of the World Conference on Human Rights, U.N. Doc. A/CONF. 157/AFRM/I4 (1992).
30. U.N. A/CONF. 157/ASRM/8.
31. Tracy Higgins (n 4) 89.
32. Fawcett (n 1) 4.
33. Steve Forster, *Human Rights and Civil Liberties* (3rd edition, Pearson Education Limited) 66.
34. *Handyside v United Kingdom* (1976) 1 EHRR.
35. Mutua enumerates a number of practices among the Akan and Akamba people of Kenya that demonstrate that the concept of rights informed the notion of justice and supported a measure of individualism. See Mutua, "The Banjul Charter," 348.
36. Mutua, "The Banjul Charter," 352.
37. Rhoda Howard, "Evaluating Human Rights in Africa: Some Problems of Implicit Comparisons" (1984) 6(2) *Human Rights Quarterly* 174–175.
38. Keba M'Baye and Ndiaye Birame, "The Organization of African Unity (OAU)" in Karel Vasak (ed.) *The International Dimensions of Human Rights* (Greenwood Press 1982).
39. Thaddeus Metz, "African Values and Human Rights as Two Sides of the Same Coin: A Reply to Oyowe" (2014) 14 *African Human Rights Law Journal* 306–321; Thaddeus Metz, "Ubuntu as a Moral Theory and Human Rights in South Africa" (2011) 11 *African Human Rights Law Journal* 532–559.
40. Metz, "Ubuntu," 540.
41. Rhoda Howard-Hassmann, *Human Rights in Commonwealth Africa* (Rowman & Littlefield 1986) 23.
42. Samuel Asante, "Nation Building and Human Rights in Emergent African Nations" (1969) 2 *Cornell International Law Journal* 72.
43. Rhoda Howard-Hassmann, *In Defense of Universal Human Rights* (Polity Press 2018).
44. Arjun Appadurai, *Modernity al Large: Cultural Dimensions of Globalization* (University of Minnesota Press 1996) cited in James Ferguson, *Global Shadows: Africa in the Neoliberal World Order* (Duke University Press 2006).
45. See Peter Geschiere and Janet Roitman, *The Modernity of Witchcraft: Politics and the Occult in Postcolonial Africa* (University of Virginia Press 1997).
46. James Ferguson, *Global Shadows: Africa in the Neoliberal World Order* (Duke University Press 2006) 32.

47. Before the advent of Christianity in the early nineteenth century, the birth of twins in some Southern Communities in Nigeria was considered an abomination. Twins were either killed at birth or abandoned to die in the evil forest. See, for instance, Derek Asiedu-Akrofi, "Judicial Recognition and Adoption of Customary Law in Nigeria" (1989) 37 *African Journal of Comparative Law* 571.
48. Howard-Hassmann, *In Defense*, 9.
49. This is the charter establishing the OAU and should be distinguished from the African Charter on Human and Peoples' Right referred to as the African Charter in this work.
50. Obinna Okere, "The Protection of Human Rights in Africa and the African Charter on Human and Peoples' Rights: A Comparative Analysis with the European and American Systems" (1984) 2 *Human Rights Quarterly* 141, 142.
51. The first paragraph of the Charter's Preamble reads: 'It is the inalienable right of all people to control their own destiny.'
52. For instance, the secessionist struggles of Biafra, Eritrea, and Somaliland. See Bjørn Møller, *The African Union as a Security Actor: African Solutions to African Problems?* (Crisis States Research Center 2009), accessed June 9, 2014, http://eprints.lse.ac.uk/28485/.
53. Chidi Odinkalu, "Implementing Economic, Social and Cultural Rights Under the African Charter on Human and Peoples' Rights" in Malcolm Evans and Rachel Murray (eds.) *The African Charter on Human and People's Rights: The System in Practice, 1986–2000* (Cambridge University Press 2002) 181.
54. Victor Dankwa, "The Promotional Role of the African Commission on Human and People's Rights" in Malcolm Evans and Rachel Murray (eds.) *The African Charter on Human and People's Rights: The System in Practice, 1986–2000* (Cambridge University Press 2002) 352.
55. Odinkalu, "Implementing," 182.
56. Richard Gittleman, "The African Charter on Human and Peoples' Rights: A Legal Analysis" (1982) 22 *Virginia Journal of International Law* 667, 676–677.
57. Mashood Baderin, "Recent Developments in the African Regional Human Rights System" (2005) 5(1) *Harvard Rights Law Review* 117, 148.
58. Christopher Mbazira, "Enforcing the Economic, Social and Cultural Rights in the African Charter on Human and Peoples' Rights: Twenty Years of Redundancy, Progression and Significant Strides" (2006) 6 *African Human Rights Law Journal* 333, 342.
59. Beyani, "Reconstituting," 149.
60. Frans Viljoen, *International Human Rights Law in Africa* (Oxford University Press 2012) 282.
61. Shivji, *The Concept*, 20.

62. Ferguson, *Global Shadows*, 30.
63. Sakah Mamud, "The State and Human Rights in Africa in the 1990s: Perspectives and Prospects" (1993) 15 *Human Rights Quarterly* 485, 489.
64. Binder, "Cultural Relativism," 221.
65. Shivji, *The Concept*, 94.
66. Ibid.
67. African (Ratification and Enforcement) Act cap 10, Laws of the Federation of Nigeria, 1990.
68. Abacha v. Fawehinmi [2001] African Human Rights Law Report 172.
69. [2001] African Human Rights Law Report 138.
70. See Viljoen, *International*.

CHAPTER 3

# Human Rights and Duties Under the African Charter

This chapter aims to ascertain and delineate the conceptual underpinnings of the Charter in order to set the stage for future evaluations of its implementation. This analysis of the Charter is split into two parts:

- Discussion on rights, duties and responsibilities including references to the additional protocol on women: This part examines the normative contents of the African Charter with emphasis on its subdivision of rights, namely civil and political rights, socio-economic rights, and peoples' rights and also the additional protocol on women's rights that makes specific provisions for rights tailored to the particular situation of women in Africa. The concept of duties will also be briefly examined to highlight the distinctive communal spirit of the Charter.
- Discussion on the machinery for the protection of these rights: This part sets out the regional machinery charged with promoting and protecting these rights. These include the African Commission and the African Court.

## 3.1 Human and Peoples' Rights in the Charter

Human rights discourse can be said to have, over the years, developed three classifications of rights, namely: civil and political rights; economic, social and cultural rights; and group rights. This classification is based on the chronological development of these rights in international discourse,



A. Uwazuruike, *Human Rights under the African Charter*,
https://doi.org/10.1007/978-3-030-41739-0_3

as well as the relative perceived ease with which they could be protected. With regard to the latter point, it was argued that civil and political rights were generally easier to legislate for, whereas social, economic and cultural rights (sometimes referred to as 'socioeconomic' rights) generally required a long-term approach and 'the injection of financial and technical aid to the economy of the state concerned'.[1] The International Covenant on Economic, Social and Cultural Rights (ICESCR) makes a strong point of this by charging each state party to take steps 'to the maximum of its available resources' towards a progressive realisation of those rights. Interestingly, a similar charge is not made in the counterpart International Covenant on Civil and Political Rights (ICCPR). However, as Smith argues, this distinction is questionable given that many civil and political rights also require considerable financial resources from states and hence progressive realisation. For example, a state would need to build courts and pay judges for the right to a fair trial to have any practical meaning. The state also has a positive duty to protect life by establishing an effective police force to protect residents. Furthermore, it is not exactly clear how the 'ease of protection' distinction would apply to group rights. On this note, therefore, it is perhaps easier to distinguish these rights by referring to their respective chronological development in international human rights jurisprudence as well as applying a literal interpretation to each term. Going by this literal interpretation, civil and political rights would be seen as those rights that owe their development to centuries of civil and political movements against dictatorship, discrimination, and repression. As such, they encompass such rights as the right to equality, right to life, right to liberty, freedom of expression, freedom of association, freedom from torture and prohibition of arbitrary execution. Accordingly, socio-economic rights are those rights that directly address the social, economic and cultural well-being of persons. They include the right to health, right to education and right to work. Group rights would be those rights accruing to a collective or group of people such as the members of a community or tribe. They include the right to self-determination and the right to economic, social and cultural development.

It appears, from the time of the Universal Declaration, that initial priority was accorded to first-generation civil and political rights. This chronology of rights was especially demonstrated in the dual approach to human rights protection adopted by the United Nations General Assembly in the drafting of an International Bill of Rights in 1966. The original idea had been for the creation of an International Bill of Rights comprising a Declaration, a Covenant, and Measures of Implementation. However, member states could not agree on this goal especially regarding the equal status of civil and political rights and socio-economic rights, resulting in the drafting of two distinct instruments: the ICCPR and the ICESCR. This bifurcation, clearly captured in the creation of two covenants, appeared to group human rights into those requiring immediate implementation (civil and political rights) and those that needed to be realised progressively depending on the individual capacity of the member states (economic, social and cultural rights). It is difficult to argue against this interpretation from an examination of the provisions of the two covenants. While the ICCPR mandates state parties to give immediate effect to the rights recognised in the Covenant, the ICESCR provides for progressive realisation of the rights contained therein thereby highlighting the relative lack of urgency in the implementation of that group of rights.

The African Charter adopts a different approach to the issue of generations or hierarchy of rights. Rather than highlighting the difference in these rights, such as through provisions subjecting socio-economic rights to the availability of resources, the African Charter stressed the harmony and synergy of the different generations of rights. In its Preamble, the African Charter states that civil and political rights cannot be dissociated from economic, social and cultural rights in their conception as well as universality. Also, the satisfaction of economic, social and cultural rights, in the Charter's view, was necessary for the enjoyment of civil and political rights.

There is no express distinction, in the African Charter, between generations or classes of rights such as civil and political rights, socio-economic rights and group rights. All rights contained therein come under the heading 'Human and Peoples' Rights'. The only remote sign of a division could be in the adopted order of listing the rights. One notices that the traditional civil and political rights are provided for before socio-economic and group rights. But even here, the latter two appear to be fused such that most group rights are only extensions of socio-economic rights to groups and peoples. The significance of the Charter's approach will be examined in later parts of this chapter. To set the stage for this and other analysis, a general overview of the normative contents of the Charter is necessary. Articles 2–14 provide for the right to freedom from discrimination, right to equality before the law and equal protection of the law, right to life, prohibition of torture and cruel, inhuman and degrading treatment, right to fair trial, right to freedom of conscience, freedom of expression, right to freedom of association, right to free movement, right to participate in government, and right to property. From Article 15, the Charter provides for socio-economic and group rights. These include the rights to work, health, education, self-determination; economic, social and cultural development; and free disposal of wealth and natural resources. As earlier observed, the latter three rights have elements of both second- and third-generation rights in that they are practically socio-economic rights owed to collectives or groups rather than individuals. The near lack of distinction between these two groups of rights, it is argued, is a strong testament to the Charter's jettisoning of the generational classification of rights.

The next sections will briefly examine the content and meaning of some of these rights and then proceed to analyse some of the distinctive features of the Charter and what they mean for the development of the region's normative human rights framework.

### *3.1.1 Civil and Political Rights*

The African Charter provides for individual civil and political rights. As discussed in Chapter 2, the inclusion of these rights was invariably influenced by the existence of international treaties guaranteeing them as well as pressure from the Western and international communities on African countries to stem human rights abuses which were often in the form of violations of individual civil and political rights. Some of these rights are examined below.

#### *3.1.1.1 Equality and Non-discrimination*

Article 2 of the African Charter provides that every individual shall be entitled to the enjoyment of the rights and freedoms recognised and guaranteed in the Charter without distinction of any kind such as race, ethnic group, colour, sex, language, religion, political or any other opinion, national and social origin, fortune, birth or other status. Furthermore, Article 3 guarantees equality before the law by stating that every individual is equal before the law and shall be entitled to equal protection of the law. These interlinked provisions are natural offshoots of the universal human rights doctrine that rights accrue to every person by virtue of his or her existence as a human being. Their importance in the African context is evidenced by the need to abolish discriminatory Caste systems and protect members of minority groups as well as women and children. Complementing this provision, Article 12(5) of the Charter prohibits the mass expulsion of non-nationals whether aimed at national, racial, ethnic or religious groups. The African Commission has had the opportunity to apply this principle in the 1996 case of *Rencontre Africaine pour la Defense des Droits de L'Homme v. Zambia*[2] where 517 West Africans were expelled from Zambia some of whom had been kept in administrative detention for over two months. The Commission held that the mass deportation of the individuals, including their arbitrary detention and deprivation of the right to have their cause heard, constituted a flagrant violation of the Charter.

In the 2016 case of *Ezzat & Enayet v Egypt*,[3] the complainants contended that the official Egyptian policy of having citizens register under one of three religions—Christianity, Islam or Judaism—was discriminatory. The complainants, adherents of the Baha'i faith, had applied to list their three daughters on the mother's passport. They were, however, summoned by the Egyptian Civil Status Intelligence Unit which seized their identity documents on the grounds that they had to identify with one of the three Abrahamic religions. The Egyptian Court agreed with this policy ruling that the state was not obliged to issue identity cards recognising the Baha'i faith on the basis that the freedom of religion could be restricted on the grounds of respecting public order and morals. The mentioning of the Baha'i faith in identity documents, the Court ruled, violated public order and could, therefore, be prohibited by the state. The Commission held that such a legal regime was discriminatory as it offered benefits to a few religious sects while denying them to others. Despite the non-recognition of the Baha'i faith, the respondent state still had a duty to ensure that adherents of the faith enjoyed the right to equal protection of their marriages under a law that is neutral of any religion.

#### *3.1.1.2 Right to Life, Dignity and Integrity*

Article 4 of the Charter provides that every person shall be entitled to respect for his life and the integrity of his person. The Commission has stated that the right to life is the fulcrum of all other rights and the fountain through which other rights flow. Any violation of this right without due process amounts to an arbitrary deprivation of life.[4] Thus, in a case,[5] the African Commission held that a flawed trial which resulted in the conviction and execution of three army lieutenants was a violation of the right to life.

The Commission has adopted a more pragmatic step of holding a state in violation where a person's life is endangered even though death has not resulted. For instance, in a case against Nigeria,[6] the denial of medication to a prisoner to the extent that his life was seriously endangered was considered to be a violation of the right to life, even though this had not caused his death. Also, in *Kazeem Aminu v. Nigeria*,[7] it was held that a series of arrests and detentions could in themselves constitute a violation of Article 4 even though there was no actual loss of life. Such an approach is significant in the African context given, as will be seen in the next chapter, the penchant for dictatorial regimes that naturally seek to silence perceived opposition groups and individuals through arrests and detentions.

#### *3.1.1.3 Prohibition of Torture and Inhuman Treatment*

Article 5 of the Charter grants every individual the right to the respect of the dignity inherent in a human being and to the recognition of his or her legal status. All forms of exploitation and degradation of man particularly slavery, slave trade, torture, cruel, inhuman or degrading punishment and treatment are prohibited. In Sudan Human Rights Organisation and Centre for Housing Rights and Evictions v Sudan,[8] the Commission set out the elements that would need to be satisfied for torture to be established. These include that severe pain or suffering be inflicted and that such pain or suffering be for a specific purpose such as to obtain information, punish or intimidate, on discriminatory grounds, or at the instigation, consent or acquiescence of state authorities. The protection of this right, the Commission has stated, should be interpreted to 'extend to the widest possible protection against abuse, whether physical or mental'. Thus, in *Hadi & Ors v Republic of Sudan*,[9] it was held that holding a person in detention under conditions that are not in keeping with his dignity and pose a threat to his health would amount to cruel, inhuman and degrading treatment. In that case, the applicants were kept in incommunicado detention, received death threats, denied access to medical care and adequate toilet facilities.

The importance of this freedom is further emphasised by the shifting, in many cases, of the burden of proof to the respondent state. Thus, in the 2015 case of *Armand Guehi v Tanzania*,[10] the African Court held that where the applicant is in custody and unable to prove his allegation because the means of verifying same are likely to be under the control of the state, the burden of proof will shift to the respondent state, and the applicant would only need to make a prima facie case of violation.

In its interpretation of this freedom, the Commission has been willing to consider the decisions of other regional bodies. One such example was in the 2003 case of *Curtis Francis Doebbler v. Sudan*[11] where security agents and policemen beat up and arrested some students who were having a picnic by a riverbank. The students were alleged to have violated public order contrary to national laws[12] for not being properly dressed and acting in an immoral manner. They were convicted and sentenced to fines and/or lashes, a popular type of punishment in Sudan. It was alleged, on behalf of the students, that this punishment was grossly disproportionate and constituted cruel, inhuman and degrading treatment. The Commission found the acts of the Sudanese police to be in violation of Article 5 of the Charter and recommended the abolition of the penalty of lashes. In reaching this decision, the Commission considered, inter alia, the decision of the European Court of Human Rights in the 1978 case of *Tyler v. United Kingdom*,[13] where it was held that even lashings that were carried out in private, with appropriate medical supervision, under strict hygienic conditions, and only after the exhaustion of appeal rights violated the rights of the victim. The Commission stated that there was no right for individuals, and particularly the government of a country, to apply physical violence to individuals for offences. Such a right, in its view, would be tantamount to sanctioning state-sponsored torture under the Charter.

The impact of this decision is crucial not only in assessing possible violations but also in appreciating the Charter's role, as interpreted by the Commission, in ensuring regional standards and regulating national legislation. It is also worth noting the reference to the European Court of Human Rights signifying a more general (or 'universal') leaning as far as the interpretation of civil and political rights is concerned. On face value, this may initially signify a departure from African cultural norm. However, it may be argued that such an approach is permitted, or even envisaged, by Article 60 of the Charter which allows the Commission to 'draw inspiration from international law on human and peoples' right'. Thus, regardless of the religious backgrounds of some of its countries which apply Sharia law (like Sudan in this case), the Commission appears more inclined to adopt and apply the more liberal and modern views on such issues as corporal punishment. Just as was argued in the previous chapter, it is clear from this case that such an approach is to avoid, or at least curtail, the excesses of brutal regimes that have blighted Africa's recent past. The allusion to the dangers of permitting 'state-sponsored torture' clearly shows the strong reluctance of the Commission to allow states any room for discretion on such an important and frequently abused right regardless of cultural or religious practices in those states. As seen in the broad interpretation of the right to life, the Commission appears committed to emphasising the sanctity of the person and enforcement of democratic norms.

The above analysis should not in any way suggest that the principles of Islamic law are contrary to the spirit or intentions of the Charter. Quite to the contrary, it has been argued by Baderin that, instead of seemingly jettisoning Islamic law in this particular case, the Commission could have found Sudan in violation of the Charter based on a harmonious interpretation of the Charter and Islamic law, the latter being one of the continent's 'principal legal traditions'.[14] Baderin points out the emphasis of the AU, with regard to the selection of judges to the African Court, that preference be given to candidates with experience in more than one of the principal legal traditions of Africa, namely Civil Law, Common Law, Islamic Law, Custom and African Customary Law. This, he argues, is to ensure that the court is conversant with, and able to harmonise misunderstandings in the relationship between human rights, on the one hand, and the principal legal traditions, on the other. This view is therefore not a criticism of the Commission's ultimate decision but of the rationale or method of reaching that decision which appears to raise questions about the compatibility of the Charter's provisions with general principles of Islamic law.

The freedom from torture also entails a positive duty on the part of the state to investigate and try, with due diligence, those alleged to have committed acts of torture, inhumane or degrading treatment.[15]

#### *3.1.1.4 Right to Liberty*

Article 6 provides that every individual shall have the right to liberty and security of his or her person. In particular, no one may be arbitrarily arrested or detained. In defining arbitrariness, the Commission has stated that this would include elements of inappropriateness, injustice, lack of predictability, and lack of due process of law. Thus, an arrest or detention may be legal according to domestic law but arbitrary (and therefore illegal) by reason of its inappropriate, unjust or unpredictable nature.[16]

Accordingly, the Commission has held that the massive and arbitrary arrests of office workers, trade unionists, Roman Catholic bishops and students violated this article.[17] As seen in the elaboration on Article 2, such persistent arrests may also amount to violations of the right to life.

In another case, the court held that there was arbitrary deprivation of liberty where the victims were indiscriminately arrested *en masse* without any measures taken to ascertain the likelihood that they had individually been involved in committing an offence.[18]

#### *3.1.1.5 Right to Fair Trial*

Article 7 provides for the right to have one's cause heard including the right to an appeal, presumption of innocence, right to defence and right to be tried within a reasonable time by an impartial court or tribunal. This article also prohibits retroactive legislation. Given Africa's history of military coups and dictatorships, this right has been important in ensuring the functioning of the judiciary. In *Civil Liberties Organisation v. Nigeria*,[19] the military government of Nigeria enacted a decree which not only suspended the country's constitution but also ousted the jurisdiction of the courts and provided that no decree promulgated after December 1983 could be examined in any Nigerian Court. The Commission ruled that the ousting of the jurisdiction of the Nigerian courts constituted an attack of 'incalculable proportions' on Article 7. The Commission stated that an attack of this sort on the jurisdiction of the courts was 'especially invidious' because, while being a violation of human rights in itself, it permitted other violations of rights to go unredressed.

The contents of this right are expatiated in the document 'Principles and Guidelines on the Right to a Fair Trial and Legal Assistance in Africa' adopted by the Commission in 2003. This declaration, among others, provides for fair and public hearings, equality of access by women and men to judicial bodies, adequate opportunity to prepare a case and entitlement to legal representatives and interpreters. The Commission made reference to these guidelines in holding that the state of Sudan violated the rights of detainees who were not promptly informed of the reason for their arrests nor allowed access to a lawyer.[20] The African Court also referenced the guidelines in the 2015 case of *Evarist v Tanzania*[21] in deciding that Tanzania had violated the rights to fair trial of an indigent suspect who was unable to hire a lawyer. The Court held that where an indigent client is charged with a serious offence, such as rape in this case—which carried a severe penalty of thirty years imprisonment—such a person was entitled to free legal aid.

However, positive duties like the provision of interpreters and legal aid are only imposed where the suspect actually needs them and not as standard guarantees. The Court made this clear in the case of *Armand Guehi v Tanzania* where the applicant claimed that his right had been violated because he was not provided with an interpreter and a lawyer during trial. The Court found that the absence of an interpreter or lawyer did not affect the applicant's ability to defend himself as he had sufficient knowledge of the language in which he was interviewed. He was also afforded the opportunity to access a lawyer but declined to do so and had met with a lawyer on the day of his arrest and before making his statement.

The duration of trial could also engage this right especially where it can be shown that delays are caused by the prosecution. Thus, in *Guehi's* case above the African Court held that the duration of the domestic proceedings which meant that the applicant was remanded in prison custody for two years and six months before the commencement of trial was a violation of his rights.

The Commission has established the correlation between this right and the principle of judicial independence. In *Lawyers of Human Rights v Swaziland*,[22] the Swazi Proclamation of 1973 and Decree of 2001 which vested judicial power in the king and ousted the jurisdiction of the court in certain matters were held to be in violation of the right to a fair trial. The Commission pointed out, in that case, that the essence of the principle of separation of powers was to ensure that no organ of government became too powerful. Thus, the right to a fair trial under Article 7 is clearly linked to the state's duty to guarantee the independence of the courts under Article 26.[23]

#### *3.1.1.6 Freedom of Conscience and Religion*

Freedom of conscience and the profession and free practice of religion are guaranteed under Article 8 of the Charter. In *Amnesty International and Others v Sudan*,[24] the Commission held that Tribunals that applied only Sharia law were not competent to judge non-Muslims and that everyone had a right to be tried by a secular court if they so wished. The Commission has, however, noted that the right to act on one's religion is by no means absolute. In *Prince v South Africa*,[25] the complainant alleged infringement following the state's proscription of the sacramental use of cannabis without religious exemption for the Rastafari. It was argued that as the Rastafari religious belief involved the sacramental use of cannabis, such restriction was in breach of their freedom of religion. The Commission, however, disagreed with this position holding that South Africa's restriction was a general one in the interest of society—cannabis being an 'undesirable dependence-producing substance'—and that the Rastafari were only incidentally (de facto) affected. It noted Article 27(2) of the Charter which is to the effect that the rights and freedoms contained therein are to be exercised with due regard to the rights of others, collective security, morality and common interest. Such limitations must, however, be strictly proportionate with and absolutely necessary for the desired objectives.

It is important to note that some states were allowed to enter reservations with regard to this right. For instance, upon ratifying the Charter, Egypt entered a reservation with regard to Article 8 stating that it was going to implement that article in accordance with Islamic law. Following this reservation, the Commission could not hold Egypt in violation of this right in the already discussed case of *Ezzat & Enayet v Egypt*. However, as previously shown, Egypt was held to have violated the right to equality and freedom from discrimination.

#### *3.1.1.7 Freedom of Expression*

Article 9 guarantees every individual the right to express and disseminate his or her opinions within the law. This is one of the few provisions in the Charter with a clawback clause and without further provisions on the limit of such clause. No doubt sensing the danger in such a wide provision and the further need to strengthen freedom of expression the African Commission, in 2002, adopted the Declaration of Principles on Freedom of Expression in Africa.[26] This declaration was intended to supplement the provisions of Article 9 and make more detailed provisions on the ingredients of the freedom of expression and right to information. In contrast to the earlier provision allowing derogation 'according to law', the Declaration states that restrictions to this freedom must be provided by law, serve a legitimate interest and be necessary in a democratic society. This provision is not as detailed as its European equivalent as contained in Article 10(2) of the European Convention on Human Rights which provides for limitations in the interests of national security, territorial integrity or public safety, for the prevention of disorder or crime, for the protection of health or morals, for the protection of the reputation or rights of others, for preventing the disclosure of information received in confidence or for maintaining the authority and impartiality of the judiciary. This notwithstanding the declaration at least tackles the ambiguity in Article 9 which, at first sight, may appear to make the freedom subject to any national law. Also, it may be argued that the specific conditions listed in the European Convention come under the declaration's umbrella provision.

It is rather interesting that the Charter itself did not expound on this right given the importance of the freedom of expression in democratic societies and the fact that the Charter was a direct response to the ills of autocratic African governments. Such lacuna has necessitated a proactive stance by the Commission which has ruled that references to 'law' in this and similar provisions are allusions to international law as opposed to national law. The Commission made this clarification in the 1998 case of *Media Rights Agenda and Others v Nigeria*,[27] where the Military government of Nigeria proscribed two magazines and ten newspapers and embarked on frequent seizures of copies of magazines critical of the government's decisions and arrest of newspaper vendors selling such magazines or papers. In its decision, the Commission stated:

> According to Article 9.2 of the Charter, dissemination of opinions may be restricted by law. This does not mean that national law can set aside the right to express and disseminate one's opinions; this would make the protection of the right to express one's opinions ineffective. To allow national law to have precedent over the international law of the Charter would defeat the purpose of the rights and freedoms enshrined in the Charter. International human rights standards must always prevail over contradictory national law. Any limitation on the rights of the Charter must be in conformity with the provisions of the Charter.[28]

It is commendable that the Commission has stepped in to clarify this and other clawback provisions. This, of course, is the only logical interpretation as the reverse would amount to subjecting this freedom to possible tyrannical legislations some of which are examined in future chapters.

The African Court has also lent its voice to the development and interpretation of this provision. In *Konaté v Burkina Faso*,[29] the Court held that, for a restriction to be acceptable, it must serve a 'legitimate purpose' and must be 'proportionate to and absolutely necessary for the benefits to be gained'. The basis for such measurement, the Court pointed out, is Article 27(2) which provides for individual rights to be exercised 'with due regard to the rights of others, collective security, morality and common interest'. The Court further stated that, going by the content of the declaration above, any question as to whether a restriction is absolutely necessary must be assessed within the context of a democratic society. In the instant case, the applicants contended that penal laws punishing defamation of the judiciary, army and other constituted authorities with imprisonment of up to 15 years were in violation of the freedom of expression.

In its assessment, the Court found that the disputed Burkinabé legislation served a legitimate purpose. However, it ruled that the limitation was not necessary to achieve the set objective. In the Court's view, the freedom of expression in a democratic society must be subject to a lesser degree of interference when it occurs in the context of public debates relating to public figures. This was especially the case as public figures must face a higher degree of criticism than private individuals. On the prescribed punishment, the Court noted that the respondent state had failed to show how a penalty of imprisonment was a necessary limitation in order to protect the reputation of the members of the judiciary. Such punishment, the Court noted, also had to be proportional to the stated aim.

The Court cited with approval the view of the European Court of Human Rights that criminal defamation laws should only be used in exceptional circumstances such as the use of hate speech or incitement to violence.[30] Accordingly, the Court held that the legal provisions violated Article 9 of the Charter.

#### *3.1.1.8 Freedoms of Association and Assembly*

Article 10 of the Charter makes provision for the individual's right to free association provided that such individual abides by the law. Considering the apparent ambiguity of this provision and the possible room for violation, the Commission, in 1992, adopted the Resolution on the Freedom of Association.[31] The resolution requires that state authorities refrain from enacting provisions that would limit the exercise of this right and other fundamental rights. In Civil Liberties Organisation v Nigeria,[32] the Commission stated that, at its core, this freedom required the state to refrain from interfering with the free formation of associations. A duty would also exist to prevent state harassment and clampdown on members of a group. In *Malawi Africa Society & Ors v Mauritania*,[33] supporters of the Ba'ath Arab Socialist Party were imprisoned for belonging to a criminal association. The Commission held that, as the government did not provide any argument to establish the criminal nature or character of these groups, there was a breach of the freedom of association. Also, in *Law Offices of Ghazi Suleiman v Sudan*,[34] Mr. Suleiman who was billed to deliver a public lecture was prohibited from travelling by security officials who threatened to arrest him if he embarked on the trip. The Commission held that this amounted to a violation of his freedom of association.

Freedom of association would go beyond state restriction of individuals' membership of a group to also include cases where such individuals are compelled to join a group. Thus, in *Tanganyika Law Society v Tanzania*,[35] the African Court held that the national requirement for a citizen to be sponsored by a political party before he or she could contest elections was an infringement of the freedom of association. In the Court's view, the freedom of association is essentially negated where an individual is forced to associate with others.

Closely linked to the freedom of association is the freedom of assembly. Article 11 of the Charter provides for every individual to have the right to assemble freely with others. Thus, in the case above, Sudan was also held to be in violation of Mr. Suleiman's freedom of assembly by preventing him from delivering the public lecture. By way of distinction, it appears that while the freedom of association refers to one's right of membership of an organisation, freedom of assembly refers to the right to congregate, partake and participate in the activities of that organisation. Thus, the latter right will expectedly cover ancillary rights such as the right to protest.

Much like the freedom of association, there is some ambiguity as to the exact extent of this right given that the Charter provides that the right shall be subject to 'necessary restrictions provided for by law, in particular, those enacted in the interest of national security, the safety, health, ethics and rights and freedoms of others'. The Commission has held that the principles in its Resolution on the Right to Freedom of Association should also apply to other rights including the freedom of assembly. Accordingly, national authorities are not to override constitutional and international provisions for human rights in its restriction of this freedom.[36]

#### *3.1.1.9 Freedom of Movement*

Article 12 of the Charter guarantees the individual's right to freedom of movement and residence within the borders of a state. The individual also has the right to leave any country including his or her own and to return to that country subject however to restrictions provided for by law for the protection of national security, law and order, public health or morality. It is important to note here, in light of earlier discussions on the freedom of expression, the relatively specific contents of the permissible derogations from this freedom. In *Huri-Laws v Nigeria*,[37] the Commission held that the arrest and detention of the victims at the border was a violation of this freedom.

It would be interesting to know the Commission's view on whether a member state can deny re-entry to a citizen who had joined, say, a jihadist organisation in his or her time abroad. This is relevant in the context of recent debates in countries like the UK and Canada over the return of jihadist fighters from Syria. These debates took an interesting turn in 2019 when the UK formally withdrew the citizenship of Shamima Begum, a teenager who fled to Syria, aged 15, to join the Islamic State in Syria (ISIS). Begum, at the time in a refugee camp, was seeking to return to the UK after four years in the war-torn state of Syria. The UK's decision was especially controversial given that it had the potential effect of rendering Begum stateless under international law. Bangladesh, the country that the UK had claimed Begum could claim citizenship in, repeatedly and vehemently stated that it would not accept her in the country.

It may be argued, in the context of the African Charter, that states could potentially restrict movement in this way provided that such restriction met the Charter's conditions namely that it is "provided for by law for the protection of national security". However, such national provisions may be subjected to further scrutiny including whether they are consistent with international and other human rights obligations, such as fair hearing, as will be shown in the case of *Good v Botswana* below.

The right to freedom of movement would not only be infringed where a person is hindered from leaving or entering a country but could also be engaged where that person is forced into exile or hiding. This, in the 1999 case of *Rights International v Nigeria*[38] where a person was forced to flee the country and take on refugee status abroad due to threats of abduction by perceived agents of the government, it was held by the Commission that his freedom of movement had been infringed.

Freedom of movement would also be violated where a state unlawfully expels non-nationals. By virtue of Article 12(4), such expulsions must be done 'in accordance with the law'. In *Good v Botswana*, the Commission was faced with the task of determining the meaning of the term 'in accordance with the law'. The respondent state argued that its expulsion of the victim, Mr. Good, was done in accordance with the domestic law of Botswana and, therefore, met the Charter provision. In its decision, the Commission agreed that the term 'in accordance with the law' referred to the domestic laws of states parties, in this case the Botswana Immigration Act. It, however, pointed out that the mere existence of a law by itself would not be sufficient as such law would need to be consistent with the provisions of the Charter as well as other international human rights instruments to which the state is a party. These instruments require states to provide the forum for such deportees to be heard or present possible defences against their expulsion. The Commission, therefore, held that Botswana was in breach of this right for deporting the complainant without giving him the opportunity to plead his case before the national courts.

It is interesting that the Commission, in interpreting these rights, does not limit itself to the provisions of the Charter. By requiring that states abide by other international instruments which they have ratified, the Commission assumes the position of a continental arbiter overseeing the implementation of member states' human rights commitments.

As has already been hinted above, the Commission is often willing to consider the provisions of these international instruments in interpreting the Charter. Thus, it may not be critical to a case that the respondent state has not ratified the necessary international instruments as the Commission may interpret the Charter such that it complies with that instrument. The Commission finds legal basis for this in Article 60 of the Charter which provides for the Commission to 'draw inspiration' from international law on human rights particularly from the provisions of other African instruments, the Charter of the United Nations and the Universal Declaration of Human Rights. Indeed, in *Modise v Botswana*,[39] the Commission held that granted that the decision on deportation was the function of national authorities, such decision must have due regard to 'acceptable international norms and standards'. The Commission has therefore been known to draw inspiration from UN treaties, the jurisprudence of the European Court of Human Rights and even standards of the International Bar Association. For instance, in *Masuku v Swaziland*,[40] the Commission cited Article 30 of the International Bar Association Minimum Standards of Judicial Independence in deciding whether Swaziland had breached principles of separation of powers.

#### *3.1.1.10 Right of Political Participation*

Article 13 of the Charter provides for the citizen's right to participate freely in the government of his or her country, either directly or through freely chosen representatives in accordance with the provisions of the law. Furthermore, the individual is entitled to equal access to the public service and public property of his or her country. The Commission has defined this provision as entailing, among other entitlements, the right to vote for the representative of one's choice. Thus, the June 1993 annulment by the Nigerian government of elections internationally adjudged as free and fair was held to be a violation of the rights of the Nigerian people.[41] Similarly, in *Lawyers of Human Rights v Swaziland*,[42] the Commission held that the King's Proclamation outlawing the formation of political parties was a violation of the Swazi peoples' right to participate in the government.

The right would also be infringed where a person is unjustly prevented from standing for office. Thus, in *Jawara v The Gambia*,[43] where former ministers and members of parliament were banned from political activity by the new regime, the Commission held the ban to be in contravention of Article 13. The African Court got an opportunity to develop the Commission's interpretation in the 2011 case of *Tanganyika Law Society and Mtikila v Tanzania*.[44] In that case, the applicants contended that certain articles of the Tanzanian constitution which required candidates for presidential, parliamentary and local government elections to be members of registered political parties were a violation of Article 13 as it did not allow for independent candidature.

On its part, Tanzania argued that the issue of independent candidature was a political, rather than, legal one. The Court agreed with the applicant's proposition that the requirement for a candidate to belong to a political party was a derogation from the provisions of Article 13 allowing citizens to participate in governance. In reaching this decision, the court pointed out that Article 13 protects 'individual' as against 'group' rights meaning that they are not necessarily meant to be enjoyed as a group through, for instance, political parties. However, the court needed to determine whether the restriction was permissible under Article 27(2) of the Charter which provides for rights and freedoms to be exercised 'with due regard to the rights of others, collective security, morality and interest'.

The court held that the respondents had not satisfactorily demonstrated that restriction of independent candidacy was proportionate to attaining stated aims of collective security and interest. The court was of the view that any law that required citizens to belong to political parties before aspiring to offices was an 'unnecessary fetter' to the citizen's right of direct participation as guaranteed under Article 13.

#### *3.1.1.11 Right to Property*

The right to property is one of the few rights protected in the UDHR but not in its accompanying ICCPR and ICESCR. By Article 17 of the UDHR, everyone may own property individually or collectively and may not be 'arbitrarily deprived' of such property. However, the UDHR does not state what may amount to arbitrary deprivation. The African Charter goes a step further by providing the circumstances when this right may be lawfully infringed.

Article 14 of the Charter provides thus:

> The right to property shall be guaranteed. It may only be encroached upon in the interest of public need or in the general interest of the community and in accordance with the provisions of appropriate laws.

Giving the limited definition of this right and its broad qualifications, it is not a surprise that the Commission has gone to some length to interpret it. Such interpretations may appear straightforward as in the case of *Malawi Africa Association and others v Mauritania*,[45] where the confiscation, looting, destruction and expropriation of land and property belonging to Black Mauritanians—actions also held to be discriminatory—were held to constitute violations of their right to property.

However, there are cases where the Commission has had to hold that infringements are lawful. In *Gabriel Shumba v Zimbabwe*,[46] the complainant argued that the respondent state's confiscation of some of his belongings (including a cell phone and some documents) in the course of arrest amounted to a violation of his right to property. In disagreeing with this position, the Commission stated that competent authorities may rightfully search a suspect and seize any articles which it believed may present evidence of the commission of an offence. The Commission's position was further motivated by the belief that the framers of the Charter did not envisage the temporary seizure of a mobile phone or diary 'as part of the property rights that should be robustly defended by Article 14'.

The provision for states to limit this right in line with the public interest is certainly not a carte blanche. The Commission has stated that such limitations be determined in the light of the principle of proportionality. To this end, any interference must be 'proportional to a legitimate need and represent the least restrictive measure possible'.[47] The state would also be required to pay adequate compensation as determined by a competent court where an individual is deprived of their property.[48]

The right to property not only precludes invasion or encroachment upon one's property. It also includes the right to 'undisturbed possession, use and control of such property however the owner deems fit'.[49] Unnecessary interference with a person's enjoyment or use of such property, even where not precluding the owner's use of it, would therefore amount to a violation of the Charter.

The Commission has also stated, in the *Ogoni* case,[50] that the rights to 'adequate housing' or 'shelter', even though not expressly provided for in the Charter, would effectively come under Article 14. However, an examination of the Commission's decision shows that this is not necessarily to be viewed from the lens of a positive duty on the state to provide housing. Rather, the Commission's definition of a right to housing, in that case, focusses on the prohibition of 'wanton destruction' of housing or the obstruction of efforts by individuals or communities to rebuild lost homes.

It is not clear why the Charter does not expressly provide for a right to housing as done in both the UDHR and ICESCR, and even national constitutions like South Africa's. It has however been argued that this right is implicit in the totality of the right to enjoy the best attainable standard of mental and physical health, the right to property and the protection of the family.[51]

### *3.1.1.12 General Points on Civil and Political Rights*

The Charter's approach to civil and political rights mirrors the general position in the Universal Declaration and ICCPR. To this extent, therefore, there is little distinction in the approach and content of this group of rights except, perhaps, from the Commission's arguably modern definition of the content of some rights such as the right to life. By upholding these rights, at least theoretically, through the ratification of the African Charter, as well as judicially, through Court pronouncements, African countries demonstrate their acceptance of these universal principles as well as their importance in ensuring the future development of the continent. There are, however, a number of concerns that have been raised on the Charter's content of civil and political rights. Aside from the already addressed issue of clawback clauses, the Charter has been criticised for its lack of clarity on certain provisions and even failure to provide for some important rights. For instance, it has been argued that the formulation of Article 7 of the Charter—right to a fair trial—is inadequate. The Charter, it is argued, leaves the answer to the question whether many of the crucial aspects of a fair trial need to be observed up to the creative interpretation of the Commissioners.[52] The article merely includes the right to a defence, appeal, presumption of innocence and trial within a reasonable time. However, Heyns argues that crucial aspects of a fair trial like the right to a public hearing, the right to interpretation, the right against self-incrimination and the right against double jeopardy need to have been included. The Commission has however interpreted the Charter to include some of these elements. Also, as pointed out above, the Commission has adopted resolutions detailing the content of such rights.

Attention has also been drawn to Article 14 which guarantees the right to property. The Charter provides that this right may only be encroached upon 'in the interest of public need or in the general interest of the community and in accordance with the provisions of appropriate laws'. Gittleman argues that by not restricting the state's ability to call virtually anything in the 'public need', nor setting forth guidelines clarifying the situation in which a government may exercise eminent domain, the Charter allows a state to take property absent local law to the contrary.[53] However, as has been demonstrated above, the Commission has, in its interpretation of that and other similar articles, pointed out that such qualifications are subject to the provisions of the Charter as well as other general principles of international human rights law. The Charter's equivocation on a number of substantive issues therefore appears to have been effectively met by a proactive Commission which by its procedures and jurisprudence define the nature and delimitations of these rights. An example of one such case is in the Commission's interpretation of the clause 'according to the law' explained above. Another instance is the Commission's view on the absence of a derogation clause in the Charter. In *Commission Nationale des Droits de l'Homme et des libertes v. Chad*,[54] the Commission interpreted the absence of a derogation clause from the Charter to mean that the Charter did not permit derogations.

Apart from the issue of ambiguity, the Charter has also been criticised for failing to make any provisions for certain rights. For instance, it has been pointed out that the Charter fails to provide for the right of citizens to vote,[55] a rather conspicuous absence given the prevalence of autocratic and unelected regimes at the time the Charter was drafted. It is argued, however, that this right is adequately protected under Article 13 which allows every citizen the right to participate freely in the government of his country whether directly or through freely chosen representatives. Given its willingness to accommodate otherwise unprotected rights such as the 'right to food' and 'right to adequate housing' under existing provisions of the Charter, it is difficult to envisage a human right that will not be accommodated under the existing provisions of the Charter. For instance, with regard to the right to food, the Commission asserts that that right is implicit in such provisions as the right to life, the right to health, and the right to economic, social and cultural development. In the *Ogoni* case,[56] the Commission held that the right to food was inseparably linked to the dignity of the human being and was essential to the enjoyment of other rights such as the rights to health, education, work and political participation.

### 3.1.2 Socio-Economic Rights

The Charter provides for a number of socio-economic rights owed to either individuals or groups. With regard to the former, the Charter makes provisions for only three rights: the right to work, the right to health and the right to education. On the latter side are the right to self-determination; right to dispose of wealth and natural resources; the right to economic, social and cultural development; right to security and peace; and the right to a satisfactory and favourable environment. The first group of rights are briefly discussed below while the latter group will be examined in discussions on group and peoples' rights. It is also worth noting that these rights have been subsequently elaborated by the 2004 Pretoria Declaration on Economic, Social and Cultural Rights in Africa (Pretoria Declaration).[57] This declaration, aside from reaffirming the continent's commitment to protecting socio-economic rights, explains the contents of the rights protected under the Charter and the responsibilities of member states under each right. These elaborations will be highlighted under the relevant right below.

*3.1.2.1 Right to Work*

Article 15 of the Charter confers on individuals the right to work 'under equitable and satisfactory conditions' and the entitlement to equal pay for equal work. This concise definition was expanded by the Pretoria Declaration which provides that the right to work includes the following:

a. Equality of opportunity of access to gainful work, including access for refugees, disabled and other disadvantaged persons;
b. Conducive investment environment for the private sector to participate in creating gainful work;
c. Effective and enhanced protections for women in the workplace including parental leave;
d. Fair remuneration, a minimum living wage for labour and equal remuneration for work of equal value;
e. Equitable and satisfactory conditions of work, including effective and accessible remedies for workplace-related injuries, hazards and accidents;
f. Creation of enabling conditions and taking measures to promote the rights and opportunities of those in the informal sector, including in subsistence agriculture and in small-scale enterprises activities;
g. Promotion and protection of equitable and satisfactory conditions of work of women engaged in household labour;
h. The right to freedom of association, including the rights to collective bargaining, strike and other related trade union rights;
i. Prohibition against forced labour and economic exploitation of children, and other vulnerable persons;
j. The right to rest and leisure, including reasonable limitation of working hours, periodic holidays with pay and remuneration for public holidays.

In *Institute for Human Rights and Development in Africa v Angola*,[58] 14 foreign mineworkers were arrested and deported on the grounds that foreigners were not permitted to engage in mining activities in Angola. This was despite the fact that the victims had the necessary official documents such as passports, visas, work and residence permits and were even mandated to make monthly payments for their work permits. The Commission held that their abrupt expulsion without due process compromised the victims' right to work under equitable and satisfactory conditions.

The Commission would also find a violation where a person has lost their job as a result of unjustifiable government policies. For instance, the Commission found that the Zimbabwean government violated the right to work in a case where the state closed down newspaper offices and confiscated printing equipment.[59] Similarly, in *Elgak and others v Sudan*,[60] the complainants lost their jobs following the respondent state's arbitrary closure of the Khartoum Centre for Human Rights and Environment Development. It was held that the state had violated their right to work. Much like the qualified rights discussed above, the right to work is not absolute. However, the state must not arbitrarily interfere with it. Thus, in the case of *Garreth Prince v South Africa*,[61] it was held that the state's restriction of the use and possession of cannabis which affected the complainant's work was not an infringement of the right to work. The right to work would not guarantee a free pass to avoid legitimately instituted restrictions. The complainant by choosing to confront those restrictions had chosen to disqualify himself.

The Commission has also stated that Article 15 imposes an obligation on the state to create a conducive environment for the employment of individuals within the state.[62] A government policy that has the effect of unduly affecting jobs may therefore be held to be in violation of this provision.

### *3.1.2.2 Right to Health*

By Article 16 of the Charter, every individual shall have the right 'to enjoy the best attainable state of physical and mental health'. Furthermore, states are to take 'necessary measures' to protect health and ensure that people receive medical attention when they are sick. Thus, the Commission has held in a case that the failure of the government to provide safe drinking water and medicines amounted to a violation of this provision.[63]

The expression 'best attainable state of physical and mental health' however poses the challenge of interpretation as the Charter does not set out its meaning. It has therefore been argued that this provision provides little guidance on the exact obligations of the state and appropriate expectations by individuals.[64] The Commission has however determined that this provision imposes an obligation on states to take 'concrete and targeted steps', while taking full advantage of their available resources, to ensure the full realisation of this right.[65] In its explanation of the right to health, the Pretoria Declaration further provides that this right entails:

a. Availability of accessible and affordable health facilities, goods and services of reasonable quality for all;
b. Access to the minimum essential food which is nutritionally adequate and safe to ensure freedom from hunger to everyone and to prevent malnutrition;
c. Access to basic shelter, housing and sanitation and adequate supply of safe and potable water;
d. Access to reproductive, maternal and child health care based on the life cycle approach to health;
e. Immunisation against major infectious diseases;
f. Education, prevention and treatment of HIV/AIDS, malaria, tuberculosis and other major killer diseases;
g. Education and access to information concerning the main health problems in the community including methods of preventing and controlling them;
h. Training for health personnel including education on health and human rights;
i. Access to humane and dignified care of the elderly and for persons with mental and physical disabilities.

The duties on a state would be even more stringent in cases of prisoners or other persons in their care. In *Malawi Africa Association and others v Mauritania*,[66] the prison conditions were so poor that four prisoners died of malnutrition and lack of medical care. Some were so weak that they could not stand and had to crawl on all fours. There was poor hygiene in the prison cells which were infested with lice, bedbugs and cockroaches. The Commission ruled that Mauritania had breached Article 16 as the state was directly responsible for the state of the prisons. The Commission stated that the state's responsibility in cases of detention was 'more evident' as such detention centres are within its exclusive preserve. Thus, the physical integrity and welfare of detainees are the state's responsibility.

Even where the state's neglect is not as extreme as the case above, the Commission may still find violation where the state has not done enough to provide for the particular health challenges of the detainee. Thus, in *Elgak and others v Sudan*,[67] the Commission held that the complainant's right to health was infringed where the medication given to him for his high blood pressure was not 'adequate to guarantee his health'. This was the case at such treatment still left him in a life-threatening situation. It was also held in that case that subjection to torture and other forms of ill-treatment resulting in physical and psychological harm would amount to violation of Article 16.

#### *3.1.2.3 Right to Education*

Article 17(1) of the Charter simply states that everyone shall have the right to education. There is no further expatiation of this right making it difficult to ascertain whether, for instance, like the ICESCR, states are obliged to make primary education compulsory and secondary/tertiary education only 'generally available and accessible'.[68] The Pretoria Declaration attempts to fill this gap by providing that this right entails the:

a. Provision of free and compulsory basic education that will also include a programme in psycho-social education for orphans and vulnerable children;
b. Provision of special schools and facilities for physically and mentally disabled children;
c. Access to affordable secondary and higher education;
d. Accessible and affordable vocational training and adult education;
e. Addressing social, economic and cultural practices and attitudes that hinder access to education by girl children;
f. Availability of educational institutions that are physically and economically accessible to everyone;
g. Development of curricula that address diverse social, economic and cultural settings and which inculcate human rights norms and values for responsible citizens;
h. Liberty of parents and guardians to choose for their children schools, other than those established by the public authorities, which conform to such minimum educational standards as may be laid down by the state, and to ensure the religious and moral education of their children in conformity with their own convictions;
i. Continued education for teachers and instructors including education on human rights and the continuous improvement of the conditions of work of teaching staff;
j. Education for development that links school curricula to the labour market and society's demands for technology and self-reliance.

It is important to note that the protection of this right is not limited to positive duties and provisions by the state as the latter is further required to refrain from taking steps that could infringe on it. Thus, in *Free Legal Assistance Group v Democratic Republic of Congo*, the Commission held that the closure of universities and secondary schools amounted to a violation of this provision.

Article 17(2) of the Charter further provides that every individual may freely take part in the cultural life of his community. It is not clear why this provision has been inserted alongside the right to education. It may be argued that the Charter is here recognising the individual's right to be educated in the culture of that community. It may also impose a duty on states not to abolish traditional systems of education in favour of solely modern or Western ones.

In the *Endorois* case,[69] the complainants alleged that government activities, which included the construction of a game reserve, violated the Endorois cultural rights. This, they contended, was due to systematic restrictions of access to cultural sites and interferences with their pastoralist way of life. In agreeing with their submissions, the Commission stressed the need for states to respect and protect religious and cultural heritage essential to a group's identity thus recognising Article 17's dual nature as both an individual and collective right. Interestingly, the Commission recognised this right as one allowing for very limited, if any, exceptions. This position was largely based on the absence of a clawback clause in the provision.

In any event, were the construction of a game reserve even to constitute a legitimate infringement of that right, the state's failure to secure access, as of right, for the celebration of the complainants' cultural festivals and rituals was deemed disproportionate. It would therefore appear, from the Commission's decision, that the limitation threshold is high so long as the group's cultural activities do not pose harm to the ecosystem.

### *3.1.3 Socio-Economic Rights: Enforceable or Not?*

Having identified the socio-economic rights protected under the Charter, an important issue that arises is their level of enforceability. Thus, can it be said that these rights are justiciable? It would appear that the Charter intended for them to be so. Two reasons justify this position. First, the Charter makes no express classification of rights. As a matter of fact, the drafters of the Charter had done away with a first draft that distinguished between socio-economic and other rights.[70] This in itself shows a strong intent against such classifications. Second, the Charter clearly states in its

Preamble that civil and political rights cannot be dissociated from socio-economic rights as the latter are necessary for the fulfilment of the former.

Since the adoption of the African Charter, commentators have presented divergent views on the extent of enforceability of socio-economic rights as envisaged under the Charter. While many have lauded the Charter's approach as welcome in light of deplorable conditions of living of many Africans, there have been reservations about the practical enforcement of this approach. Thus, while praising the merits of this position, it has been often opined that given the realities of economic development in most African countries, socio-economic rights in the Charter may be regarded as merely exhortatory.[71]

On the other hand, it has been argued that socio-economic rights are as unequivocally justiciable as any other rights in the Charter.[72] The African Commission would undoubtedly be granting states a great latitude if civil and political rights were promoted at the expense of socio-economic rights as it is the Commission's aim to strike a healthy balance between the two.[73] This is because the African Charter has already undone the tripartite division of rights by including rights from all three generations in one document. Rather than seeing the poor economic state of African countries as impeding justiciability, Viljoen opines that the Charter's position is a response to the prevailing situation of dire poverty and 'exploitation by kleptocratic elites'.[74] The justiciability of economic rights, he argues, was an acknowledgement that accountability through the law was part of the solution to Africa's economic woes.

That the Charter does not make the fulfilment of any of its provisions dependent on 'available resources' or 'progressive realisation' has been put forward as an argument for the justiciability of socio-economic rights. Unlike the ICESCR, the African Charter avoids the incremental language of progressive realisation in guaranteeing socio-economic and cultural rights except in Article 16(1) which guarantees the best attainable state of physical and mental health.[75]

In a direct criticism of the view that socio-economic rights be only promotional based on economic crises of African states, Agbakwa argues strongly that recognition and enforcement of these rights catalyse development and are inextricable from it. Poor economic conditions of many African states, he contends, do not justify outright non-enforcement of economic, social and cultural rights. Even if underdevelopment were to become a huge impediment, it would merely affect, in his view, the extent to which these rights can be realised and not justify outright non-justiciability. Most armed conflicts in Africa, he argues, are caused by the denial of socio-economic and cultural rights to the people who then embark on armed struggles to fight for these rights.[76]

The seeming 'uncertainty' by some commentators about the enforceability status of socio-economic rights is not very convincing given the Charter's obvious attempt to downplay any classifications of rights. In the absence of a special tag or exemption clause, it is reasonable to infer that the Charter intended for them to be enforceable. Evidence of such an intent may also be gleaned from the Commission's Concluding Observations on state reports where state parties are continually tasked on the improvement of living conditions regardless of the economic conditions of these states. This view is backed by the 2009 decision of the Economic Community of West African States (ECOWAS) Court of Justice (ECCJ) in a case against Nigeria.[77] The Nigerian government had, in addressing a complaint on its failure to adequately implement the country's Basic Education Act, argued that the educational objective in the national constitution was non-justiciable. However, the ECCJ dismissed this position pointing out that it was 'well established' that the rights guaranteed by the African Charter were justiciable. Thus, while the argument against the enforceability of these rights based on the economic situation of many African countries has its merits, it is argued that this should be seen only as a challenge and not as defining the intended status of these rights. Accordingly, for the purpose of measuring compliance, states must be seen as having a duty to implement these rights. Whether this feat is achievable as well as the most practical ways of achieving it will be addressed in subsequent chapters.

### *3.1.4 Peoples' Rights*

The Charter is unique in its approach to peoples' rights. These are contained in Articles 19–24 and provide for various rights that accrue to 'all people'. The Charter makes the collective the holder of these rights rather than the individual. Thus, the 'people' as rights holder may be a community, a population of the country as a whole or even everyone living on the continent.[78] The Commission, as will be seen in cases below, has been active in applying provisions on peoples' rights to indigenous populations in Africa. The Commission describes indigenous peoples as groups whose cultures and ways of life differ considerably from the dominant society, those cultures being under threat, in some cases to the point of extinction.[79] Such threat may come in the form of discrimination, domination and marginalisation such that they are unable to actively participate in decisions regarding their future. The survival of such groups would often depend on access and rights to their traditional lands and the natural resources thereon. Examples of indigenous groups in Africa are the Endorois, Ogiek and Maasai in Kenya; the Ogoni in Nigeria; and the San in South Africa and Zimbabwe.

The concept of peoples' rights, and the significant portion of the Charter dedicated to it, is reflective of the communal and people-oriented nature of Africa. It also reflects the multiethnicity and cultural diversity present in most African countries. For instance, Nigeria alone has over 250 ethnic groups[80] while Cameroon has more than 230.[81] By providing for a whole range of peoples' rights, the African Charter can be seen to fulfil, at least to some extent, this clamour for communitarianism and oneness. By giving room for their application in cases where indigenous and ethnic populations in Africa seek to establish their rights as a collective within the state, the provisions on peoples' rights serve the 'vital purpose' of accommodating class actions and recognising such claims as the right to self-determination within a sovereign state.[82] The following sections examine these collective rights.

#### *3.1.4.1 Rights of Peoples to Equality and Rights*

Article 19 of the Charter guarantees equality to all peoples. By this provision, all peoples shall enjoy the same respect and rights and shall be free from domination by another group. Granted that this provision may have originally been inspired by the continent's colonial history, the Commission has been quick to point out that this protection extends to both internal and external domination. Therefore, in a case against the government of Sudan,[83] the Commission found a violation of this article and stated that the people of Darfur did not deserve to be dominated by a people of another race in the same state. In that case, residents of Darfur had been subjected to large-scale killings, forced displacements and bombings by military fighter jets in the government's attempt to contain an insurgency. In finding a violation of this right, the Commission stated that the people of Darfur did not:

> deserve to be dominated by a people of another race in the same state. Their claim for equal treatment arose from the alleged underdevelopment

> and marginalization. The response by the Respondent State, while fighting the armed conflict, targeted the civilian population, instead of the combatants.

The Commission will also find a violation of this right where it appears that a government has adopted policies that have adverse effects on the economic well-being of a people or tribe. In *Kevin Gunme and others v Cameroon*,[84] the respondent state relocated some major economic projects, including a seaport, from Anglophone to Francophone Cameroon. The Commission found that such relocation, which negatively impacted on the economic well-being of Southern Cameroon, constituted a violation of Article 19. The Commission was particularly not satisfied with Cameroon's explanations on the need to relocate the port due to security and customs concerns.

#### *3.1.4.2 Right to Self-Determination*

By Article 20, all peoples shall have an 'unquestionable' and 'inalienable' right to self-determination. They shall have the freedom to freely determine their political status and pursue their economic and social development according to the policy that they have freely chosen. No doubt inspired by the continent's colonial history, the Article goes on to state that 'colonised or oppressed peoples shall have the right to free themselves from the bonds of domination by resorting to any means recognised by the international community'. Furthermore, such people shall have the right to assistance of other state parties to the Charter in their liberation struggles. In *Democratic Republic of Congo v Burundi, Rwanda and Uganda*,[85] the Commission found that the occupation by the Respondent state of territories in the complainant state was a 'flagrant violation' of the latter's inalienable right to self-determination.

Interestingly, however, the Commission has been reluctant to extend this right to secessionist movements despite their conspicuous presence in many parts of Africa. For instance, in *Congrès du peuple katangais v Democratic Republic of Congo*,[86] the Commission stated that the right to self-determination must be exercised taking into consideration other 'recognised principles' such as sovereignty and territorial integrity. It appears from the language of the Commission that principles of sovereignty and territorial integrity would only be jettisoned where there is concrete evidence of violation of human rights to the point where the territorial integrity of a state is threatened and denial, towards a particular people, of the right to participate in government. In the instant case, the Commission stated thus:

> In the absence of concrete evidence of violations of human rights to the point that the territorial integrity of Zaire should be called to question and in the absence of evidence that the people of Katanga are denied the right to participate in government as guaranteed by Article 13(1) of the African Charter, the Commission holds the view that Katanga is obliged to exercise a variant of self-determination that is compatible with the sovereignty and territorial integrity of Zaire.[87]

It is not clear how, and in what circumstances, the Commission would reach the conclusion that human rights violations have reached the point where a state's territorial integrity is 'called into question'. It also remains to be seen whether the Commission would uphold a right to secession in those circumstances.

#### *3.1.4.3 Right to Free Disposal of Wealth and Natural Resources*

Article 21 provides that all peoples shall freely dispose of their wealth and natural resources. In the *Ogoni case*, which concerned the impact of oil development activities on the Ogoni people living in the Niger Delta area of Nigeria, the Commission found that the Nigerian Government violated, *inter alia*, the right of the Ogoni people to freely dispose of their wealth and natural resources. It articulated the scope of Article 21 in a way that resonated with separate provisions, notably in relation to property, health and the environment, and recognised substantive rights which were not expressly mentioned in the Charter, such as the right not to be subjected to forced evictions.[88]

The Article also presupposes a duty on the state to protect against interferences with the enjoyment and free disposal of wealth. Thus, in the instant case, the Commission bemoaned the Nigerian government's failure to checkmate the devastating effects of the extraction and other exploration actors in Ogoni land.

#### *3.1.4.4 Right to Economic, Social and Cultural Development*

By Article 22, all peoples shall have the right to their economic, social and cultural development with due regard to their freedom and identity and in the equal enjoyment of the common heritage of mankind. In the

*Endorois* case,[89] the Commission provided a first comprehensive interpretation of the right to development by a supranational adjudicatory body. The complaint surrounded the Kenyan government's eviction of hundreds of Endorois families from their land around the Lake Bogoria area in the Rift Valley to create a game reserve for tourism. The Endorois, an indigenous people had been promised compensation and benefits, but these were never fully implemented, and the community's access to the land was restricted to the discretion of the Game Reserve Authority. This prevented the community from practising their pastoralist way of life, using ceremonial and religious sites and accessing traditional medicines. The Commission found that the Kenyan government had violated the Endorois' rights to religious practice, property, culture, the free disposition of natural resources and development as variously protected under the African Charter.[90] The Commission stated that the lack of consultation with the community, the subsequent restrictions on access to the land and the inadequate involvement in the process of developing the region for use as a tourist game reserve had violated the community's right to development. Also, the Commission found that the Kenyan Government's Trust Land System violated the Endorois' right to property. The system allowed gradual encroachment onto Endorois land and, even though it allowed for compensation, it nevertheless violated property rights by effectively causing forced evictions. For these violations, the Commission recommended that the government recognise the right of ownership of the Endorois people, restitute to the Endorois their ancestral lands, compensate their losses and ensure that the Endorois benefit from the royalties and employment opportunities within the game reserve.[91]

In *African Commission on Human and Peoples' Rights (Ogiek) v Kenya*,[92] the African Court decided that the Kenya government's 30-day eviction notice to the Ogiek community inhabiting Kenya's Mau Forest was contrary to the Charter as it posed huge threats to the survival of the Ogiek people. In another case, the Commission held that the forced displacement of the residents of Darfur denied them the right to engage in economic, social and cultural activities.[93]

## 3.2 Communitarian Duties

A peculiar feature of the African Charter is its imposition of duties on states and individuals. In its Preamble, the Charter provides that the enjoyment of rights and freedoms implies the performance of duties on the part of everyone. This declaration subscribes to the communitarian perspective of rights and attendant duties. The communitarian philosophy is based on the premise that rights have limits and involve concomitant responsibilities. It has, therefore, been described as 'the sane middle ground' between the 'extremes' of authoritarianism and libertarianism.[94] While communitarians support basic civil liberties, they fear that the ability to confront societal problems effectively is compromised by the claims of 'radical individualists' who would subordinate the needs of the community to the absolute fulfilment of individual rights. Thus, in addition to recognising individual human dignity, the communitarian also recognises the 'social dimension' of human existence and proposes an agenda to advance commonly held social values without unduly compromising individual rights. The African Charter's provision and emphasis on duties can be interpreted as an adoption and development of this communitarian doctrine. Instead of a purely individualistic document that focusses on the individual and his/her rights, the African Charter stresses the importance of the family, social and community values by making provisions for duties owed to the family and state.

It has been correctly argued that the notion of duties originates in the American and Universal Declaration and is therefore not the novelty of the African Charter.[95] However, these duties are spelt out more elaborately in the African Charter than anywhere else.[96] The African Charter has also certainly improved and developed the concept of rights and corresponding duties.

Article 1 requires member states to recognise the rights, duties and freedoms enshrined in the Charter and adopt necessary legislative measures to give them effect. In Lawyers of Human Rights v Swaziland, a 1973 Proclamation which preceded the adoption of the Charter was held to violate the rights to a fair trial and political participation. Even though the Proclamation had been enacted prior to Charter's coming into force, the Commission held that the respondent state had a duty to ensure its conformity with the Charter after ratifying the latter. By failing to amend its laws to comply with its responsibilities under the Charter, Swaziland had failed to abide by its duty under Article 1.

The Charter also provides for specific duties to the family. By Article 18, the state has a duty to assist the family in the latter's role as the custodian of morals and traditional values. The Commission has defined this duty to entail a negative obligation to refrain from violating the rights and interests of the family. It has therefore been held that the sudden deportation and unjustified deportation of a man in the knowledge that he would be separated from his minor daughter was a violation of this duty.[97] Similarly, in the *Mauritania* case, it was held that holding people in solitary confinement before and during trial deprived them of the right to family life.

Article 18 also requires the state to ensure the elimination of every discrimination against women and to protect the rights of women, children, disabled and aged persons.

Article 25 of the Charter imposes on state parties the duty to promote and ensure through teaching, education and publication, the respect of the rights and freedoms contained in the Charter. There is also the duty to guarantee the independence of the courts and 'to allow the establishment and improvement of appropriate national institutions entrusted with the promotion and protection of the rights contained in the Charter'. It is not clear what are the exact delimitations of the phrase 'to allow' and whether this entails merely creating an enabling environment for these institutions to operate or some more positive exertions like funding them.

Article 27 provides that every individual shall have duties towards his family and society, the state and other legally recognised communities and the international community. The Article does not state what exactly these duties are although these can be inferred from Article 29 which sets out duties of the individual. These are examined below.

### 3.2.1 *Individual Duties in the Charter*

The Charter provides for individual duties to the family, community and state. Article 29 provides that the individual has the duty to preserve the harmonious development of the family and to work for the cohesion and respect of the family; to respect his parents at all times; and to maintain them in case of need. He or she also has to serve the community by placing his or her physical and intellectual abilities at its service.

There is also an emphasis on maintaining social and cultural values. An individual is therefore required to preserve and strengthen 'positive African cultural values' in his relations with other members of the society, in the spirit of tolerance, dialogue and consultation and, in general, to contribute to the promotion of the moral well-being of the society. It is interesting to note the Charter's reference to 'positive' African values thereby implying the existence of 'negative' ones. The latter may be observed in practices that have routinely been condemned by the Commission such as female genital cutting and widow inheritance some of which are highlighted throughout the book.

Duties owed the state include not to compromise the security of the state whose national or resident he is; to work to the best of his abilities and competence, and to pay taxes imposed by law; and to preserve and strengthen the national independence and the territorial integrity of his country and to contribute to its defence in accordance with the law. It has been pointed out that the duties of the individual are traditionally 'moral' and generally not enforceable.[98] It is, however, important to note that some of these duties like the payment of tax and preservation of territorial integrity often carry the full force of the law.

The communitarian perspective adopted by the Charter has not gone unchallenged. It has been suggested, for instance, that the chapter on duties (Articles 27–29) represents perhaps the most elaborate limitations of the rights contained in the Charter.[99] Shivji describes the representation of duties as an ideological reflection of the authoritarian character of the African neo-colonial state.[100] Also, Mutua argues that the language of duties in the Charter underplays the force of rights because it emphasises the duty of the individual, rather than that of the state.[101] In a similar vein, Ankumah posits that being vaguely defined, the language of duties could be used to suppress individual rights such as freedom of conscience.[102] Furthermore, Hatem Ben Salem, at the time a member of the African Commission, suggested amending the Charter given the imposition of such 'heavy duties' on individuals.[103]

While they vary in their degrees of criticism, the above opinions appear to be anticipations of a potential conceptual clash between the provisions for rights on the one hand and duties on the other. The case has however been made for the compatibility of liberal and communitarian ideas. For instance, Scott[104] argues against the notion that liberal theory and communitarian morality are essentially incompatible. While liberal theory places a high value on personal choice and circumscribes the use by the state of its coercive powers to enforce communal norms, it does not follow that 'autonomous, liberal selves will [not] choose lives filled with deep commitment, lasting relationships, and social responsibility'. She, therefore, argues that communitarian values and liberalism are not mutually exclusive and share important commonalities.

Buttressing this point Pityana argues that, far from creating an environment for a gratuitous invasion of rights, duties should be understood as reinforcing rights. It is, therefore, necessary, in his view, to make reference to duties because, in the modern global environment, the key performers are not necessarily the states but non-state actors. Also, the African Charter spells out duties in order to save the African system of human rights from over-dependence on individualism.

In conclusion, it is opined that the provisions for duties reflect the communal and familial nature of the traditional African state and show that the Charter was specially crafted to reflect a pan-African identity as opposed to a holistic, uncritical adoption of Western liberalism. Much as has been pointed out in the previous chapter, the provision for duties reflects the moderate relativist approach of the Charter which, in adopting liberal conceptions of individual civil and political rights, interspersed these with other provisions reflecting the continent's communal traditions and philosophy. It is such provisions as these that give the Charter its African flair and uniqueness.

## 3.3 The Protocol to the African Charter on Human and Peoples' Rights on the Rights of Women in Africa

The Protocol to the African Charter on Human and Peoples' Rights on the Rights of Women in Africa (Women's Protocol) was drafted in 2003 as part of the work of the African Commission's Special Rapporteur on the Rights of Women in Africa. Even though women are equally addressed under the African Charter, it was thought to create a distinct instrument for them because:

> Despite the ratification of the [African Charter] and other international human rights instruments by the majority of States Parties, and their solemn commitment to eliminate all forms of discrimination and harmful practices against women, women in Africa still continue to be victims of discrimination and harmful practices.[105]

Much like the African Charter, the Women's Protocol makes provisions for civil and political, socio-economic and group rights. It also, remarkably, became the first international treaty to provide for a range of sexual and reproductive rights. For instance, Article 14 mandates states parties to protect the reproductive rights of women by allowing medical abortion in cases of sexual assault, rape and incest, and where the pregnancy endangers the health of the mother or child. This interestingly was the first time an international treaty recognised abortion as a woman's human rights albeit under limited circumstances.

The Women's Protocol reiterates some of the rights contained in the Charter such as elimination of discrimination, right to dignity and rights to life, integrity and security of the person, 'though from the particular perspective of the lived experience of women and girls, which often tends to differ from that of men and boys'. It also provides for rights that apply mainly to women within the African context including the elimination of harmful practices such as female genital mutilation; equality in marriage, health and reproductive rights; the right to inheritance; political participation; and widows' rights.

The Women's Protocol is modelled to address particular issues facing women in Africa and, as is the case with the Charter, reflects particular African cultures and traditions. One instance of this is in the Protocol's approach to polygamous marriages. The 'universal' position as expressed by both the UN Human Rights Committee and CEDAW Committee is that polygamous marriages are incompatible with the woman's right to equality with men.[106] However, the Women's Protocol does not adopt such outright prohibition. Instead, while encouraging states to enact laws that 'encourage' monogamy as the 'preferred' form of marriage, Article 6(c) of the Protocol provides that 'the rights of women in marriage and family, including in polygamous marital relationships' must be promoted and protected. In further explaining this approach, Baderin states:

> Practically, it would be very difficult, if not impossible, to enforce a sweeping prohibition of polygamous marriages within most African societies, especially amongst the rural communities. The African states have, therefore, under the African Women's Protocol, opted for the practical alternative of encouraging monogamy rather than prohibiting polygamy.[107]

In 2011 the Commission, for the first time, reached a decision on the merits in a case concerning the violation of women's rights.[108] The complaint was filed on behalf of four women who were sexually abused during a demonstration in Cairo regarding a referendum on the amendment of the Egyptian Constitution. The complainants claimed that the first victim's clothes were torn, documents seized and her private parts fondled. The second, third and fourth victims, all journalists covering the protest, were beaten and sexually harassed by unidentified men and security officers. It was also alleged that, when the victims lodged their complaints, they received threats to withdraw the case. Their complaints were subsequently rejected on the basis that the offenders could not be identified. The Commission held that the physical, mental and sexual harm inflicted on the victims affected their physical and mental well-being in violation of the right to health. The Commission ordered Egypt to conduct an investigation into the violation and to pay adequate compensation to each of the victims.[109]

The African Court has also elaborated on some of the provisions of the Women's Protocol such as consent and the minimum age of marriage. In an application brought against Mali,[110] the applicants argued that Malian law which set the minimum age for girls to marry at 16 contravened Article 6 of the Protocol which stipulates a minimum age of 18. The Court agreed and held Mali to be in violation of that provision. The Court also held that the Malian law which allowed religious minister and civil registry officials to perform marriages without verifying the parties' consent to such marriages was contrary to the spirit of the Protocol which prohibits forced marriages. With regard to inheritance, the Court ruled that the prevailing customary law which allowed a woman to only inherit half as much as a man was contrary to Article 21 of the Protocol which provides for widows to be entitled to an equitable share in the inheritance of their husbands' properties. The article further provides that women and men shall have the right to inherit their parents' properties 'in equitable shares'. It is interesting that the Protocol adopts the wording 'equitable' as opposed to 'equal' thereby leaving room for female children to inherit less than their male counterparts.

## 3.4 Conclusion

The African human rights system has created a comprehensive network of human and peoples' rights captured in the African Charter, the Court's Protocol and the Women's Protocol. While there have been subsequent AU human rights protocols, like the Charter on the Rights and Welfare of the Child and Convention Governing Specific Aspects of Refugee Problems in Africa, it can be argued that they, like the Women's Protocol, mainly develop the rights guaranteed under the African Charter in relation to certain affected groups within African societies. The African system has taken advantage of its comparative recent existence to draw from the experiences and conceptions of other climes thus creating a hybrid system of rights that has at its core, the spirit and flair of Africa. This is clearly demonstrated in the protection, both in Charter provisions and by the decisions of the Commission, of socio-economic and cultural rights as well as peoples' rights.

The Charter's clear attempt to enthrone the enforceability of socio-economic rights is reflective of the situation in the region and the need to build a society of general well-being. Its provisions and positive decisions of the Commission in defence of peoples' rights demonstrate the true 'Africanness' of the Charter and underline the need to protect the diverse identities and cultures of many minorities and oppressed groups on the continent. The Charter does not draw any express distinction between these rights and other civil and political rights in the area of justiciability. This characteristic increases the burden of implementation on member states, and future chapters will examine just how much member states have implemented and enforced these rights.

Additionally, there is the concept of peoples' rights which makes the collective the holder of the right as opposed to the individual. This further shows the distinctiveness of the African Charter as opposed to, say, the European Convention, which appears to place greater emphasis on the individual with little or no mention of group rights. The uniqueness of the Charter is also evident in its approach to duties owed both by the states and by individuals. This further reflects the Charter's communitarian and collective stance.

The additional protocol on women's rights is a step taken to protect this marginalised group whose history has been tainted with abuses and exploitations. Thus, far from being an unnecessary duplication of rights already contained in the Charter, this Protocol addresses and buttresses very germane issues that affect women and the girl child such as sexual health and child marriages. The next chapter will further demonstrate the importance of some of these provisions.

In summary, this chapter has shown the presence of a unique and dynamic normative human rights framework in Africa—one that involves a blend of civil and political rights, group rights, socio-economic rights, duties and responsibilities. Future chapters will examine the implementation of these rights as well as the operation of the African institutional human rights framework.

## Notes

1. See Rhona Smith, *Textbook on International Human Rights* (Oxford University Press 2013) 48.
2. Communication No. 71/92 (1996).
3. Communication No. 355/07 (2016).
4. *Forum of Conscience v. Sierra Leone*, Communication No. 223/98 (2000).
5. Consolidated Communication Nos. 54/91-61/91-96/93-98/93-164/97. *Malawi African Association & Others v Mauritania.*
6. *International PEN and Others v Nigeria*, Communication No. 137/94 (1998).
7. Communication No. 205/97 (2000).
8. Communication Nos. 279/03-296/05.
9. Communication No. 368/09.
10. Application No. 001/2015.
11. Communication No. 236/2000 (2003).
12. Criminal Law of 1991, Article 152.
13. Application No. 5856/72, European Court of Justice (1978).
14. Mashood Baderin, "Recent Developments in the African Regional Human Rights System" (2005) 5(1) *Harvard Rights Law Review* 133–137.
15. *Thomas Kwoyelo v Uganda*, Communication No. 431/12 (2018).
16. *Article 19 v The State of Eritrea*, Communication No. 275/2003 (2007).
17. *Achutan (on behalf of Banda) and Amnesty International (on behalf of Orton and Vera Chirwa) v. Malawi*, Communication Nos. 64/92, 68/92, and 78/92 (1995).
18. *Hadi & Ors v Republic of Sudan*, Communication No. 368/09.
19. Communication No. 129/94 (1995).
20. *Hadi & Ors v Republic of Sudan*, Communication No. 368/09.
21. Application No. 001/2015.
22. Communication No. 251/02.
23. Article 26 provides thus: "States parties to the present Charter shall have the duty to guarantee the independence of the Courts and shall allow the establishment and improvement of appropriate national institutions entrusted with the promotion and protection of the rights and freedoms guaranteed by the present Charter."
24. Communication Nos. 48/90, 50/91, 52/91, 89/93 (1999).
25. Communication No. 255/02.
26. African Commission, Declaration of Principles on Freedom of Expression in Africa, accessed April 29, 2016, https://www1.umn.edu/humanrts/achpr/expressionfreedomdec.html.
27. Communication Nos. 105/93, 128/94, 130/94 and 152/96 (1998).

28. Media Rights Agenda and Others v. Nigeria, African Commission on Human and Peoples' Rights, Communication Nos. 105/93, 128/94, 130/94 and 152/96 (1998) para 66.
29. Application No. 004/2013.
30. *Cumpana and Mazare v Romania*, Application No. 33348/96 (2004).
31. African Commission, accessed March 17, 2017, http://www.achpr.org/sessions/11th/resolutions/5/.
32. Communication No. 101/93.
33. Communication Nos. 54/91, 61/91, 98/93, 164/97_196/97 and 210/98.
34. Communication No. 228/99 (2003).
35. Application No. 009/2011.
36. *Lawyers of Human Rights v Swaziland*, Communication No. 251/02.
37. Communication No. 225/98.
38. Communication No. 215/98 (1999).
39. Communication No. 97/93.
40. 444/2013.
41. Constitutional Rights Project and Civil Liberties Organisation v. Nigeria, Communication No. 102/93 (1998).
42. Communication No. 251/02.
43. Communication Nos. 147/95 and 146/96.
44. Application Nos. 009&011/2011.
45. Communication Nos. 54/91-61/91-96/93-98/93-164/97_196/97-210/98.
46. Communication No. 288/04.
47. *Centre for Minority Rights Development (Kenya) and Minority Rights Group International on behalf of Endorois Welfare Council vs. Kenya*, Communication No. 276/2003, para 211.
48. *Dino Noca vs Democratic Republic of the Congo*, Communication No. 286/2004.
49. *Gabriel Shumba v Zimbabwe*, Communication No. 288/04.
50. *Social and Economic Rights Action Center, Center for Economic and Social Rights vs. Nigeria*, Communication No. 155/96.
51. Icelandic Human Rights Centre, The Right to Adequate Standard of Living, accessed June 2, 2019, http://www.humanrights.is/en/human-rights-education-project/human-rights-concepts-ideas-and-fora/substantive-human-rights/the-right-to-an-adequate-standard-of-living.
52. Christof Heyns, "The African Regional Human Rights System: In Need of Reform" (2001) 1 African Human Rights Law Journal 155.
53. Richard Gittleman, "The African Charter on Human and Peoples' Rights: A legal Analysis" (1982) 22 *Virginia Journal of International Law* 667, 700.
54. Communication No. 74/92.

55. Gittleman, "African Charter," 699.
56. Communication No. 155/96.
57. African Commission, accessed March 17, 2017, http://www.achpr.org/instruments/pretoria-declaration/.
58. 292/04.
59. *Zimbabwe Lawyers for Human Rights & Associated Newspapers of Zimbabwe v. Zimbabwe*, 284/03.
60. Communication No. 379/09.
61. Communication No. 255/02.
62. *Elgak and others v Sudan*, Communication No. 379/09.
63. 25/89-47/90-56/91-100/93: Free Legal Assistance Group, Lawyers' Committee for Human Rights, Union Interafricaine des Droits de l'Homme, Les Témoins de Jehovah/DRC.
64. Shedrack Agbakwa, "Reclaiming Humanity: Economic, Social, and Cultural Rights as the Cornerstone of African Human Rights" (2002) 5 *Yale Human Rights and Development Law Journal* 177, 193.
65. *Purohit and Moore v. The Gambia*, 241/01. See Sect. 6.4.2.
66. 54/91-61/91-96/93-98/93-164/97_196/97-210/98.
67. Communication No. 379/09.
68. International Covenant on Economic Social and Cultural Rights, Article 13.
69. *Centre for Minority Rights Development (Kenya) and Minority Rights Group (on behalf of Endorois Welfare Council) v Kenya*, Communication 276/03.
70. Frans Viljoen, *International Human Rights Law in Africa* (Oxford University Press 2012) 215.
71. Obinna Okere, "The Protection of Human Rights in Africa and the African Charter on Human and Peoples' Rights: A Comparative Analysis with the European and American Systems" (1984) 2 *Human Rights Quarterly* 141.
72. Viljoen, *International*, 218; Chidi Odinkalu, "Implementing Economic, Social and Cultural Rights Under the African Charter on Human and Peoples' Rights" in Malcolm Evans and Rachel Murray (eds.) *The African Charter on Human and People's Rights: The System in Practice, 1986–2000* (Cambridge University Press 2002); Agbakwa, "Reclaiming," 177.
73. Gittleman, "African Charter," 687.
74. Viljoen, *International*, 214.
75. Odinkalu, "Implementing Economic," 195.
76. Agbakwa, "Reclaiming," 177.
77. See Socio-Economic Rights and Accountability Project (SERAP) v. Federal Republic of Nigeria and Universal Basic Education Commission, No. ECW/CCJ/APP/0808.

78. Viljoen, *International*, 226.
79. African Commission International Workgroup for Indigenous Affairs, *Indigenous Peoples in Africa: The Forgotten Peoples?* (Transaction Publishers 2006) 10.
80. World Bank, Nigeria: Socio-Economic Overview (2014), accessed June 8, 2016, http://www.worldbank.org/content/dam/Worldbank/Feature%20Story/japan/pdf/event/2014/Africa-Business-Seminar-100314.pdf.
81. Republic of Cameroon, *Third Periodic Report of Cameroon Within the Framework of the African Charter on Human and Peoples' Rights* (2013) 142, accessed December 15, 2015, http://www.achpr.org/files/sessions/54th/state-reports/3-2008-2011/staterep3_cameroon_2013_eng.pdf.
82. Barney Pityana, "The Challenge of Culture for Human Rights in Africa: The African Charter in a Comparative Context" in Malcolm Evans and Rachel Murray (eds.) *The African Charter on Human and People's Rights: The System in Practice, 1986–2000* (Cambridge University Press 2002) 232.
83. 279/03-296/05: Sudan Human Rights Organisation & Centre on Housing Rights and Evictions (COHRE)/Sudan.
84. Communication No. 266/03.
85. Communication No. 227/99.
86. 75/92.
87. Ibid., para 6.
88. Gaetano Pentassuglia, "Indigenous Groups and the Developing Jurisprudence of the African Commission on Human and Peoples' Rights: Some Reflections" (2010) 3 *University College London Human Rights Review* 150, 155–156.
89. Centre for Minority Rights Development (Kenya) and another on behalf of the Endorois Welfare Council v. Kenya, Communication No. 276/2003.
90. Articles 8, 14, 17, 21 and 22, respectively.
91. International Network for Economic, Social and Cultural Rights, accessed July 8, 2014, http://www.escrnet.org/docs/i/1216218.
92. Application No. 006/2012.
93. Sudan Human Rights Organisation & Centre on Housing Rights and Evictions (COHRE)/Sudan, 279/03-296/05.
94. Robert Ackerman, "Tort Law and Communitarianism: Where Rights Meet Responsibilities" (1995) 30(4) Wake Forest Law Review 649.
95. Chaloka Beyani, *Reconstituting the Universal: Human Rights as a Regional Idea* (Cambridge University Press 2012) 179.
96. Pityana, "The Challenge," 229.
97. *Good v Botswana*, 313/05.

98. Michelo Hansungule, "The African Charter on Human and Peoples Rights: A Critical Review" (2000) 8 *African Yearbook of International Law* 265, 294.
99. Pityana (n 61) 229.
100. Shivji, *The Concept*, 98.
101. Makau wa Mutua, "Savages, Victims, and Saviors: The Metaphor of Human Rights" (2001) 42 *Harvard International Law Journal* 201.
102. Evelyn Ankumah, "Towards Effective Implementation of the African Charter" (1994) 8(3) *Interights Bulletin* 8, 60 cited in Barney Pityana (n 61).
103. Pityana (n 61) 229.
104. Elizabeth Scott, "Rehabilitating Liberalism in Modern Divorce Law" (1994) *Utah Law Review* 687.
105. Women's Protocol, Preamble.
106. See HRC General Comment 28, Equality of Rights between Men and Women, Article 3 UN Doc. CCPR/C/21/Rev.1/Add.10 (2000); UN Committee on the Elimination of Discrimination Against Women (CEDAW), CEDAW General Recommendation No. 21: Equality in Marriage and Family Relations, 1994, accessed June 22, 2016, http://www.refworld.org/docid/48abd52c0.html.
107. Mashood Baderin, "Modern Muslim States Between Islamic Law and International Human Rights Law" (PhD thesis, University of Nottingham 2001) 123.
108. *Egyptian Initiative for Personal Rights and Interights v Egypt*, Communication No. 323/06.
109. Magnus Killander and Bright Nkrumah, "Human Rights Developments in the African Union During 2012 and 2013" (2014) 14(1) *AHRLJ* 275, 281.
110. APDF & IHRDA v Republic of Mali, Application No. 046/2016.

CHAPTER 4

# Implementation and Compliance with the Charter Rights

## 4.1 Introduction

> The existence of constitutional provisions for specific civil and political rights is a necessary but insufficient condition for the legal protection of these rights… the question should always be whether the government is open and legally accountable to its citizens.[1]

> Today, it is generally agreed that there is no shortage of human rights norms. The most pressing problem is the implementation of these norms at the 'grass roots' and making them meaningful in people's lives.[2]

Having explored the substantive provisions of the African Charter, it is pertinent to examine its practical implementation and the level of compliance by states. Thus, do African states abide by the norms and duties prescribed by the Charter? Also, do the institutions charged with the promotion and protection of those rights and duties effectively play their roles as stipulated by the Charter? In simpler terms, while the previous chapter examined the 'ought' (i.e. the situation envisaged by the Charter), this chapter will examine the 'is' (i.e. what is the reality on the ground? What is the system in practice?).

In examining compliance with the Charter, the book will rely on two main types of reports. The first consist of state reports and Concluding Observations exchanged between the Commission and state parties. Article 62 of the Charter mandates state parties to submit, every two years,



A. Uwazuruike, *Human Rights under the African Charter*,
https://doi.org/10.1007/978-3-030-41739-0_4

a report on the 'legislative or other measures' taken to give effect to the rights in the Charter. Concluding observations, on the other hand, are assessments by the treaty body, in this case the African Commission, of the implementation of a treaty (in this case the African Charter) by a state. The second, which will be cursorily examined in the later part of this chapter, are reports of Special Rapporteurs and NGOs that work in partnership with the Commission.

State reports, as will be observed from the analysis below, are important given that they examine compliance with most of the rights explained in the previous chapter (i.e. including socio-economic and peoples' rights). On the other hand, NGO and Special Rapporteur reports appear to focus more on first-generation civil and political rights and are, therefore, important for drawing attention to the violation of those rights. This group of results are also necessary given the likelihood of states exaggerating compliance in the state reports.

## 4.2 Analysing Compliance Through State Reports and Concluding Observations of the Commission

The examination of state reports has been described as the core of the Commission's promotional mandate.[3] This is because it offers the Commission a direct means of engaging in a formal and constructive dialogue with states on their implementation of human rights and an avenue for making necessary reform proposals. The examination of state reports has further been identified as 'the most important means of monitoring compliance' with instruments at the international level.[4] It must however be noted, as will be seen in later sections, that such monitoring does not necessarily translate to the ability to change a state's behaviour and that the Commission does indeed lack coercive power.

The analysis of state reports and Concluding Observations is crucial for a credible assessment of the African human rights system in practice. This is because the exchange of reports and observations captures essential information that is mostly missed in other reports, namely the positive steps and policies that have been put in place by states to improve and comply with human rights obligations. This is a different approach from NGO and other reports which generally tend to ignore these positive human rights developments with the focus being almost exclusively on violations. While states would usually attempt to highlight their achievements in the reports, the Commission in their own feedback (Concluding Observations) would, while acknowledging whatever positive developments there are, still draw the states' attention to important violations and lapses. For instance, state reports reveal a host of legislative, executive and judicial human rights measures that have been initiated by state parties, ignorance of which would impair any credible assessment of compliance with the Charter provisions. Also, it is important to point out that the Charter, aside from requiring states to protect rights, also tasks them with the promotion of rights through teaching, education and publications.[5] It is ideally through such state reports that the Commission may set about gauging how effectively these rights are being promoted and make further recommendations on how promotional and other obligations may be better observed. This process can thus be likened to a system of self-assessment and subsequent objective feedback.

Also, state reports and Concluding Observations create a more complete and holistic assessment of the human rights situation in individual countries. This they do by addressing most of the relevant areas and sections of the African Charter and its accompanying Protocols. They, therefore, address the implementation of the different classes of rights: civil and political, socio-economic and peoples' and women's rights. This is important in determining whether there is a balance in the treatment of the different categories of rights or whether there is more focus on particular rights or categories at the expense of others.

In analysing the content of state reports, this book will focus on the reports of states from each of the following sub-regions of the continent: East, West, Northern, Central and Southern Africa. The aim is to ensure a geographical spread and to avoid the possibility of concentrating analysis on just one part of the continent. The countries selected in that order are: Uganda, Nigeria, Sudan, Cameroon and Malawi. The factors taken into consideration for selection include states with the most up to date submissions, geographical size, population, volatility and high level of criticism for human rights infringements.

Nigeria was chosen largely for its size and for having up-to-date reports. With a population of over 200 million people, Nigeria is, by far Africa's most populous state. Its sheer size is all the more noticeable within West Africa—a subregion of just under 400 million people. Cameroon was selected as the only Central African state, at the time of commencing research for this book, with complete state reports on the

African Commission's website. With over 23 million inhabitants, it is the third most populous state in the subregion. Sudan was chosen to represent Northern Africa owing to having a relatively recent state report and also for the human rights issues that have arisen due to the crisis and political instability in that country. It is important to point out that the term 'Northern Africa' as used in this book is distinct from 'North Africa' whose definition remains disputed and is, in political spheres, taken to refer to four countries, namely Morocco, Tunisia, Libya and Algeria. Like Cameroon above, Uganda and Malawi were selected for having more recent state reports at the time of research. While focus will be on the reports of these countries, due regard is other had to sources from other African countries such as Kenya, South Africa and Libya.

Understandably, analyses of the chosen countries cannot literally be said to be representative of the human rights situations in those regions. They, first and foremost, represent the human rights situation in those countries for the periods covered in the reports. However, it is necessary, for practical purposes, to examine a representative sample of states as it would be quite onerous and verbose to undertake an examination of each of the 55 states in Africa. On the whole, it is envisaged that the sum total of analyses would give an indication of the general practice of human rights across the continent.

Analysis of the state reports will be subdivided into civil/political rights, socio-economic rights and group rights with emphasis on the most recurrent violations. Special attention will also be paid to women's rights as covered under an additional protocol to the Charter.

### *4.2.1 Civil and Political Rights*

An examination of the state reports and Concluding Observations shows an emphasis on the following rights and freedom: the right to life, freedom from torture and the right to a fair trial.

#### *4.2.1.1 Right to Life (Article 4)*

The Commission's Concluding Observations highlight instances of extrajudicial killings, maintenance of the death penalty and cases of arbitrary arrests. It will be recalled, as regards the latter, that the Commission has held that a series of arrests and detentions could in themselves constitute a violation of the right to life even though there was no actual loss of life.[6] On the death penalty, the Charter does not expressly forbid its practice although, as will be seen, the Commission has constantly pushed for its abolition.

In its observations on Nigeria's 2014 4th periodic report covering the period 2011–2014, the Commission expressed concerns over cases of extra-judicial killings in the country.[7] These concerns expectedly heightened following even more allegations of extrajudicial killings against the Nigerian government in its fight against Boko Haram.[8] For instance, the Associated Press reports that in June of 2013 (30 days) the Nigerian Army delivered 1795 bodies to a single mortuary in Maiduguri, the birthplace of Boko Haram.[9] In November 2016, Amnesty International reported that over 150 persons were killed in a vicious government crackdown on members of a secessionist movement, the indigenous people of Biafra.[10] That same year a judicial inquiry concluded that Nigerian troops should be prosecuted for the 2015 killing of 349 Shia Muslims in the northern city of Zaria. The Shiites were reportedly killed and buried without family members' permission.[11] A military source had reportedly explained the motivation behind the brutal army crackdown as 'intended to teach the Shia a lesson' after members of the group had stopped the convoy of the army's Chief of Staff in Zaria.[12]

The Commission, in its observations, had directed Nigeria to enact a law criminalising torture and appoint a commission to investigate and make public the findings of all extrajudicial executions and enforced disappearances. However, in its most recent observation, the Commission noted that Nigeria had not reported on any steps taken to investigate and prosecute alleged perpetrators of these violations from among its military personnel.[13]

Nigeria responded to the Commission's enquiries on Boko Haram in its 2018 report covering the period 2015–2016. It acknowledged official records that showed that over 100,000 people had died as a result of the Boko Haram insurgency while 2.1 million others had been displaced. It reported that the government had secured the release of 103 kidnapped schoolgirls and resettling over 2 million internally displaced persons. The report goes further to state that the country's National Human Rights Commission (NHRC) had inaugurated a Nigerian Military Human Rights Dialogue aimed at promoting human rights awareness and ensuring the 'speedy resolution' of allegations of human rights violations against the Nigerian army. The Dialogue had, among other resolutions, recommended that the Human Rights Institute of the NHRC play a leading role both in ensuring that human rights education forms a core part of the military training curriculum and investigating violations by military units and personnel.

Another state that caused concerns with regard to police killings was Malawi. In its 2014 report covering the period 1995–2013, the Malawian government admitted to experiencing difficulties in curbing the arbitrary killing of citizens, especially during protests. It cited the example of the events of July 2011, where nationwide demonstrations organised by civil society organisations resulted in the death of 20 people, 19 of whom died from gunshot wounds inflicted by the police while one person suffocated from inhaling tear gas.[14]

On the issue of the death penalty, there is an almost general violation by all the states examined. The Commission's observations have called on Uganda, Nigeria and Sudan to observe moratoriums on the death penalty with a view to abolishing it. In Cameroon's case, the observation noted that the country maintained the death penalty despite a de facto moratorium since 1997.[15] The Commission's observations also highlighted cases of arbitrary arrests and detentions largely permitted by Sudan's National Security Act of 2010, the content of which will be examined presently.

In their reports, the states generally express disagreement with the Commission's stance on the death penalty while often retaining hope for reform. For instance, Uganda, while reiterating the constitutional provision allowing the practice, drew the attention of the Commission to a 2009 Supreme Court ruling upholding the argument that it was unreasonable to keep an inmate on death row for more than three years, after which time their sentence must be commuted to life imprisonment. It stated that as of April 2013, 224 inmates on death row had had their sentences commuted to life imprisonment.[16] In its response to the Commission, Nigeria simply maintained the constitutionality of the death penalty pointing out that this position had been upheld by the Nigerian Supreme Court.[17] Similarly, the Sudanese government, in disagreeing with the Commission, maintained that the death penalty would be applied in the case of 'very serious crimes in accordance with the law'.[18]

It must be stated that the Charter itself does not expressly forbid the death penalty with the only driving force being resolutions adopted both by the African Commission and the United Nations.[19] The Commission has however gone a step further by adopting, in 2015, a 'draft protocol to the African Charter on Human and Peoples' Rights on the Abolition of the Death Penalty in Africa' which was subsequently brought before the African Union.[20] Until this draft Protocol goes through the necessary process of adoption and ratification whereby it becomes a part of the Charter, member states may argue, not without some validity, that they are not in violation of the Charter by allowing the death penalty in their laws. In any case, it should be pointed out that more countries have either abolished or initiated a moratorium on the death penalty than not. As of 2019, all but 13 African countries had either abolished or issued a moratorium on its practice.

#### 4.2.1.2 *Freedom from Torture, Cruel, Inhuman and Degrading Treatment (Article 5)*

Another human right that features prominently in both the reports and observations is the freedom from torture, cruel, inhuman and degrading treatment. Violations of these are usually in the form of police torture of crime suspects, prison overcrowding and harassment of detainees. For instance, the Commission called attention to the use of torture by Nigerian and Sudanese officials, harsh prison conditions in Sudan and prison overcrowding in Cameroun. In Sudan's case, the Commission noted that there was no law criminalising torture in the country. Rather, Sudan's laws provided for several forms of corporal punishment such as stoning, amputation, cross-amputation and whipping. Some of these punishments were routinely meted out, particularly against women from marginalised backgrounds, following summary trials. These forms of punishment, the Commission stated, were cruel, inhuman and degrading. The Commission also expressed disappointment on the rise of police brutality in Uganda and urged the Ugandan government to speed up the process for the adoption of its Anti-Torture Bill.

In their reports, the states have revealed legislative and other measures taken to tackle these practices. For instance, Uganda reported the initiation of legislative measures against torture including the passing of the Prohibition and Prevention of Torture Bill as previously recommended by the Commission. Similarly, Nigeria, following the Commission's recommendation, passed the Anti-Torture Act 2017 into law. Another state in need of such legislative measure is Malawi which, in its last submitted report, acknowledged the existing legislative loophole whereby torture had not been criminalised such that alleged perpetrators could only be charged with offences such as assault, or causing grievous bodily harm.

With regard to administrative measures, the Nigerian government reported that its NHRC was investigating cases of torture and that a committee had previously been established to review complaints of torture in police cells although, as the Commission subsequently noted, the said committee had not yet made any reports more than six years since its creation. Similarly, Uganda reported the establishment of a Professional Standards Unit and a Human Rights Desk to deal with complaints from the general public regarding the conduct of members of the police force. The Uganda Prisons Service even had an Assistant Commissioner tasked specifically with handling human rights issues of prisoners. In a similar vein, Malawi, in 2014, reported the recent creation of an Independent Complaints Commission to investigate complaints of brutality, deaths or misconduct at the hands of the police. There were also provisions for a Lay Visitors Scheme whereby a team of local people would inspect conditions of police stations and places of detention. Importantly, however, the government cast doubt on its ability to enforce these based on available resources and capacity. It also acknowledged the lack of adequate mechanisms for reporting incidents of alleged torture either at the hands of the police officers or prison authorities.

The significance of such concessions as the above, in the context of states' ability to protect and implement rights, will be discussed more thoroughly in the next chapter. At this stage, it is only necessary to observe that these states often do not have the capacity to implement policies even where they exist. This is significant because it shows that failure to observe rights is not always solely attributable to dictatorial or legislative factors as the existence of laws or democratic governments may not in themselves guarantee human rights protection where the government is incapacitated through the lack of adequate finance and infrastructure.

#### *4.2.1.3 Right to Fair Trial (Article 7)*

The state reports and Concluding Observations also highlight violations of the right to fair trial especially the right to be tried within a reasonable time by an impartial court or tribunal. It must be pointed out here that, as discussed in the preceding section, failure to implement this right did not owe solely to the lack of appropriate legislations as most of the states studied had the requisite provisions for bringing suspects before the courts. Rather part of the problem lay with governments' incapacity to cope with the demand for these services. For instance, Malawi noted that despite provisions to arraign suspects in court within 48 hours, this was not always feasible given the lack of courts in some localities and the poor police-citizen ratio. Also, the criminal justice system was so overwhelmed that criminal cases, especially serious ones like homicides took a long time to be decided.

However, it was not always the case that appropriate laws were in place to safeguard these rights. One clear case of this is Sudan's National Security Act 2010 which allows security officials to detain suspects for up to four and a half months without judicial review before charges are levied. The said Act also provided members of the National Intelligence and Security Service and their associates with immunity from criminal and civil procedures for acts connected with the official work of the member. The Commission observed that this Act had been the basis of several human rights infringements including incommunicado detentions and called for the Sudanese government to repeal the offending articles.

### *4.2.2 Socio-Economic Rights*

This section will cover individual socio-economic rights, namely the rights to health and education. Other collective socio-economic rights will be discussed under the heading 'peoples' rights'.

#### *4.2.2.1 Right to Health (Article 16)*

This area is extensively covered in all of the reports with the major cited challenges being the prevalence and high mortality rates from malaria and HIV, and the lack of access to basic health facilities. The various reports detail governments' steps in tackling these challenges and ameliorating their general negative impact. For instance, Uganda stated that the government spent about $43 per capita on health, which was 'about the same as its low-income country peers'.[21] The latter part of this statement is important for future discussions on the role of finance and infrastructure in implementing these standards. Furthermore, Uganda reported that steps had also been taken to increase the number of health centres and workers through the construction of six regional health centres with fully functional mental units. According to the Uganda National Household Survey 2009/2010, government health units and traditional birth attendants were reported to be the nearest health facilities/providers to the communities. On its part, the Sudanese government highlighted the features of the country's health insurance scheme which applied to state employees, the private sector and retirees. By this scheme, the medical and healthcare expenses of its beneficiaries and their families would be met.

These steps notwithstanding, the reports acknowledge a general poor state of health especially with respect to fighting malaria which remains the leading cause of death in the continent followed by HIV/AIDS. In Sudan alone, malaria accounted for 17.5% of deaths/morbidity in all outdoor patients according to the state report. The baseline of HIV prevalence in 15–24-year-old pregnant women in Malawi was as high as 24.1% in 2000 though the country reported improved figures of 12% in 2011. Cameroon reported an uneven distribution of health personnel across the country and the unequal access to quality health care between the urban and rural areas.[22] In addition, the Commission noted that there was 'limited free medical coverage' for children below five years and pregnant women, and a high rate of maternal and child mortality despite government efforts. In explaining the extent of its 'free health care', Cameroon stated that this was provided for some diseases and target persons such as malaria in children below five and expectant mothers.

The question that ordinarily arises is whether, with regard to its 'limited free medical coverage', a country like Cameroon is adequately fulfilling its duty under the Charter to protect the health of its people. It would be recalled that Article 16 of the Charter entitles every individual, and not just a few, to the best attainable state of physical and mental health. However, as already highlighted in Chapter 3, the Commission has interpreted this provision to mean that states must take 'concrete and targeted steps' while taking full advantage of their available resources, to ensure the full realisation of this right. This would be similar to the position of the United Nations Committee on Economic Social and Cultural Rights that state parties to that Covenant strive to ensure the widest possible enjoyment of the rights under their respective prevailing circumstances.[23] Given this interpretation, it may reasonably be argued that Cameroon's limited provision for malaria in expectant mothers and children below five years would amount to 'concrete and targeted steps'. This may also satisfy the requirement for the state to take full advantage of its available resources if it were shown, for instance, that the country could not afford to extend such services to other affected age grades and groups. However, the challenging bit is in the last part of the Commission's interpretation to 'ensure the full realisation' of the right. It may be argued that a literal interpretation of this latter provision is incompatible with the condition to take full advantage of available resources and must, therefore, be interpreted in the light of that condition. 'Full realisation' would, therefore, be dependent on the specific situation of each state and the resources available to it. To this end, it may be posited that Cameroon is well within its duties to provide health care as long as it has taken 'full advantage' of its available resources, the latter being an assessment that must be left to the appropriate judicial authority.

However, the important question for the purpose of the chapter is whether to adjudge a state, say Cameroon in this instance, as having fulfilled its duty to protect health under the Charter because it has used its available resources to protect a tiny section of the populace while the majority is denied this protection. It is argued that this approach would defeat the essence of the Charter. In order to give full meaning to the dictates of the Charter, there is the need to add a further 'majority test' to the availability criterion. By this test, an adequate section (or majority) of the populace must be afforded protection according to the state's available resources for that state to be judged as having fulfilled its duty under the Charter. Where a majority of the populace is not protected, then that state must be adjudged to have failed in its duty whether it lacks the available resources or not. This, of course, would impose a huge task on states that lack the resources to adequately protect these rights but is important to create a more accurate picture and measurement of the protection of that right. Thus, the absence of resources should mainly be seen as a challenge to the implementation of rights and not as the main criterion for measuring compliance. It is only after the 'real' state of implementation has been accurately determined that a proper and effective solution can be proposed and implemented. Accordingly, the studied countries, given their statistics on mortality from malaria and HIV and general lack of access to adequate healthcare, should be rightly adjudged to have failed in fulfilling their duties under the right to health regardless of the amount of resources available to those countries.

It is also important to state that, as is the case for some infringements discussed above, the exercise of the right to health could also be affected by certain cultural and religious beliefs. In one instance, Sudan reported that some parents refused to vaccinate their children against the measles outbreak because of their religious beliefs. In the ensuing court case,[24] 11 of such parents were convicted and fined for failure to provide necessities of life for their children. Similarly, the Commission has expressed worry over Nigerian laws criminalising homosexual unions as this had the potential 'to drive this group of persons vulnerable to HIV/AIDS underground' thereby making it difficult to effectively address the HIV pandemic in the state. It, accordingly, recommended review of the legislation and tasked Nigeria to ensure the protection of sexual minorities.

The Commission's bravery in raising this issue deserves commendation especially given the wide support such legislation has across African states such as Nigeria. The Nigerian government's response, in 2018, to the Commission's recommendation was rather cryptic: 'Nigeria notes this recommendation'. Such a terse response would appear to emphasise the country's strong stance against same-sex unions. More than the subject of capital punishment covered above, legalisation on same-sex unions would appear to be a red line for the Nigerian state. Again, the state reporting system is able, not only to raise questions on the subject, but also to capture the country's disposition to it.

#### *4.2.2.2 Right to Education (Article 17)*

As pointed out in Chapter 3, the Charter does not elaborate on the contents of this right but merely provides that everyone shall have the right to education. However, from the issues raised by both the Commission and states, one can deduce some of the contents and responsibilities covered under this right. One of these is the provision of free primary school education. Thus, the Commission has consistently called on states to provide free and compulsory primary education, especially for the girl child. Also, the states have generally taken to running free primary school education programmes even though the quality and sustainability of these programmes are often in doubt given the paucity of resources. Uganda reported that access to free primary education increased by almost 180% from 3.1 million pupils in 1996 to about 8.7 million in 2010, further improving to 9.2 million pupils in 2012. Nigeria and Malawi also reported the operation of free primary school education in their respective countries.

States have also made strong attempts to extend free education beyond the primary level to secondary and even tertiary levels. For instance, Uganda reported the initiation of a Universal Secondary Education Programme which saw the award of free tuition to at least four 'secondary school going children' per family. Nigeria also reported the construction of junior girls' model secondary schools in 13 states of the federation aimed at addressing the high rate of girls who were out of school. Malawi reported a 'heavily subsidised' university education which had seen the literacy rate improve from 68% in 2000 to 84% in 2011.

Interestingly, the prevailing situation is similar to previously discussed rights despite the steps taken by states. Uganda has stated that in spite of the high enrolment in schools, retention rates, especially for the girl child, remained poor due to social, economic and cultural pressures. Similarly, Malawi stated that the millennium development goal of achieving universal primary education by 2015 was unlikely to be met due to economic constraints. In Nigeria, only about 44% of children of primary school entry age (age 6) were attending the first grade of primary school. North–South disparity was noticeable here with up to 92% attendance in the South-West and only 48% in the North-East signifying a link between attendance and other factors such as culture and poverty. The economic status of families was yet another indicator with the primary school net attendance ratio for children in rich households standing at about 94% compared to 34% in the poorest households.

### *4.2.3 States' View on Enforcement of Socio-Economic Rights*

It is not clear from the state reports whether states view socio-economic rights as having the same status as negative rights, especially as regards enforceability. One can, however, glean a view more in line with 'progressive realisation'. This is more so the case given that most African countries do not grant enforceability to these rights in their constitutions. Thus, despite what may appear as the clear dictates and intent of the Charter, member states appear to have taken the easy route. With the exception of South Africa and, more recently, Kenya there is little indication of indivisibility in the jurisprudence of domestic courts across the continent.[25] For example, the Nigerian Court of Appeal has held that 'the arbiter for any breach of the Objectives and Directive Principles of State Policy is the legislature itself or the electorate'.[26] This precludes judicial intervention and suggests that the only way to guarantee these rights is for citizens to vote out incompetent governments—an unsatisfactory remedy given the long time it takes between elections and massive electoral malpractices that characterise many African elections. It has been argued that by relegating socio-economic rights to non-justiciable directive principles of state policy, states contradict one of the core principles of the African Charter.

## 4.3 Peoples' Rights

As has already been discussed in previous chapters, Africa is peculiar for the multi-ethnicity and vast cultural disparities in several of its countries. Consequently, there is the need to protect 'all the peoples' of Africa especially indigenous groups and populations who may be at risk of suppression by more dominant groups. Chapter 3 has already highlighted exemplary decisions by the Commission in the *Ogoni* and *Endorois* cases.

Of the five countries studied, the Commission made observations on this group of rights for three countries, namely Cameroon, Uganda and Nigeria. Analysis of these will be done under the following two headings: right to free disposal of wealth and natural resources with allusions to the right to economic, social and cultural development, and the right to a general satisfactory environment.

### *4.3.1 Right to Free Disposal of Wealth and Natural Resources and the Rights to Social and Cultural Development (Articles 21 and 22)*

The Commission identified serious breaches of this right by Cameroon. It criticised the delay in finalising the study on the identification of indigenous communities and lack of concrete steps taken to enact a law on indigenous populations as previously recommended both by the Commission and the United Nations Committee on the Elimination of Racial Discrimination. In its recommendations, the Commission directed Cameroon to enact, with the participation of the indigenous people, a specific law recognising the latter's rights of ownership over their ancestral lands. A similar directive had previously been issued both by the Commission, in its previous Concluding Observation of 2010, and the United Nations Committee on the Elimination of Racial Discrimination.[27] Indigenous populations were also to be allowed effective participation in all ongoing and future legislative and political reforms having an impact on their rights. The Commission also recommended the adoption of a quota system or co-optation for university graduates from indigenous communities to facilitate their participation in decision-making institutions.

In its report, Cameroon stated that it had begun discussions on the identification of indigenous populations in the country and also taken steps to ensure socio-economic inclusion of indigenous populations. The latter was accomplished through vocational training and consideration of the interests of indigenous populations in the forestry policy and hydro-electric projects.

In Uganda's case, the Commission identified the need to establish laws that protect land rights and natural resources of indigenous populations. Legislative measures like Uganda's Forest Bill did not, in the Commission's view, take into adequate account the rights of indigenous peoples. Overall, indigenous populations were not fully aware nor effectively involved in decision-making processes on issues that directly affected them such as land and forest law reforms. Other expressed areas of concern on peoples' rights include: the expansion of agriculture and extractive industries which threatened the rights of indigenous populations to their ancestral lands, through the granting of land concessions for development projects without the prior, free and informed consent of the indigenous people; the lack of an appropriate legal framework to eliminate the discrimination and marginalisation of indigenous populations, particularly by ensuring that their customary ownership rights are promoted and protected under the law; and the absence of schools and health centres in close proximity to indigenous populations thereby limiting their access to basic social services.

In response to the Commission's recommendation to establish laws that protect land rights and natural resources of indigenous populations, Uganda stated that Article 244 of its constitution provided for the enactment of legislation by parliament to regulate the exploitation of mineral and the sharing of royalties. Despite having already passed two laws on exploration, refining and gas processing, the Ugandan Parliament was yet to pass the draft Public Finance Bill which envisaged the payment of royalties to districts.

### *4.3.2 Right to a General Satisfactory Environment (Article 24)*

Of the states studied, Nigeria was the most criticised in this regard. This was largely due to environmental degradation and damage caused by large-scale oil exploration and extraction. One such example is the case of the Ogoni people which has been briefly discussed in Chapter 3.

In its observation, the Commission directed Nigeria to take all necessary steps to ensure that companies in the extractive industry lived up to the high standards of human rights as espoused in the Charter. This, in the Commission's view, could be done by, for example, revoking the licences of companies that failed to live up to such standards. In its response to the Commission's recommendation on environmental degradation, the Nigerian government stated that it had established the Nigeria Extractive Industries Transparency Initiative (NEITI) which was empowered to promote due process, transparency and accountability in extractive industries and to prosecute defaulters of the NEITI Act. The report, however, stated that greater political will and staff capacity building were the twin challenges that needed to be addressed before NEITI could perform credibly. These added challenges of political will and human resources will be duly considered in Chapter 5.

## 4.4 Women's Rights

It would be recalled that an additional protocol to the Charter, in the form of the Women's Protocol, was adopted in order to better protect the rights of women in the continent. As such, the Commission has taken to calling member states' attention to violations of these rights. It should, however, be noted that, unlike the Charter, the Women's Protocol does not have near unanimous ratification. As of March 2019, only 36 out of 54 states have ratified the Protocol.[28] Of the five states studied, only Sudan has defaulted in this regard which inevitably raises the question of whether Sudan can rightly be assessed based on the provisions of the Protocol. While it should ordinarily be the case that Sudan would not be bound by the provisions of this Protocol not having ratified it, it should be considered that many of the Protocol's provisions can rightly be argued under the provisions of the Charter. What the Women's Protocol has mainly done, in essence, is to flesh out the rights in the Charter taking into particular consideration the peculiar situation and experiences of women in the continent. Accordingly, the Commission has taken to highlighting perceived violations in Sudan even though it has not ratified the Protocol, and Sudan has in turn routinely replied and addressed such observations.

The major recurrent themes under which these rights will be discussed are violence against women, poor representation in government and inequality in marriage.

### 4.4.1 *Violence Against Women (Articles 3, 4 and 5)*

These are often either in the form of domestic violence or harmful practices such as female genital mutilation (FGM). With regard to the latter, Nigeria reported that 27% of its women aged 15–49 years had one form of genital cutting or the other. Here, results varied across geopolitical zones with 48% of such women coming from the South-West and only 3% from the North-East of the country. The distinction across zones is important in illustrating the role of culture and religion in either increasing or reducing this practice. Incidentally, FGM appears to be a popular practice among some African countries with the Commission further identifying its prevalence in Sudan and Cameroon.

Domestic violence was also identified in some of the countries studied with both the state reports and Concluding Observations highlighting instances of violations in Nigeria, Sudan, Cameroon and Malawi. Some instances of infringements were no doubt influenced by cultural perceptions of the superiority of the male gender, especially within the marriage setting. In its report, Nigeria detailed the results of a survey wherein 48% of women felt that their husbands or partners had a right to hit or beat them for at least one reason[29]; 48% of these were married women while 37% had never been married. Such dispositions, especially by the perceived victims of such actions, show that member states have failed in their duty to create awareness and sensitise the local populations on the rights of women.

While it may well be argued that the prevalence of these practices is clear evidence of failure on the part of the member states, it has to be pointed out that some of these practices have flourished in spite of the efforts of governments. For instance, while highlighting the continued practice of FGM in Cameroon, the Commission stated that this was the case 'despite government efforts to eradicate it'. The Sudanese government reported the existence of a special unit within its Council of Ministers for combating violence against women and children. On its part, Malawi adopted policies and laws aimed at addressing some of the challenges affecting the family unit. One example is the Prevention of Domestic Violence Act which seeks to protect persons affected by domestic violence. Other legislative measures include the Domestic Violence Act, Employment Act 2006, Trafficking in Persons Act, 2009, and the Prohibition of Genital Mutilation Act, 2010. Similarly, Nigeria passed the Gender and Equal Opportunities Act 2015, which prohibits FGM and domestic violence against women. There was no such luck, however, in passing the Gender and Equal Opportunities Bill, which effectively seeks to domesticate the Women's Protocol. The Nigerian Senate rejected the bill on the grounds that it was not in line with the religious and cultural beliefs of the people. Granted that the impact of local culture on the implementation of Charter will be discussed in the next chapter, it is necessary to point out here a clear conflict between the country's executive that has ratified the Women's Protocol and the Senate that believes that some of its provisions are incompatible with native religion and customs. Indeed, it has been argued that the Senate's position only reflects patriarchal norms and the general perception of male superiority in the country.[30]

### *4.4.2 Inequalities in Marriage (Article 6)*

Article 6 of the Women's Protocol directs state parties to ensure that women and men enjoy equal rights and are regarded as equal partners in marriage. Some of the ingredients of such equality are the free and full consent of both parties before a marriage can take place, a minimum age at marriage of 18 years for women, and the right of a woman to hold property in her name during and after the marriage.

The reports show that early and forced marriages are rather common across the selected countries. In the case of Cameroon, the Commission observed the continuous practice of early and forced marriages among young indigenous girls which invariably affected their reproductive health. In its report, Nigeria provided statistics that showed that about 20% of young women aged 15–19 years were married with 8% being from the urban areas and 18% from rural areas. Only 6% of these had secondary education while 72% had no education at all. Again, the numbers varied across geopolitical zones with 52% of women in the North-West and only 2% in the South-East in early marriages. It has to be pointed out here that Nigeria is split into six geopolitical zones, namely the South-East, South-West, South-South, North-East, North-West and North-Central.

Eighteen per cent of women were married before age 15 while 40% married before age 18, failing to meet the minimum standard set by the Women's Protocol. About 52% of married women aged 15–19 were married to men 10 or more years older, many of which marriages were polygamous. The report pointed out that the results were significantly different between zones in the North and South as well as urban and rural areas.

Again, this draws attention to custom and literacy levels. The education of women was also identified as an important determinant.

The reports show that some states have taken steps to enhance the protection of women's rights within marriage by recognising rights such as the right to own property. For instance, Uganda drew attention to its Marriage and Divorce Bill which was brought before parliament in May 2011. The Bill addresses women's rights during marriage including the right to own property both during and after the dissolution of a marriage. On its part, Malawi pointed out that its constitution makes copious provisions for family and marriage rights. For instance, Section 24 of the country's Constitution specifically provides for the rights of women granting them equal protection under the law and capacity to enter contracts, acquire property and retain custody of children, among others. However, the state conceded that it faced challenges in ensuring equality of rights and responsibilities within the marriage due to a clear discrepancy between the declaration of equality in the Constitution and the actual relationship that exists between men and women. This was primarily due to cultural practices that favoured men over women and the male child over the female. Examples of such cultural practices were where a woman was forced to marry her brother-in-law following the death of her husband, or where a male child was given financial support to go to school while the female child was made to stay at home and look after the family. To tackle some of these challenges, a comprehensive review of laws on marriage and divorce was conducted which resulted in the Marriage and Divorce Bill. A Prevention of Domestic Violence Act was also passed to deal with cases of violence against women.

### *4.4.3 Political Participation (Article 9)*

Another important area that the Commission has tasked the states on is in the political representation and participation of women. Article 9 of the Women's Protocol requires state parties to take 'specific positive action' to promote participative governance and the equal participation of women in the political life of their countries. The reports show a mixed result with some states having a relatively good level of female participation in government and other states having less. For instance, the Commission commended Uganda on its 30% representation of women councillors and women in parliament. The situation was slightly different in Cameroon.

In its Initial Report of 2004, the government had presented information that showed a steady decline in the proportion of female members of parliament. From 14.5% in 1987, representation had fallen to 5.5% in 1997.[31] However, the country's subsequent report showed an increased female representation of 13.89% in 2008.[32] This notwithstanding, the Commission has recommended the enactment of a quota law and adoption of a 50% quota for women in order to increase their representation in decision-making. In its later report, the Cameroonian government stated that even though the prescribed 50% quota had not been attained, initiatives like the National Gender Policy were going a long way in guaranteeing the enjoyment of the same rights by both men and women.

One may argue that the Commission's proposed 50% quota for women is ambitious given that only three countries in the world—Rwanda, Bolivia and Cuba—have reached this mark according to a World Bank 2018 report.[33] It should also be pointed out that an African country, Rwanda, has the highest proportion of women in parliament at 61%.

While none of the states studied had met the 50% goal set by the Commission, steps were at least taken to carve out places for women in government. For instance, in Sudan, women were encouraged to participate in politics with the allocation of 25% of the legislative seats (in addition to other seats) in the 2008 Elections Act. As at the time of the report, women occupied 28% of seats in parliament and their number in the National Legislature Council had risen from 7% in 2004 to 25% in the 2010 elections. Nigeria also noted the increase in women's representation in governance with 33% of female appointments at the federal executive level. Meanwhile, Malawi reported that women in the National Assembly had increased from 5.65% in 1994 to 22.85% in 2009. Also, many women had regularly vied for political positions with quite a few getting elected. For instance, in the country's 2009 General Elections, 237 women contested for elected positions and 43 were elected. The only female contestant in the presidential race came fifth out of seven candidates.[34]

An interesting observation was made by Cameroon which, in its initial report, noted that even though 30.6% of public employees were women, they were mostly concentrated at the lower levels of the public service hierarchy. Interestingly, the report states that one of the determinants of female distribution in the public service was whether men were willing to allocate certain roles to women. Just as with some of the cases highlighted above, one can detect the influence of cultural and patriarchal leanings in the exercise and implementation of this right.

## 4.5 Special Rapporteur Statements

Special Rapporteurs oversee specialised areas of human rights and as such can only offer an overview of those areas. However, their appointments are a strong pointer to the areas of human rights which the Commission views as problematic and needing extra attention. These areas are the treatment/harassment of human rights defenders (HRDs), freedom of expression, women's rights, rights of prisoners and refugee rights. From the available reports, there appears to be a strong focus on the harassment of HRDs and restrictions on freedom of expression and assembly. An examination of some of the affected countries shows that these violations mostly occur in volatile areas experiencing electoral or armed conflicts. For instance, the Special Rapporteur on Refugees, Asylum Seekers, Internally Displaced Persons and Migrants in Africa expressed concerns about the decision of the Republic of Sudan to expel international and national humanitarian organisations and their personnel from Darfur, in the wake of the ICC indictment of President Omar El Bashir. It should be pointed out that Sudan has been embroiled in years of civil war and conflict that have seen its leadership accused of gross human rights violations and war crimes. Attention has also been drawn to increasingly disturbing situation of refugees owing to sustained conflicts across the continent especially in the Central African Republic, South Sudan, Somalia, Nigeria and the Democratic Republic of Congo.[35]

The Special Rapporteur on HRDs has consistently drawn attention to the persecution of human rights activists. One such report highlighted the assassination of HRDs in the Democratic Republic of Congo. Another report raised concerns on the plight of the women HRDs in Zimbabwe known as Women of Zimbabwe Arise (WOZA) with the Special Rapporteur detailing acts of violence and harassments against that group. In 2015, the Special Rapporteur met with HRDs to discuss the achievements and challenges recorded in the past ten years. On the conditions of HRDs, the Special Rapporteur stated:

> As they continue to function in volatile environments their operations and officers continue to suffer from harassments, premises clamped down and face arbitrary arrests and detentions, while allegations of forced disappearances, summary, and extrajudicial executions remain reported in great numbers.[36]

She also cited reports of violations and harassment of women HRDs including unfavourable working environments, patriarchal customs and national laws 'which deny women HRDs the full enjoyment of their rights'. There were also reports of sexual violence and murder of women HRDs who defend variations in sexual orientation (i.e. LGBT rights) and 'gender identity' both of which were reportedly perceived as Eurocentric norms. It needs to be pointed out that many African states have laws prohibiting LGBT acts and unions. More recently, in 2019, the Special Rapporteur on HRDs issued a press release on the arrest of over 200 opposition party members in Cameroon.[37]

Special Rapporteurs have also called states' attention to potential infringements such as in Kenya where the Special Rapporteur called on the state to reject proposed bills that conflicted with the Charter's provisions on the freedom of expression.[38] This particular plea was heeded with Kenyan lawmakers rejecting the bill by 83–73 votes, with eight MPs abstaining.[39] More recently, in 2019, the Special Rapporteur on Freedom of Expression and Access to Information has expressed concerns over recurrent cases of government shutdown of the internet in Chad, Sudan, the Democratic Republic of Congo, Gabon and Zimbabwe. The rapporteur also called on the Nigerian government to take necessary steps to ensure full implementation of the country's Freedom of Information Act.

## 4.6 NGO Statements

Much like the Special Rapporteurs, NGO statements focus mainly on civil and political rights especially the freedom of expression, freedom of assembly and association and the treatment of HRDs and NGOs. This comes as no surprise given that human rights NGOs in fledgling democracies tend to focus more on basic civil and political rights.

The harassment and ill-treatment of HRDs dominated early NGO statements which set out challenges faced by these activists in mostly North and Southern African countries such as Algeria, Egypt and Malawi. For instance, at the Commission's 51st Session, the Cairo Institute for Human Rights Studies (CIHRS) called the Commission's attention to the 'worrying situation' of HRDs in Algeria. It stated that HRDs continually suffered police and judicial harassment in the form of arrests, interrogations and malicious prosecutions. It cited examples such as the arrest of a member of the Algerian League for the Defence of Human Rights after she had announced a hunger strike and sit-in protesting human rights violations in Algeria. Two members of the National Committee for the Defence of the Rights of the Unemployed were convicted for participating in 'unauthorised' demonstrations and sentenced to one year in prison. The sentence was later overturned on appeal.

Similarly, with regard to Egypt, the report highlighted the deprivation of the right to liberty of HRDs through arbitrary arrests. CIHRS pointed out that there has been a crackdown on independent civil societies and HRDs. For instance, within just a few months, over 17 NGO offices had been raided by security forces. There was also a government-led smear campaign aimed at defaming these groups before the Egyptian public as foreign agents whose objective was to cause public instability and division within Egypt.

Another NGO, the International Commission of Jurists reported similar violations in the Democratic Republic of Congo, Malawi, Senegal, Swaziland, Uganda and Zimbabwe. These included arbitrary arrests, degrading treatment of HRDs in prison custody, physical assaults, death threats and extra-judicial executions.[40] These persistent violations, the group noted, often arose in the context of elections and were perpetrated by state actors who were hardly ever held to account.

Closely related to the harsh treatment of HRDs are the restrictions on the operation of NGOs. The reports note that certain states have adopted laws and policies that limit or frustrate the operation of human rights NGOs. Such restrictions, it was noted, generally infringed on the freedom of conscience and association. For instance, with regard to Algeria, CIHRS pointed out that the Algerian law No 12-06 of 2012 increased governmental restrictions on human rights NGOs. Article 39, in particular, gave the government broad discretion to refuse to register associations and failed to provide these associations with an adequate remedy to appeal a rejection of their registration request. Under that provision, the government could refuse to register an association whose purpose or goals are deemed contrary to basic national values and to law and order, public morality and the provisions of existing laws and regulations. The new law also tightened governmental control over funding by providing a shortlist of authorised national funding sources. International funding required prior authorisation and was forbidden to Algerian associations without officially established relationships of cooperation with the Ministry of Interior. Due to difficulties occasioned by the new law, some organisations were forced to close down.[41]

In a similar vein, Amnesty International, at the Commission's 51st Ordinary Session, drew attention to Ethiopia's Charities and Societies Proclamation of 2009 which placed 'excessive restrictions' on the work of human rights organisations. Top of these was the restriction on such organisations from receiving more than 10% of their funding from foreign sources which resulted in at least 17 organisations changing their mandate from human rights. In a retroactive application of the law, two organisations had their assets frozen, amounting to over $500,000 each.[42] The report pointed out the excessive powers of interference and surveillance granted to the Charities and Societies Agencies such as the power to suspend licences and confiscate and transfer the assets of any organisation. Also, the Agency had the power to demand any document in an organisation's possession invariably including the testimonies of victims of violations thereby contravening principles of confidentiality and further endangering the victims. Furthermore, some organisations were forced to remove certain areas of work from their mandates such as election monitoring and even change their names before they could be registered under the new law. Amnesty International claimed that the intended effect of this law was to restrict and effectively stifle critical voices as well as limit the level of scrutiny of the government thereby limiting civil and political rights such as freedom of association, freedom of speech and the right to participate in government.

## 4.7 Conclusion

The aim of this chapter has been to examine state implementation of the Charter through the instrument of state reporting. Attention has also been paid to the general themes of NGO and Special Rapporteur statements. On a whole, the reports showed that the implementation of civil and political rights, in the states covered, was generally characterised by state repression. Socio-economic and peoples' rights were poorly implemented, and women's rights implementation had not reached the desired level of the Women's Protocol. This is not to say that the states had not taken fruitful steps to abide by their Charter duties and implement its provisions. Quite to the contrary, it was found that states had often taken very direct and commendable steps towards protecting the rights guaranteed in the Charter and promoting the equality canvassed under the Women's Protocol. For instance, with regard to the latter, Sudan had allocated 25% of legislative seats to women in order to encourage their involvement in politics. Thus, while they could have a higher level of representation, 25% was the minimum threshold. Both Nigeria and Cameroon, at the time of those reports, had female representations of over 30% in the federal executive and legislative governments respectively. Such direct attempts had also been made in areas of socio-economic rights where states had strived to make direct impacts in the health and educational sectors. It is believed that an acknowledgement of such positive efforts should characterise future assessments of human rights implementation in Africa. It has however been concluded that, despite these efforts, the member states have not been able to meet the required thresholds of the Charter. Thus, these efforts often amounted to a part-fulfilment of responsibilities which often left glaring gaps in implementation.

The NGO and Special Rapporteur reports showed a degree of high-handedness and undemocratic tendencies on the part of the identified states. The harassment of HRDs also signalled a low commitment to the ideals of the Charter. While the reports are by no means comprehensive in the sense of covering every member state, they call attention to the challenges facing NGOs and HRDs in many African states that tend to be intolerant of any form of opposition or dissent. These reports also paint a picture of the general disposition of some African states towards the observance of basic democratic and human rights values.

In examining the state of compliance with the Charter, this chapter identified key themes and reasons for the state of partial or non-fulfilment of states' obligations. These themes have been consistently identified throughout the progress of the chapter and include the lack of political will, lack of human and financial resources, poor economic conditions, cultural inclinations and stereotypes, poverty, ignorance and illiteracy. Care has been taken not to digress into analysis and discussions of these challenges as this is done in the next chapter.

In summary, therefore, the practice of human rights in the continent is certainly a mixed bag. While there have been many positive legislative and other measures taken to promote these rights, there are still a number of entrenched practices and other lapses that create an overwhelmingly negative picture. As seen in the final summations above, states seriously default in all of the categories studied. While some of these defaults are owing to poor economic conditions and entrenched customary practices, others, especially in the civil and political rights category, boil down to undemocratic tendencies and lack of political will. This raises questions on the commitment of states to their obligations under the Charter. Thus far, there is still a huge gap between the theory of human rights, as contained in the Charter, and its practice by states.

## Notes

1. Abdullahi An-Na'im, *Human Rights Under African Constitutions* (UPP 2003) 18.
2. George Mugwanya, "Realising International Human Rights Norms Through Regional Human Rights Mechanisms: Reinvigorating the African System" (2000) 10 *Indiana International and Comparative Law Review* 35, 39.
3. Frans Viljoen, *International Human Rights Law in Africa* (Oxford University Press 2012).
4. Dejo Olowu, *An Integrative Rights-Based Approach to Human Development in Africa* (Pretoria University Law Press 2009) 35.
5. Article 25.
6. *Kazeem Aminu v. Nigeria*, Communication No 205/97 (2000).
7. Federal Republic of Nigeria, *Nigeria's 5th Periodic Country Report 2011–2014 on the Implementation of the African Charter on Human and Peoples' Rights in Nigeria* (June 2014), http://www.achpr.org/files/sessions/56th/state-reports/5th-2011-2014/staterep5_nigeria_2013_eng.pdf.
8. See Human Rights Watch, "World Report 2014: Nigeria: Events of 2013" (2014), accessed September 15, 2018, http://www.hrw.org/world-report/2014/country-chapters/nigeria.
9. Michelle Faul, *Nigeria's Military Killing Thousands of Detainees* (Lagos: Associated Press, October 18, 2013).
10. Amnesty International, "At Least 150 Peaceful Pro-Biafra Activists Killed in Chilling Crackdown" November 24, 2016, accessed June 20, 2018, https://www.amnesty.org/en/latest/news/2016/11/peaceful-pro-biafra-activists-killed-in-chilling-crackdown/.
11. BBC, "Mass Graves for '300 Shia Nigerians' in Zaria," accessed June 20, 2018, https://www.bbc.co.uk/news/world-africa-35168211.
12. BBC, "Nigeria Shia Killings, Army Should Be Prosecuted," accessed June 20, 2018, https://www.bbc.co.uk/news/world-africa-36941986.
13. African Commission, "Concluding Observations and Recommendations on the 5th Periodic Report of the Federal Republic of Nigeria on the Implementation of the African Charter on Human and Peoples' Rights (2011–2014)" (2016), http://www.achpr.org/files/sessions/57th/conc-obs/5th-2011-2014/concluding_observations_nigeria_5th_sr_eng.pdf.
14. Republic of Malawi, *Report to the African Commission on Human and Peoples' Rights: Implementation of the African Charter on Human*

*and Peoples Rights 1995–2013 and the Protocol to the African Charter on Human and Peoples Rights on the Rights of Women 2005–2013* (2014) para 65, http://www.achpr.org/files/sessions/56th/state-reports/1-1995-2013/malawi_state_report_eng.pdf.

15. African Commission, "Concluding Observations on the 3rd Periodic Report of the Republic of Cameroon" (2014) para 51.
16. Republic of Uganda, *5th Periodic Report by the Government of the Republic of Uganda to the African Commission on Human and Peoples' Rights* (2013) 16.
17. The Report cites the 1998 case of *Kalu Onuoha v The State.*
18. Republic of Sudan, the 4th and 5th Periodic Reports of the Republic of the Republic of the Sudan in accordance with art 62 of the African Charter on Human and Peoples Rights 2008–2012 (2013) para 83.
19. The African Commission adopted a resolution calling on states to observe a moratorium on the death penalty at its 44th Ordinary Session in Abuja, 2008. See Amnesty International, "African Commission Call for a Moratorium on the Death Penalty" (2008), https://www.amnesty.org/en/latest/news/2008/12/african-commission-calls-moratorium-death-penalty-20081205/.
20. World Coalition Against the Death Penalty, "African Commission Adopts on Draft Protocol on Abolition" (2015), http://www.worldcoalition.org/Abolition-of-the-death-penalty-at-the-heart-of-African-Commission-session.html.
21. Uganda, "5th Report," 9.
22. Republic of Cameroon, *3rd Periodic Report of Cameroon within the Framework of the African Charter on Human and Peoples' Rights* (2013) para 248, accessed October 13, 2015, http://www.achpr.org/files/sessions/54th/state-reports/3-2008-2011/staterep3_cameroon_2013_eng.pdf.
23. Athew C. Raven, *The International Covenant of Economic, Social and Cultural Rights* (Clarendon Press 1995) 138.
24. *The Republic v. Jamison Ofesi and 10 others* (Criminal Cause No. 64 of 2010).
25. Frans Viljoen, *International Human Rights Law in Africa* (Oxford University Press 2012) 218.
26. *Archbishop Okogie v The Attorney-General of Lagos State* (1981) 2 Nigerian Constitutional Law Reports 350 paras 7–8.
27. See African Commission, "Observation on Cameroon".
28. African Commission, http://www.achpr.org/instruments/women-protocol.
29. Some of these reasons include if the women neglect the kids or go out without telling their husbands.

30. Makinde et al., "Rejection of the Gender and Equal Opportunities Bill in Nigeria: A Setback for Sustainable Development Goal Five" (2017) 32(3) *Gender in Management: An International Journal*, 234–240.
31. Republic of Cameroon, *Cameroon's Initial Report* (2004) 120, accessed October 23, 2015, http://www.achpr.org/files/sessions/31st/state-reports/1st-state-report/achpr31_staterep_cameroon_2002_eng.pdf.
32. Cameroon, "3rd Report," 48.
33. World Bank, Proportion of seats held by women in national parliaments (%), accessed July 3, 2019, https://data.worldbank.org/indicator/SG.GEN.PARL.ZS.
34. See Republic of Malawi, "Report," para 159.
35. Special Rapporteur of the African Commission on Human and Peoples' Rights on Human Rights Defenders in Africa, "Press Release: Assassination of the Journalist and Human Rights Defender Serge Maheshe" (2007), http://www.achpr.org/press/2007/06/d28/.
36. Statement by the Special Rapporteur on Human Rights Defenders in Africa, Africa Day' (2015), http://www.achpr.org/news/2015/05/d183.
37. African Commission, http://www.achpr.org/fr/press/2019/03/d446/.
38. African Commission, "Press Release on the NGO and Media Bills in Kenya" (2014), accessed 25 October 2015, http://www.achpr.org/press/2014/04/d198/.
39. Agence France-Presse, "Kenya Parliament Block Controversial NGO Bill" (2013), http://www.capitalfm.co.ke/news/2013/12/kenya-parliament-blocks-controversial-ngo-bill/.
40. ICJ Oral Intervention on the Human Rights Violations Affecting HRDs (HRDs) in Africa, accessed October 14, 2015, http://www.achpr.org/sessions/51st/ngo-statements/14/.
41. The International Centre for Not-for-Profit Law, "NGO Law Monitor: Algeria," accessed October 14, 2015, http://www.icnl.org/research/monitor/algeria.html.
42. Amnesty International, "Oral Statement at the 51st Ordinary Session of the Commission," accessed October 14, 2015, https://www.amnesty.org/download/Documents/16000/afr250032012en.pdf.

CHAPTER 5

# Challenges to States' Protection of Human Rights

## 5.1 Introduction

The previous chapter examined states' implementation of the Charter through the prisms of the state reporting system, NGO and Special Rapporteur reports. On a whole, these reports chronicle systematic and other violations over the years. The latter two have particularly decried the poor state of human rights implementation across several African countries. This chapter examines the reasons for the relatively poor implementation of the Charter. It does this under two main headings, namely civil and political rights, on the one hand, and socio-economic rights, on the other, with women's and group rights subsumed under those headings.

## 5.2 Protection of Civil and Political Rights

The previous chapter, after an analysis of relevant reports, concluded that there were serious lapses in the observance of civil and political rights. These violations persisted despite often clear provisions of the states' laws except in a few instances where local laws allowed for their perpetuation. Both of these instances are examined below.



A. Uwazuruike, *Human Rights under the African Charter*,
https://doi.org/10.1007/978-3-030-41739-0_5

### 5.2.1 *Violations of Charter and National Provisions*

It was found that many violations existed despite Charter provisions and even domestic laws. The Special Rapporteur and NGO reports found several cases of harassment of human rights defenders (HRDs), violations of women's rights, rights of prisoners and refugee rights. While some of these actions were backed by national laws, many of them, such as the shooting of protesters and assassination of HRDs, were in flagrant violation of both regional and domestic laws. Similar findings were made by the Commission in its Concluding Observations on state reports. For instance, Nigeria had been reprimanded by the Commission for its use of torture and extrajudicial killings even though both practices were indefensible under Nigerian law. Human Rights Watch had also raised similar concerns about arbitrary arrests, torture and extrajudicial killings.[1] Such was the gravity of these concerns that the Associated Press reported that, in one single month (June) of 2013, the Nigerian Army delivered 1795 bodies to a single mortuary in Maiduguri, in its bid to flush out the militant group Boko Haram.[2] In Uganda, the Commission's Concluding Observations recorded a prevalence of police brutality. In Cameroon, the government still maintained the death penalty despite the observation of a de facto moratorium since 1997. In Sudan, the practice of female genital mutilation(FGM) and the recruitment of child soldiers remained prevalent despite restrictive national laws.

In analysing the reasons for states' violation of the Charter, this chapter will particularly examine the challenges that have been identified by the defaulting states themselves in their various country reports. Some of these reasons have already been established in the previous chapter and will be further expounded here. The importance of examining the challenges that have been revealed by the state reporting process is twofold. First, that these reasons have been cited by the states themselves mean that there is little need to make assumptions on the reasons for violations except, of course, where the sincerity of such concession is called into question. Secondly, the fact that these reasons have been highlighted from the internal system of the Charter also sidesteps the potential allegation of imperialism that trails other external (mainly Western) analyses.

### 5.2.2 *Reasons Adduced by States for the Violation of Rights*

A study of the state reports reveals the following as the main challenges to implementing civil and political rights as identified by these states: lack of financial and human resources (which is arguably a matter of capacity building), culture and traditional practices, Illiteracy and lack of knowledge. These are discussed below.

#### 5.2.2.1 *Lack of Financial and Human Resources*

This is the most cited challenge, by states, to the implementation of the rights and standards of the Charter. Member states strongly make the case that they lack the financial, human and other resources to effectively guarantee and implement rights. As a result, many institutions and machinery created to implement these rights are underfunded and understaffed thereby limiting their impact and leaving room for unaddressed violations. In its report, Malawi identified 'the lack of resources and capacity' as its chief challenge in implementing the rights guaranteed under the Charter.[3] This lack of resources was felt in such key institutions of justice as the Police Force, Office of the Directorate of Public Prosecutions (DPP) and the office of the Ombudsman. For instance, the police-to-population ratio was as low as 1: 6455 in rural areas, making such areas very difficult to police. The absence of such an important organ like the police in these areas invariably translates into poor protection of vital rights to life and property. Furthermore, the office of the DPP had offices in only three major cities making the supervision of police prosecutors in several other locations difficult thereby compromising the right to a fair trial.

The lack of decentralised grass-roots structures was also a challenge for the office of the Ombudsman as it meant that many local indigenes did not have access to this body. Other factors that affected the performance of the Ombudsman include inadequate staff and funding, obsolete equipment and a huge backlog of cases due to absences and unavailability of the Ombudsman. On the whole, the government stated that the criminal justice system was so overwhelmed that even serious crimes like homicide took a long time to finalise thereby compromising the right to a fair trial. This situation was attributed almost entirely to the lack of human resource capacity and a large staff turnover.

The situation appears even direr in Nigeria where there was a high level of 'awaiting trial prisoners' in the system, a situation that seriously compromised the right to a fair trial. The country's report stated that of

47,508 prisoners in custody, 30,629 were awaiting trial, some for more than 17 years. A similar situation of backlog of cases was reported by the Ugandan government. The Sudanese government also highlighted the lack of financial and human resources, a huge chunk of these having been previously deployed towards restoring security and order in the aftermath of heavy armed conflicts. After cessation of conflicts, establishment and maintenance of peace required a huge amount of resources resulting in deficits in the country's budgets.

These assertions and complaints by the states are supported by independent research. For instance, in an earlier study of 10 African countries,[4] it was found that the judicial systems of all the countries studied suffered from 'a lack of resources across the board'. Materials and equipment such as typewriters and stationery were lacking, court dockets were crowded, courtroom facilities were inadequate, delays were frequent, and there was a general lack of access to case reporters and other sources of legal precedent necessary for adequate judicial performance. Access to the legal system was challenging especially for poor and rural dwellers as lawyers were expensive and literally beyond the reach of most potential litigants. Public defenders, when they existed, were only available for criminal defendants in serious cases.

It is interesting to note that in the decade after these findings were made, these challenges still exist and are routinely cited by states as inhibiting protection of rights. This shows the important connection between the economic situation of states and their ability to protect human rights.

#### *5.2.2.2 Culture and Traditional Practices*

Another major challenge to the implementation and enforcement of civil and political rights is the existence of entrenched customary practices that are inimical to the practice of human rights. Such practices include the practice of female genital cutting, disinheritance of women. So ingrained are some of these customs that the existence of regional and national laws does little to affect their application. For instance, the Malawian government reported that it faced challenges in ensuring equality of rights and responsibilities within marriage. This was due to cultural practices that favoured men over women such as where a woman was forced to marry her brother-in-law upon the death of her husband or where a male child was awarded academic sponsorship and the female child made to stay at home. The situation was similar in Nigeria. Here, the government reported that, despite signing to 'an array of international human rights instruments' affirming women's rights, there were other 'laws reflecting aspirations in direct variance to what these international instruments espouse'.[5] These were in the form of customary laws that provided institutional support for practices such as early marriages, early and 'unspaced' childbearing, FGM, widowhood rites and laws that exclude women from inheritance. The government went on to state that even where statutory laws outlawed some of these practices, evidence abounded to show that the enforcement level of these laws was 'negligible'. This challenge of enforcing or monitoring violations in such regions was further demonstrated in the Ugandan report.[6] The government stated therein that it was particularly challenging for the police to investigate and prosecute cases of mob justice as these often involved entire communities or villages.

As is noticeable from the above examples, women and children (especially the female child) are often affected the most by these customs. For instance, traditional systems of tenure do not generally recognise women's rights to access land in their own right. They would only usually have rights of use through marriage or through their male children.[7] Thus, on the dissolution of the marriage, the woman would usually be dispossessed of the land and made to return to her people where she is treated as a minor dependent on other male relatives. Even in many areas where some of these practices are not observed, the bureaucracy on land allocation is usually based on policies that favour men against women. Thus, most land registries in Africa would 'bear only the names of men spiced with a handful of women'.[8] While there have been steps to eradicate these practices through legislation and judicial pronouncements, some of these customs are still entrenched and widely practised. One question that arises is why these customs are still prevalent. An even more pressing question is: What can be done to curb their practice? This task is undertaken in the section below.

#### 5.2.2.3 *Resolving the Culture Imbroglio*

A number of reasons can be adduced for the proliferation and entrenchment of varying customs across the continent some of which are inimical to the practice of human rights. One reason is that most of these cultures existed in early African societies and have survived notwithstanding radical events like colonialism and adoption of human rights norms. While it is not particularly within the scope of this chapter to investigate the reasons for their survival, it has been argued that some of these customary laws (being the legal application of customs) owe their continued existence to political, economic and social features such as general and drastic instability due to civil war or insurrection in a country.[9] Another factor that has been identified is the weakness and inaccessibility of institutional resources for the legal protection of rights which have forced people into seeking alternative mechanisms for the adjudication of disputes.

Given some of the above reasons for their continued existence, it may be ambitious to create a roadmap for the outright elimination of most of these practices. Rather, the challenge is on how states can regulate their content and application in order to better protect and promote human rights. This task, it is argued, is best carried out through direct and targeted promotion. This, of course, is not an opinion that stands in isolation but one that has been canvassed and demonstrated by some commentators down the years. It has been shown that legal pronouncements alone are not sufficient and that merely proscribing harmful cultural practices does very little to curb them.

Mubangizi identifies law as only one component of a multidisciplinary approach required to halt harmful practices like FGM. Civil society, government and other role players are needed to change perceptions and attitudes through the use of human rights education, human rights advocacy, legislative measures and developing customary law to ensure compatibility.[10] He particularly applauds the techniques applied by the NGO group 'Tostan' which engages local communities through activities like theatre and role-playing such that members of the community reach a consensus themselves about how to deal with issues such as FGM. This has resulted in an FGM abandonment success rate of 77% in that community.[11]

Ibhawoh has similarly argued for an understanding of both the general nature of the tension between national human rights regimes and cultural traditions and the internal tensions between contending paradigms of cultural legitimacy. He advocates a constructive approach to promoting human rights by seeking ways of enhancing the supportive elements of culture while redressing the problematic elements in ways that are consistent with the cultural integrity of the tradition in question and the contending groups within it.[12] Thus, the interplay between national human rights standards on the one hand and local cultural orientations on the other should be a dynamic process of give and take, ideally through persuasion and dialogue, with legislation serving only to complement the process. This system of cross-fertilisation, he argues, would narrow the gap between national human rights provisions and cultural orientations. More so, constitutional rights can derive their legitimacy not only from state authority but also from the force of cultural traditions.

Like Mubangizi, Ibhawoh uses the FGM example to drive home his point. He points out that, as with most other customary practices, legislation has only been effective, in the case of FGM, where it has been integrated into other aspects of a comprehensive eradication strategy. He states that in several African countries where FGM legislation exists, it is not enforced for fear of alienating certain power bases or exacerbating tensions between practising and non-practising communities. He states:

> No African country that has banned FGM, including Senegal, Egypt, Ghana and Burkina Faso, dares enforce the law. In Guinea, FGM carries the death penalty but it has never been applied. Early attempts to enforce legislation against FGM in Sudan caused such popular outcries that enforcement was subsequently abandoned. In Burkina Faso… it has become clear that criminalising practitioners and families has only succeeded in driving the practice underground and creating an obstacle to outreach and education… [In] order for legislation to be effective it must be accompanied by a broad and inclusive strategy for community-based education and awareness raising.[13]

The above portrayal necessarily invokes concerns about the foothold of normative human rights standards in these communities. It is also important for an internal critique as it is a demonstration of an instance when peoples' actions go against national and even regional standards. However, as has been canvassed in the first chapter, the African Charter is the adopted representation of African human rights standards and necessarily supersedes other pockets of contrary practices. A viable way forward is through integrative programmes that involve local communities 'as changes in cultural attitudes and orientations can only be meaningful and sustainable if they come from within these local communities'.[14] Ibhawoh gives an example of how this has worked with regard to FGM in Kenya:

> [In Kenya] some local communities have successfully introduced 'alternative circumcision rites' to replace old traditions. Under the new procedure arrived at through communal dialogue and consensus, the people within these communities agreed to do away with the physical mutilation

> of the woman's body during the traditional female circumcision rites while retaining other harmless aspects of the circumcision rites... During the celebrations...the adolescent girls are taught the basic concepts of sexual and reproductive health and are counselled on gender issues and other customary norms. As a way of legitimising the new procedure, the girls receive certificates certifying that they have undergone the traditional rites into womanhood. These innovations have produced hopeful results where previous efforts have failed. In one of the communities where the alternative circumcision rites were introduced and where about 95 percent of the girls previously had to undergo circumcision, the rate of FGM is estimated to have gone down to 70 percent.

It is clear from the above that different actors have varying roles to play in curtailing harmful cultural practices. The courts, for instance, have to refuse to recognise customs that are repugnant to justice, equity and good conscience, while the legislature passes laws that reform obnoxious customary law. However, it has been noted that reversing particular cultural practices is difficult and akin to reversing social conventions thus necessitating a careful approach that not only promotes human rights but that is also respectful of the culture and values of particular communities.[15] It has been posited that 'outsiders' often view cultural practices from a very simplistic perspective without appreciating the complexities and meanings of such practices, and the differing and sometimes conflicting responses to them.[16] Such observation demands that care is taken not only in the approach to legal enactments and interpretations but also in the formulation of administrative policies.

In summary, therefore, the challenge of repugnant cultures cannot be solved solely through legislative means but through a fusion of soundly formulated and applied promotional measures as in the examples cited above. Such promotions require the concerted efforts of states, NGOs and the Commission alike. Applied side by side with promotional measures should be positive protective steps, for example criminal prosecution, as provided in the national laws. Thus, while the promotional measures are aimed at instilling the standards in the people thereby restraining them from violating human rights, the protective measures are aimed at protecting and providing remedies to those persons whose rights have been infringed.

### 5.2.2.4 *Illiteracy and Ignorance of Rights*

Another factor that has been highlighted by states is ignorance, on the part of the citizens, of rights and how to enforce them. For instance, Malawi pointed to a general lack of public awareness especially by vulnerable groups, of their rights and how to exercise them. Thus, even though there were some existing institutions for the protection of these rights, a proportion of the populace either had no knowledge of these or did not know how to use them. The Malawian government gave the example of the Ombudsman of which the general public, and even the respondents, had little knowledge either of its functions or mode of operation. Like Malawi, Nigeria and Uganda have also identified illiteracy and ignorance as major challenges to the practice and implementation of human rights. In the latter's case, the government states that civic education of the masses before, during and after elections continue to pose a challenge.

This need to educate is not limited to the masses but also extends to institutions tasked with protecting human rights. For instance, Malawi has noted that the 'main challenge' in terms of ensuring public peace has been the 'capacity and independence of the police'. It goes on to state that there have been cases of violation of rights by the police in the process of maintaining national peace. Thus, the police have, for instance, shot at unarmed civilians in the process of dispersing demonstrations. Such actions invariably infringed on such rights as the right to life and freedom of assembly.

The ignorance and sometimes sheer disregard for human rights by the police has led some states to incorporate human rights into their local police training. One example is Cameroon which reported that, to ensure the protection of rights and minimise abuse, the government had included human rights training in the programme of the Cameroonian national gendarmerie, with some security personnel even trained in human rights at the master's level.

There is no doubt that, for better protection of rights, the prospective victims, or those close to them, need to be aware of the existence of these rights and the duty of the state to protect them. This is because they are the ones who would have to bring complaints against the state. The level of protection would be negatively impacted where such persons are ignorant of their rights or misconstrue them as privileges. This essentially means that improving human rights protection requires an empowered citizenry. It should also be pointed out that states have a duty under

Article 25 of the Charter to educate the people on their rights and to see to it that these rights are understood.

It is again clear from the above that targeted promotional measures are needed to better educate and enlighten general populations on their rights and how to protect them. This is not to say that some such measures are not already in place. Governments, civil society and the Commission have, over the years, initiated measures aimed at educating the various strata of the society, including public organs and local populations, on human rights. It has been observed that while the government concentrated its efforts on the development of school curricula, the training of officials was left to NGOs.[17] There was also the subsequent increase in the number of national human rights commissions which became the 'main role players' in human rights education. However, much like the conclusion on the state of human rights in Africa, the issue is not whether there are some measures in place[18] or even a few success stories but whether the entire system of promotion and education has been implemented to such a level as to be adjudged to have objectively met the needs and standards of the continent. This has clearly not been the case. To resolve this challenge of ignorance (and even to some extent the cultural challenges), such promotional measures have to be proportional to the level of awareness, or lack thereof, of human rights in the continent. This necessarily entails a concerted effort by the key players, the national systems (including governments and national human rights commissions), regional system and civil society, towards the promotion of rights and education of local populations based on a viable Plan of Action. It should, however, be stressed that, while such plans may go a long way in setting the stage for improvements, other factors exist which could thwart or frustrate them. The book will demonstrate this in future discussions of the challenges to the promotional mandate of the Commission.

### 5.2.3 *Violations Aided by National Laws*

While factors such as lack of resources, cultural leanings and illiteracy can adversely affect the implementation of rights guaranteed in the African Charter by otherwise willing states, there are however many instances, some of which have been highlighted in Chapter 4, of states' unwillingness to implement these rights and even taking positive steps to truncate or undermine them. In some instances, national laws were passed which directly restricted or jeopardised the enjoyment of some rights, for instance, Sudan's National Security Act (NSA) 2010 which allowed security officials to detain suspects for up to four and a half months before being charged as well as granting security officials immunity from criminal and civil procedures for acts connected with their official work. Restrictive statutes such as the Sudan's NSA 2010 infringed the rights to liberty and fair trial, press freedom and the freedom of association. Another area of dissonance, as already discussed in the previous chapter, was in the application of the death penalty, even though here it was argued that until member states signed a Protocol abolishing same, they could not be held in violation as the Charter does not expressly prohibit the death penalty.

The wilful or careless violation by states of their human rights responsibilities raises serious implications from the perspective of an internal African critique as such actions show a flagrant disregard for the established normative standards. The pertinent question is why a state that participated in drafting, signing, ratifying and even domesticating a treaty would turn around to systematically violate it. In order to resolve this question, this section will briefly examine two cases of such positive systematic violations with a view to ascertaining the underlying causes and adduced reasons for those violations. These cases are Zimbabwe's controversial land reforms that led to the disbanding of the Southern African Development Community (SADC) Tribunal and Sudan's NSA.

#### *5.2.3.1 Zimbabwe's Land Reform Programme*

The controversial contents of this programme were contested in the case of *Mike Campbell (Pvt) Ltd and Others v Republic of Zimbabwe* where the applicants challenged the compulsory acquisition of their agricultural lands under the land reform programme of the Zimbabwean government. Such acquired land vested full title in the state without compensation to the dispossessed party, except for improvements effected on the land before it was acquired. Also, a person whose land had been acquired was barred from challenging its acquisition in a court of law with the courts also expressly prevented from hearing such matters.[19]

These provisions immediately raise serious human rights concerns. The first is the issue of fair hearing; the second more subtle concern is the freedom from discrimination. While not obvious from the provisions, the implementation of Zimbabwe's land reforms necessarily involved dispossessing white farmers of land appropriated to them prior to and even after Zimbabwe's independence. On the right to fair trial and access to the courts, the SADC Tribunal held that the constitutional provision ousting the court's jurisdiction infringed on the right to the protection of the law and to a fair hearing. In reaching this decision, the Tribunal referred, *inter alia*, to the decision of the African Commission in the case of *Constitutional Rights Project, Civil Liberties Organisation and Media Rights Agenda v Nigeria*[20] which concerned ouster clauses preventing Nigerian courts from hearing cases brought by publishers contesting the search and seizure of their premises. The Commission held, in that case, that such a practice would result in a legal situation where the judiciary could no longer provide a check on the executive branch of the government, a situation which was inimical to constitutional democracy.[21] On the issue of discrimination, the Tribunal concluded that even though there was no express mention of race, the effect of Amendment 17 was such that it would be felt almost exclusively by white farmers and was, therefore, discriminatory.

Given the weight of the issues raised and the findings by the Tribunal, one wonders why Zimbabwe, a signatory to the Charter and other human rights treaties, would enact such a provision into law. To determine this, one needs to understand the history of the country and its land reforms as well as the stated reasons for such a law.

#### *5.2.3.2 Understanding Zimbabwe's Violation*

Zimbabwe's land reform measures were instituted to address perceived problems of injustice and discrimination against the local population by European colonial and post-colonial settlers. During the country's colonial years, discriminatory agricultural policies and the alienation of most of the fertile, well-watered land to European settlers resulted in the oppression, marginalisation and impoverishment of indigenous people.[22] In 1930, an enforced racial division of land saw the country's land divided roughly equally between the African majority and a few European settlers constituting less than 5% of the total population. It was in an effort to redress these inequities that the government introduced a series of agrarian reform measures after independence and beyond. These reforms included a constitutional amendment and modified Land Acquisition Act promulgated in April 2000 to effect land designation and compulsory acquisition without compensation.

In its response to the above claim filed before the Tribunal, the government stated that the fact that the lands acquired belonged to white farmers had to be attributed to the country's colonial history, which had seen the majority of fertile land allotted to those farmers. Thus, the land reform was to be seen as a legitimate means to achieving an equally legitimate end which was to correct colonial land imbalances. Here, one notices a possible intent behind the law which was to tackle economic and social imbalances in the system, even though legitimate questions can be raised as to whether the particular farmers dispossessed were original beneficiaries of the initial favourable allocations.[23] Some doubt may be further raised on the genuineness or, at least, the implementation of this intent. This is clearly captured by Howard thus:

> While the ostensible reason for land invasions was that the whites had taken over the land while Zimbabwe was under colonial rule, in fact, over 80 percent of white-owned land had changed hands since independence. Farms offered for sale after independence had by law to be first offered to the government on a willing-seller, willing-buyer basis, and the government had refused the offers. Thus, the government could have acquired 80 percent of white-owned land to redistribute to black Zimbabweans, but had declined to do so. Moreover, many of the large farms taken over after 2000 were distributed to single black owners, not to landless peasants. Mugabe's inner circle and relatives benefited: for example, the Minister of Home Affairs was given five farms, and Mugabe's wife was given two.[24]

It is no doubt the case that many governments, even where their policies are repressive, believe that there is some justification for those policies. It would, however, defeat the purpose of human rights and the rule of law to shield such governments from accountability by silencing the national judiciary and other external tribunals. At the most basic level, human rights are essentially protection from the state with such protection to be offered through the process of adjudication when an individual perceives that his or her rights have been infringed. It is therefore not difficult to agree with the Tribunal's finding in this case.

Interestingly, this is not an isolated occurrence. Ouster clauses have already been seen in the *Constitutional Rights Project v Nigeria* case above as well as the Zimbabwean case of *Zimbabwe Human Rights NGO Forum v Zimbabwe*,[25] and while there may be some perceived 'good' intention behind these clauses and the policies they protect, they only reveal a fear of accountability and dictatorial tendencies, and even more seriously, a lack of commitment to the protection of human rights. The subsequent disbandment of the SADC Tribunal further strengthens the second-place status of human rights in the African political context. After the finding in this case, Zimbabwe pulled out of the Tribunal leading to a review of the latter's jurisdictions. The Court was subsequently disbanded. Zimbabwe's unsavoury tactics and approach led to a chain of events which ultimately resulted in the disbandment of the Tribunal.[26] In August 2014, the SADC Summit adopted a new protocol which removed the right of private access and allowed member states to withdraw from the Tribunal's jurisdiction by giving 12-months' notice. In December 2018, the South African Constitutional Court held that South Africa's decision to sign the Protocol thereby suspending the operations of the Tribunal was unconstitutional, unlawful and irrational.

#### *5.2.3.3 Sudan's NSA and Gagging of the Press*

One major area of concern for the Commission was Sudan's NSA 2010 which allows security officials to detain suspects for up to four and a half months without judicial review before charges are levied. It also provides members of the National Intelligence and Security Service (NISS) and their associates with immunity from criminal and civil procedures for acts connected with the official work of the member. This has been the basis for arbitrary arrests and incommunicado detentions.

Amnesty International detailed what appeared to be a crackdown on independent media and civil society in the run-up to the general elections in 2015. The NISS reportedly confiscated publications from at least 16 newspapers on 42 different occasions and interrogated about 21 journalists.[27] These actions were obviously sanctioned by Sudan's national laws and even exacerbated by more recent constitutional amendments passed by parliament which gave unlimited discretion to the NISS to interfere in political, economic and social issues. There have been other similar reports of pre-print censorship despite constitutional guarantees of freedom of expression and the media.[28] As in Zimbabwe's case above, the issue that arises for determination is the motive behind these laws and their general implication.

#### *5.2.3.4 Understanding Sudan's Violations*

Sudan's human rights records should be seen in the context of a nation only emerging from the bitter experience of a brutal and protracted civil war. For a country embroiled in over two decades of civil war, such practices as systematic torture of individuals, often at the hand of the NISS, were already commonplace.[29] Such was the practice of this war-torn country that changing its national security law was at the heart of reforms envisaged in the 2005 Comprehensive Peace Agreement between the two warring sides. According to this agreement and Sudan's 2005 Interim National Constitution, the existing security laws were to be radically changed with the NISS transformed into an intelligence service. However, the Sudanese government delayed these reforms only to present a new security bill in 2009 which effectively retained NISS powers and immunity from accountability. This action triggered widespread opposition by local and international observers.

Amnesty International attributes the emergence of the Act to events following the 2008 attack by Chadian armed opposition groups on N'Djamena, the capital of Chad. A number of Sudanese newspapers had reported that the Sudanese government had supported the attack to overthrow the President of Chad. In reaction to these reports, the government ordered a clampdown on the press through the reintroduction of preprint censorship and the resumption of daily visits to printing houses and newspapers by the NISS. After a failed attack on Sudan's capital, Khartoum, by an armed opposition group, more than 1000 individuals were arrested mainly by the NISS and 106 death penalties pronounced in under 2 years.[30]

The essence of the above narrative is to understand the state of affairs in Sudan and its impact on the development of legal enactments affecting human rights. It appears that the volatile and conflict-ridden state of the country has driven its leaders, who in any case are not particularly known for human rights observance, to implement draconian and unsavoury policies. One may argue whether, given its peculiar situation of civil conflicts and unrest, Sudan is not permitted to derogate from the provisions of the Charter. However, the Charter does not contain a derogation clause and the Commission has interpreted this to mean that the Charter does not permit derogations.[31] Moreover, a peace agreement with the opposition has been signed since 2005, and even though there may be occasional pockets of violence, these cannot justify a perpetual derogation. Infringements by the NISS are also systematic and lack the necessary ingredients of urgency and emergency that characterise such derogations under international law. While it may be necessary to take further steps in the aftermath of an event like the armed attack on Khartoum, it is hard to justify pre-print censorship which effectively gags the press and restricts freedom of expression. Far from seeing any justifiable reason for Sudan's dictatorial pose, Amnesty International believes that the NSA 2010 embodies the government's vision of a national security force whose function is to maintain it in power.[32] This perceived tyranny is evidenced by the issuance of an arrest warrant against Sudan's President, Omar Al-Bashir, by the International Criminal Court for war crimes and crimes against humanity.[33] Al-Bashir was eventually ousted from power in April 2019.

A number of conclusions can be drawn here. The first is that, given its protracted civil war, a number of rights were routinely violated by the Sudanese government resulting in charges of war crimes and crimes against humanity against the country's President. Now, after the cessation of conflicts, the government has apparently retained the oppressive role of its security forces. Whether this is done to maintain the still fragile peace or to maintain the government in power is an issue for debate. The main point is that the Sudanese government has little legitimate excuse for its violations of the above-stated rights. This is, therefore, one case that shows a clear disregard for the rights of the individual as contained in the African Charter of which Sudan is a signatory.

The above two case studies are instances where political and country-specific considerations have triumphed over the African Charter. Incidentally, it was such situations as these that necessitated the creation of a regional human rights system in the first place, to curtail systematic and blatant violations by states. That these situations still exist means that mere signing and ratification of treaties do not necessarily induce compliance with the provisions of those treaties even in those instances where compliance is not hindered by the lack of resources. To resolve this issue, the subject of political will in the particular context of the African Charter needs to be addressed as well as the issue of accountability through the regional institutions. The former is examined in later parts of this chapter while the latter will be addressed in Chapter 7. In the meantime, it is necessary, just as has been done with civil and political rights, to analyse the challenges confronting the protection of socio-economic rights under the Charter.

## 5.3 Protection of Socio-Economic Rights

> ...Convinced that it is henceforth essential to pay a particular attention to the right to development and that civil and political rights cannot be dissociated from economic, social and cultural rights in their conception as

> well as universality and that the satisfaction of economic, social and cultural rights is a guarantee for the enjoyment of civil and political rights.[34]

With the above words, the Charter set the basis for the importance and sanctity of socio-economic rights such as the right to work, right to health and right to education. However, after a study of relevant reports and assessments in Chapter 4, it was found that some of these basic standards had generally not been met. While there were some efforts to ameliorate the poor state of living, all of the states examined acknowledged the persistent dismal state of health, education and social services. Some of the major causes of these were the lack of human and financial resources, poverty, cultural influences, war and political instability. Each of these will be discussed briefly.

### 5.3.1 *Lack of Human and Financial Resources*

Much like civil and political rights above, the implementation of socio-economic rights has been hindered by the lack of human and financial resources of many African states. Nigeria reports that the paucity of funds has affected the ability of mainline ministries and agencies responsible for the promotion of security, socio-economic welfare and poverty eradication programmes and projects to effectively implement most of the provisions of the economic, social, cultural, environmental and developmental rights guaranteed under the Charter. For instance, the nationwide Universal Basic Education Programme which sees over 20 million children attending more than 60,000 basic education schools has been severely affected by funding and implementation challenges leaving nearly 11 million children out of school. Similarly, Uganda reports that there was limited funding for activities to implement the Charter requirements for both the health and education sectors. This challenge was worsened by the country's 'considerably high' birth rate as against its slowing economic growth rates. Kenya pointed to its worsening economic performance as having 'a profound and negative impact on the overall welfare of the people'.[35] It stated, additionally, that the government lacked adequate infrastructure and financial resources to extend its free primary education programme to secondary and tertiary institutions.

On the converse side, it must also be noted that massive corruption by government officials has arguably had some bearing on the claimed paucity of funds by many African states. For instance, in her 2018 book

Fighting Corruption is Dangerous,[36] former Nigerian Finance Minister, Ngozi Okonjo-Iweala, discloses how a financial audit of subsidy claims by private oil marketers for 2011 revealed fraudulent claims of N382 billion ($2.5 billion). The Ad Hoc Committee set up by the Nigerian Parliament to investigate the corruption in the oil sector was also mired by controversy after one marketer, Nigerian billionaire, Femi Otedola, accused the chair of the Ad Hoc Committee, Hon. Farouk Lawan, of demanding a bribe of $3 million from him to facilitate the Committee's removal of the names of Mr Otedola's oil companies from the list of those to be sanctioned. Otedola was able to show a video wherein he could be seen giving out $620,000 to Hon Farouk Lawan.

A 2013 Task Force set up by the government also revealed that there were unaccounted-for funds in the transactions of the Nigerian National Petroleum Corporation (NNPC) to the tune of nearly $12 billion from the period January 2012 to July 2013. The then Central Bank Governor, Sanusi Lamido Sanusi, tendered exhibits before the Nigerian Senate showing the unaccounted-for amount to be as high as $20 billion.[37] With regard to individual members of the Nigerian government, the late Nigerian Head of State, General Sani Abacha is recorded as looting between $3 billion and $5 billion of public funds.[38] Former Nigerian Petroleum Minister, Diezani-Alison Madueke, has also been accused of misappropriating up to $153 million dollars during her time in government. She has been made to forfeit assets including a $37.5 million apartment complex in Lagos.[39]

The corruption scourge is by no means limited to Nigeria. African countries have generally not fared well in corruption studies and indices. For instance, the Transparency International Corruption Index 2018 has only two countries, Botswana and Namibia, scoring over 50%. Countries like Somalia and South Sudan score as low as 10 and 13%, respectively, indicating very poor performance.[40] It is therefore fair to argue that, in order to free up funds for developmental projects, African states must plug leakages such as corrupt practices in the system.

Howard-Hassmann has even gone a step further in arguing that developing states should no longer hide behind the qualifier of progressive implementation of socio-economic rights especially given the enrichment of the upper and middle classes through globalisation and the turn to market economies. She argues that there is plenty of room for anticorruption campaigns and the institution of welfare and redistributes economic measures to benefit the poor in those states. The choice not to ameliorate the living conditions of citizens, she argues, is political.[41]

It is difficult to contend with this position given the level of corruption in most African countries as indicated above. Granted that some states are genuinely hampered by paucity of human and financial resources, it is argued that a lot more could be done were current resources diligently and effectively managed.

### *5.3.2 Large-Scale Poverty*

> Africa's trademark as a continent is punctuated by poverty, ignorance, diseases and a high level of underdevelopment not comparable to other continents.[42]

Extreme poverty is undoubtedly one of the main causes of poor socio-economic standards. If a majority of the population of the target countries were able to sustain themselves, then the respective governments would have relatively fewer people to worry about. However, Africa as a region has been continually plagued with poverty. 2017 World Bank figures put the rate of extreme poverty (i.e. people living on less than $1.90 a day) in sub-Saharan Africa at 41%.[43] In Liberia alone, the poverty headcount ratio stood at an alarming 89.6%, with Madagascar, Burkina-Faso, Democratic Republic of Congo and Malawi standing at 81.8, 80.5, 77.2 and 70.9%, respectively. It is no surprise then that poverty has been described as 'the greatest threat to and source of human rights violations in Africa'.[44] This challenge has unsurprisingly been echoed by states. For instance, Kenya, in its 2014 report, stated that, as 56% of its population (about 17 million people) lived below the poverty line, it had found it difficult to meet the needs of these people.[45] Malawi's report also pointed out that its poor rural dwellers being more concerned with daily sustenance, pay less attention to other socio-economic rights such as the right to education. This, the country states, has had a bearing on the literacy levels as some children, with the endorsement of their parents, drop out of school to seek jobs for sustenance. Uganda reported static school enrolment and increasing drop-out rates due to 'social, economic and cultural pressures'. Similar reports were also made by Nigeria and Ethiopia.[46]

### 5.3.3 *Cultural and Religious Influences*

While poverty and dwindling economic fortunes may be largely responsible for the poor implementation of socio-economic rights, other factors like culture and religion have played an adverse role. In one instance, the Sudanese National Council for the Welfare of the Child faced challenges in ensuring child welfare when parents refused to vaccinate their children against a measles outbreak because of their religious beliefs. In a similar vein, the Cameroonian government reported that its efforts to enrol children into school had been confronted with 'the challenge relating to people's regard for socio-cultural value linked traditions where educating the child in general, and the girl child in particular, is not considered as a priority'.[47] Much like civil and political rights above, one notices that it is vulnerable groups like women and children (particularly the female child) that are more prone to such cultural stigmatisation. Here again, the necessity of the additional instruments[48] to protect the rights of these groups is not left in doubt.

### 5.3.4 *Ignorance and Illiteracy*

Much like civil and political rights, the implementation of socio-economic rights has been affected by ignorance of the protection of this subgroup of rights on the part of the populace. Ssenyonjo states that one contributory cause for the continued marginalisation of this category of rights is the lack of awareness of the Commission's jurisprudence on these rights.[49] Where the people do not appreciate the social and developmental obligations of the government, they cannot reasonably be expected to make complaints on those grounds despite the existence of supportive decisions and interpretations by the Commission. This is further evidenced by the poor use of the Commission's communications procedure in relation to socio-economic rights resulting in its slow jurisprudential development.[50]

The general prevailing ignorance of human rights points to institutional failures both at the national and regional levels. While states have failed in their duty, under Article 25 to educate the general populace on their human rights, the regional system, through the Commission, may have also failed in its promotional duties. This will be discussed in more depth in the next chapter.

## 5.4 Evaluation of the Charter's Content on Rights—Too Ambitious?

The preceding sections have examined the reasons proffered by states for the violation of Charter rights, or in many cases, the inability to stop these violations. Of these, lack of resources, cultural influences and poverty take centre stage with the first being the most cited challenge. These identified challenges naturally raise questions on the Charter's content of rights. Thus, despite being appropriate and geared towards an egalitarian society, are these espoused standards also suited to Africa's prevailing economic and political situation or are they perhaps too ambitious and demanding of the largely developing states? This question is necessary, not only for socio-economic rights like the right to health, but also for civil and political rights.

The sections above have demonstrated that weak institutions, occasioned by the lack of human and financial resources, are one of the major challenges identified by states for non-implementation of civil and political rights. As in the examples above, the inability to build courts and pay more judges would likely result in the prolonged detention of inmates without trial thereby violating their right to a fair trial including the provision to be charged to court within a reasonable time. Lack of resources would also occasion the overcrowding of prisons and affect the right to human dignity—an often-cited challenge[51] for which the Commission has created the office of a special rapporteur. Many similar instances could be mentioned including the inability to train the police force or to site institutions in rural areas.

On the converse side are socio-economic rights which, unlike in other instruments, have been accorded an enforceable status by the Charter. Like civil and political rights, this subset of rights is affected by the lack of human and financial resources. While states have taken varied steps to improve health, education and social services, these areas remain in deplorable states. Given the poor implementation of the Charter rights and the inability of states to enforce them (in many cases), the question that arises is whether the normative standards of the Charter is too ambitious thereby requiring that expectations be scaled down. This question will be addressed in relation to both groups of rights.

### 5.4.1 *Civil and Political Rights*

Addressing the question of whether the Charter's civil and political rights are too ambitious necessarily demands knowledge of the content or substance of those rights. This exercise has already been undertaken at some length in Chapter 3. It was shown that the Charter mainly adopted basic civil and political rights as contained in the Universal Declaration and International Covenant on Civil Political Rights. Granted that the Court and Commission have proactively interpreted the content of those rights, they are not substantively distinct from standard international principles of civil and political rights from which they derive. Interpreting these rights, therefore, as too ambitious and unattainable would be tantamount to putting forward the proposition that African countries are not expected to live up to or observe even the most basic first-generation rights.

Without a doubt, the Charter as a whole was ambitious at its inception. It should be recalled that the Charter was necessitated as a result of gross human rights violations by a number of dictatorial African regimes. Efforts to draft a Charter were commenced in 1979 after three African governments, Idi Amin of Uganda (1971–1979), Macias Nguema of Equatorial Guinea (1968–1979) and Jean-Bedel Bokassa (1966–1976) of the then Central African Empire—known for their egregious violations of human rights—came to an end.[52] The then OAU saw the need for a continental human rights instrument to reinforce the human dignity and worth of Africans that had been utterly disregarded by these regimes as well as the apartheid regime of South Africa. Given the number of military dictatorships and wanton violation of rights, the implementation of civil and political rights was no doubt expected to be a challenge. It was however hoped that the Charter, through its acceptance and adoption, would usher in a period of human rights observance and respect.

Interestingly, as has been shown in the course of this book, most of the conditions that led to the creation of the Charter still exist. For instance, many African states are headed by long-serving and oppressive Heads of States under false appendages of democracy. Keen to maintain their grip on power, these governments would characteristically limit the opposition by arresting dissenters and restricting the press. Sadly, therefore, despite improvements in many quarters as in the eradication of apartheid and democratic transitions of a few African states, the contents of the Charter on civil and political rights could arguably be regarded as ambitious even 40 years after the Charter's creation. This is further amplified by the above-stated challenges particularly the lack of human and financial resources.

This adopted position is supported by the assertion that the shortcomings of the African regional system are mostly practical and political matters to which treaties are, 'to put it bluntly, irrelevant'.[53] Odinkalu lists these practical and political matters as funding, absence of compliance and supportive political will on the part of the state parties, inadequate popular awareness about the system, and the management and administration of the Commission. Some of these issues have already been addressed. With regard to political will, the question that arises is why states would sign and ratify the Charter with little intention of upholding same. Arguments proffered towards this end are analysed below.

#### *5.4.1.1 Why States Do Not Adhere to Their Commitments Under the Charter*

The question of why states do not abide by their Charter commitments is not a simple one. This is especially considering the general, even record-breaking, acceptance and ratification of the Charter. Indeed, there is substantial literature on why some states ratify these international instruments even when they have little intention of abiding by them. Some of the reasons adduced include prestige and states doing 'what they are supposed to do'.[54] An interesting argument in the African case has however been made by Hansungule.[55] Firstly, he argues that the OAU's 'open door policy' which allowed any African state to join the Charter without questions asked on its state of democracy or human rights was responsible for making the Charter 'the only human rights instrument in the world to win near universal endorsement of the potential state parties in a record time'.[56] This was unlike other instruments like the European Convention on Human Rights which operated restricted criteria that required prospective member states to be democratic and be able to respect the rule of law. Hansungule argues that the text of the Charter encourages its accession even by the most repugnant violators of human rights. This is because by creating a weak and 'timorous' institution the Charter ensured its ineffectiveness in stemming the tide of violations taking place. This was the intention of OAU states who 'worked hard' to ensure the Charter's weakness in order to protect their sovereignty. Evidence of this intent could be found in the last two provisions of the Committee of Ministers' Terms of Reference as follows:

to ensure the protection and promotion of human rights declared and accepted as such through the activities of a commission, although reserving the powers of the Assembly which must be associated with the final decisions; and

not to exceed that which African states were ready to accept in the field of the protection of human rights.

Given the above, Hansungule asserts that the system was deliberately not intended to be as strong as critics would have wanted and that criticisms of the Commission are based on an inflated expectation of a system that was not intended to deliver. States' fear of losing their sovereignty was also the reason the Court was deliberately left out of the institutional arrangements at the time. Hansungule's point is, therefore, simple: states do not comply with the Charter because they were never fully committed to doing so. It is important, at this juncture, to recall a similar argument by Shivji[57] who saw the intent behind the Charter as deceitful. He argued that after the fall of three of the continent's dictators identified above, African leaders needed to salvage their severely tainted human rights record and re-establish their qualification for Western aid, and only drafted the Charter to accomplish those aims.

While some of the issues the above commentators raise may be incontrovertible, it is hard to accept every aspect of their arguments. It is true—as briefly surmised in Chapter 3 and further demonstrated in the next chapter—that the Charter created a weak institution in order to cater to mostly new democracies which jealously guarded their sovereignties. However, rather than a being sinister plot of deception, the Charter was a steppingstone that lured these mostly dictatorial countries, albeit gradually, into the unfamiliar world of human rights. Whatever the case, with the additional protocols, especially that which established the Court, African states showed an increased willingness to gradually bind themselves to human rights. However, Hansungule's arguments still hold strong in the aftermath of the Court's creation as shown by the relatively low number of ratifications and declarations on individuals' jurisdiction. Unlike the Charter, which was quickly and generally accepted, the Court's Protocol has largely been met with indifference. It is thus not hard to agree with Hansungule that 'the enthusiasm which greeted the African Charter through the unprecedented number of ratifications in a very short time [was] for most of these states nothing but an empty gesture'.[58] The response to the Court must be seen as a more accurate representation of the states' commitment to human rights protection—reluctance to commit and an aversion to superseding judicial authority. While signing up to the Charter required minor commitments (like sending in periodic reports), ratifying and signing the Article 34(6) Declaration of the Court's Protocol allowing individual access to the Court was more than the majority of states could commit to. As of May 2019, only ten states have made this declaration with Rwanda's 2016 withdrawal effectively bringing the number down to nine. Thus, while the Charter, with its norms and weak institutions, was an initiation or birthing process, African states have shown that they are not quite ready to be weaned. The position is summed up in Heyns' cautious assessment that, 'it is not clear that the political commitment necessary to sustain an independent and impartial regional human rights court in Africa exists'.[59]

The above conclusion would mean that there are no easy policy solutions to the regional human rights system as any viable policy reform suggestions would simply not be adopted or implemented as long as they demand a level of accountability and commitment from member states. This has already been demonstrated in the example of the Court's Protocol where only seven member states have made the declaration allowing individuals and NGOs to institute cases despite constant reminders by the Commission in its various Concluding Observations on state reports. Other commonly canvassed options like the introduction of sanctions by the AU[60] against erring states are also not feasible as the AU has down the years shown an unwillingness to demonstrate such commitment. For instance in 2015, after accusing the International Criminal Court of bias against African leaders and proposing a local solution in the form of the African Court of Justice and Human Rights,[61] Heads of States voted to allow sitting leaders and senior officials immunity from prosecution in the proposed court.[62] This is despite the fact of Africa's long-serving leaders, eleven of whom, as of 2018, had been in power for at least 16 years.[63] This number has gone down in recent months owing to the deposing of the Heads of State of Zimbabwe, Angola and Sudan.

Also, apart from cases of overthrow of governments,[64] the Assembly of Heads of State has hardly sanctioned a member state for serious violations of human rights. This obvious show of camaraderie at the helm of Africa's regional structure does not bode well for human rights protection and enforcement. Here, one can notice a political impasse with little hope for progress, save there is 'a change of heart'[65] by the AU and its member states.

#### 5.4.1.2 *Facilitating a 'Change of Heart': Example from the ECOWAS Court*

While there appears to be limited political will at the regional level, there appears to be some measure of success in at least one of the sub-regions, the Economic Community of West African States (ECOWAS), in its development and sustenance of the ECOWAS Community Court of Justice (ECCJ). Originally created to adjudicate interstate disputes bordering on ECOWAS economic rules, the ECCJ has gradually metamorphosed into a human rights tribunal through the adoption of a Supplementary Protocol allowing the ECCJ to receive human rights complaints from individuals.

It is interesting to note that, while West African governments authorised the ECCJ to review human rights suits filed by individuals, the same was not the case for private actors complaining about violations of ECOWAS economic rules such as the free movement of goods and persons, a situation which had propelled the reforms in the first place. For instance, in the 2004 case of *Olajide Afolabi v Federal Republic of Nigeria*,[66] a Nigerian trader, Olajide Afolabi, who had entered into a contract to purchase goods in Benin, which were meant for transport to Nigeria, could not complete the transaction following the closing of the border between the two countries by the Nigerian government. After deliberations, the ECCJ ruled that under the Protocol, only member states could institute cases. The court restrained itself from making an expansive ruling, concluding instead that ECOWAS political bodies must expressly grant the ECCJ jurisdiction to hear suits from private actors. However, rather than simply address the issue of jurisdiction in matters relating to ECOWAS' economic integration, the 2005 Supplementary Protocol introduced new features for human rights complaints in West Africa: direct access by individuals and non-exhaustion of domestic remedies.[67] The latter feature meant that aggrieved persons could bring human rights complaints before the ECCJ in Abuja without needing to go through their national courts.

It is not easy to understand such audacious reforms for the ECCJ when the same ECOWAS member states have opposed or not complied with similar reforms at the AU level. A number of reasons have been adduced for this anomaly. One reason is that human rights NGOs lobbied hard for these features especially the omission of an exhaustion of local remedies requirement. These arguments and propositions were in turn accepted by ECOWAS officials who recognised, inter alia, that it was difficult for individuals to access national courts in human rights cases. With regard to the lack of enumerated rights, it was proposed that governments assumed that the references to the African Charter in the ECOWAS treaty and other legal texts would lead the ECCJ to view the Charter as the Community's primary source of human rights norms. Also, they viewed the absence of an exhaustion requirement as an experiment that could be revisited if the system proved to be unworkable—this especially given the fact that the Protocol entered into force on a provisional basis.

The ECCJ example is one rare demonstration of political will and commitment by African states. Unfortunately, this has not been replicated at the regional level and even other sub-regions. For instance, the SADC disbanded its Tribunal following the latter's decision against Zimbabwe. On the converse side, while there are still cases of non-implementation of the ECCJ's decisions,[68] member states have usually protected its mandate. For instance, attempts by the Gambia to restrict the Court's jurisdiction, after two decisions were made against it, were spurned by the other states parties. The ECCJ, owing to its wider jurisdiction, also has a healthy docket of cases compared to the African Court.

It may, therefore, be argued that the African Court can be developed in a fashion similar to the ECCJ. Thus, the requisite political will can be garnered by using the ECCJ as a reference point in such promotions. Also, the daring developments of the ECCJ, such as non-exhaustion of local remedies, show that despite their reservations African states could occasionally be made to conform to high, pace-setting standards.

### 5.4.2 *Socio-Economic Rights: Achievable or Ambitious?*

It may appear at first sight futile to discuss the ambitiousness of positive duties such as socio-economic provisions in the Charter when civil and political rights have been categorised as ambitious with regard to implementation. However, it must be pointed out that, as far as the system of government in place is concerned, a state may sufficiently provide for socio-economic rights while defaulting in civil and political rights. Reference may be made here to economically stable countries like Saudi Arabia and China of which, in spite of positive economic provisions, there are often reports of entrenched violations of civil and political rights such as the rights to freedom of expression, association and religion. This, however, may not be the case in Africa where, aside from running unaccountable and often dictatorial governments, there are, generally, insufficient resources to meet these rights.

The ambitiousness of the Charter with regard to socio-economic rights can be seen in their justiciability and in the absence of a 'progressive realisation' clause. The former was not the consequence of oversight as the Charter had consciously done away with a first draft that differentiated between civil and political rights on the one hand and economic, social and cultural rights on the other.[69] By according these rights the same status as civil and political rights, the Charter emphasised their utmost importance and priority regardless of the states' financial positions. Viljoen states that the justiciability of socio-economic rights was a response to the prevailing situation of dire poverty and exploitation by kleptocratic elites. Their justiciability was, therefore, an acknowledgement that accountability through the law was part of the solution.

Three different positions will be used to demonstrate the ambitious nature of the Charter's stance. They are the provisions of the International Covenant on Economic, Social and Cultural Rights (ICESCR), the South African experience and the Commission's decisions on communications. These are briefly examined below.

#### *5.4.2.1 Provisions of the ICESCR*

Article 2 of the ICESCR provides that each state party must undertake to take steps 'to the maximum of its available resources' to 'achieving progressively' the full realisation of the rights recognised in the Covenant, including particularly the adoption of legislative measures. In sharp contrast to the African Charter, this provision acknowledges the diverse economic strengths of member states and requires that they fulfil their obligations to the maximum of available resources. In interpreting this provision, the UN Committee on Economic, Social and Cultural Rights has stated that the provision for progressive realisation should not be misinterpreted as depriving the obligation of all meaningful content. While it is, on the one hand, a necessary device reflecting the realities of the real world, on the other hand, it must be read in the light of the overall objective of the Covenant which is to establish clear obligations for states parties in respect of the full realisation of the rights in question. It, therefore, imposes an obligation to move as expeditiously and effectively as possible towards that goal.[70] This would imply that even when the available resources are demonstrably inadequate, the obligation remains for a state party to strive to ensure the widest possible enjoyment of the rights under the prevailing circumstances.[71] Theoretically, this would seem to reflect the Charter's intent as it cannot reasonably be the case that the drafters intended for states to fulfil their obligations even where it was practically impossible to do so. As will be seen shortly, the Commission has adopted a similar position. In any event, the absence of any qualification in the Charter despite the existence of a precedent in the form of the ICESCR is only a pointer to its high demands and expectation.

#### *5.4.2.2 The South African Experience*

South Africa was the first of only two African states, the other being Kenya, to implement the principle of indivisibility of rights as opposed to the majority that relegated socio-economic rights to non-justiciable directive principles of state policy. The country's 1996 Constitution included a range of socio-economic rights, with the most important of these contained in Sections 26 and 27. The former provides for the right to have access to adequate housing while the latter guarantees the right to have access to healthcare services, sufficient food and water, and social security. However, both of these sections are qualified by the provision that the state must take reasonable legislative and other measures, within its available resources, to achieve the progressive realisation of these rights. Thus, while adopting the justiciability of these rights as guaranteed under the Charter, South Africa was careful to insert the 'available resources' and 'progressive realisation' clauses present in the ICESCR.

Despite these safeguards, and other supportive frameworks, the enforcement of socio-economic rights through litigation has proven to be challenging. Keightley identifies the primary underlying factor for this as 'the disjuncture between the constitutional promise to effect social justice through the enforcement of socio-economic rights, and the actual extent of the socio-economic need on the ground'.[72] The poverty gap in South Africa is huge, as well as the backlog in the provision of basic services, that it far outstrips the capacity of the state's available resources to effect delivery.[73] As such, the burden of expectation on the courts to fill the gaps through socio-economic rights adjudication is disproportionately high. This has prompted the country's Constitutional Court to interpret these rights as well as the corresponding obligations on the states in the light of the 'relevant social and historical context'. While they remain justiciable, there are clearly limitations in the area of litigation. Thus, the courts would not take over the duties of the executive and legislative arms of government whose responsibility it is to assess social and economic needs and put in place measures to fulfil these needs. While the state is required to set clear targets for the fulfilment of its socio-economic obligations and to explain its policy choices, the courts will not interfere provided the policy is reasonable and the process followed is not flawed. For instance, the question of whether the measures adopted to give effect to socio-economic rights are reasonable or not will depend to a great extent on the particular difficulties and resource challenges faced by the state.[74]

The approach of striking a balance between holding the exercise of public power accountable to the Constitution and deferring to the policy choices of the government has been adjudged to have resulted 'in very modest gains for the poor'.[75] This only goes to show the practical difficulty in enforcing these rights and placing them on the same level as civil and political rights. As the South African Court has observed, limitations must be placed on litigating socio-economic rights as the other arms of government are better placed, more so statutorily, to make such policy decisions. It would, therefore, amount to usurping the roles of these other arms for the courts to routinely overrule their decisions. As such, it has been argued that socio-economic rights 'may well promise more than they can deliver', even though the modest consequence of compelling government to justify its policy choices when they affect the poor should not be discounted.[76]

The South African example, being one instance of enforcement of socio-economic rights in Africa, goes to illustrate the practical difficulties of litigating these rights even where the 'available resources' and 'progressive realisation' clauses exist. Such an example can only demonstrate the high expectations of the African Charter which does not include these clauses.

#### 5.4.2.3 *The Commission's Position*

Perhaps the most obvious evidence of the Charter's ambitiousness is in the position taken by the Commission when deciding the relatively few complaints on socio-economic rights. Despite the obvious absence of the notions of 'progressive realisation' and 'available resources', the Commission read these into the Charter in the case of *Purohit and Moore v. The*

*Gambia*[77] (the *Purohit case*). In interpreting the state's duty under Article 16 (right to health), the Commission stated thus:

> The African Commission would ... like to state that it is aware that millions of people in Africa are not enjoying the right to health maximally because African countries are generally faced with the problem of poverty which renders them incapable [of providing] the necessary amenities, infrastructure and resources that facilitate the full enjoyment of this right. Therefore, having due regard to this depressing but real state of affairs, the African Commission would like to read into Article 16 the obligation on part of states party to the African Charter to take concrete and targeted steps, while taking full advantage of its available resources, to ensure that the right to health is fully realised in all its aspects without discrimination of any kind.[78]

The Commission's position above has been suggested to establish that the availability of resources is a relevant factor when determining whether a state is in violation of the socio-economic rights in the African Charter.[79] Thus, a state should not be held to be in violation in such cases as seen in Chapter 4 as long as it can be shown that the available resources are not sufficient to meet those needs.

In summary, the above sections have demonstrated that the expectations of the Charter with regard to socio-economic rights were and remain higher than attainable, at least to the extent of equating the delivery of civil and political rights with socio-economic rights. However, taking into consideration the South African example, it would be more pragmatic to demand their justiciability by states albeit with the qualification of 'progressive realisation' according to 'available resources'.

#### *5.4.2.4 The Importance of Justiciability for Africa*

While it is accepted that most African states cannot adequately fulfil their socio-economic obligations, it would be retrogressive to suggest that they be rid of any form of accountability for these duties. The inclusion and accordance of a relatively high status to socio-economic rights in the Charter were deliberate. As has already been argued, it was a response to the prevalent poverty in African states often occasioned by corrupt and inefficient governments. The correct progressive step was to make these rights justiciable to allow for some measure of state accountability. An enforceable system of socio-economic rights could provide a means of challenging governments' priorities and holding them accountable for the expenditure of international aid and loans.[80] Agbakwa argues that poor economic conditions do not justify outright non-enforcement but should merely affect the extent to which these rights can be realised. Rather than be seen as a clog in its wheel, the enforcement of these rights could actually catalyse development. It could also reduce the spate of armed conflicts most of which are caused by the denial of these rights to the people who believe that taking up arms against the government is the only way to fight for their enforcement. In other words, if there are no legitimate ways to enforce these rights, the people may resort to armed revolutions. This latter argument is supported by Bulto who argues that justiciability of socio-economic rights is 'perhaps the most viable means' through which marginalised and impoverished groups can voice their grievances and oppose any systematic exclusions that they face.[81] It is unfortunate, therefore, given the many arguments in favour of justiciability, that the vast majority of African states have chosen the opposite path of non-justiciability.

#### *5.4.2.5 Solution Through the Regional System*

While the most obvious path forward would be for states and national parliaments to make socio-economic rights justiciable, an argument can also be made for the regional system to take over the role of enhancing their justiciability. Generally, a complaint can only be brought before the Commission where the applicant has exhausted domestic remedies. However, given the non-justiciable nature of socio-economic rights in most African states, the Commission, it has been argued, could exercise original jurisdiction on economic and social rights since individuals cannot be expected to exhaust domestic remedies which do not exist.[82] Thus, the Commission would be examining alleged violations of socio-economic rights as a tribunal of the first instance. This would allow the opportunity of further developing the jurisprudence of these rights. Much as compliance with decisions may not be guaranteed as seen in the cases of violations of civil and political rights, such pronouncements and jurisprudential developments could set the tone for future legislative measures and precedential references. It has accordingly been pointed out that, given that the adjudication and jurisprudence of socio-economic rights have yet to take root in a great majority of domestic jurisdictions across the continent, the fate of socio-economic rights is bound up with the prospects of the African regional human rights mechanism generally.[83]

However, despite what may appear as an opportunity for the Commission, socio-economic rights have mostly been relegated to the background in terms of normative and jurisprudential development. The Commission's case law has mostly dealt with civil and political rights such as the right to a fair trial, freedom of speech, and freedom from torture, inhuman and degrading treatment. The fault is however not entirely the Commission's and largely owes to the fact that civil society actors have mostly raised issues relating to civil and political rights despite the existence of numerous socio-economic problems. After more than two decades of coming into force, the African Commission had dealt with relatively few communications dealing principally with socio-economic rights.

It becomes clear that to improve legal accountability and the justiciability of these rights, the regional system must step up its role. It must, however, be pointed out that the legal/judicial option is only an aid and not a solution to the enforcement of socio-economic rights. This conclusion can be easily garnered from the analysis of the South African experience. Supporting this argument, Keightley states that the difficulty for lawyers involved in socio-economic rights work in South Africa was that, because of the weakness in other parts of the system, 'disproportionate reliance' was sometimes placed on finding a solution through the law in order to rectify the hardships suffered by many South Africans. As has been seen above, this has not always yielded the desired results.

## 5.5 Conclusions on Governments' Enforcement of the Charter

The aim of this chapter has been to analyse the failure of implementation by states of the provisions and standards of the African Charter. Overall, the above analyses reveal two main causes of poor implementation of the Charter by member states. On the one hand is the governments' low level of commitment evidenced by occasional sheer disregard of the provisions of the Charter and the reluctance to promote judicial accountability at the regional level. On the other hand are practical challenges (such as lack of resources, poverty, obnoxious customary practices and illiteracy) that governments face when trying to implement the Charter. Thus, were it to be the case that governments were fully willing and cooperative in implementing the Charter, they would still fall short of the Charter standards. This would be true not only for socio-economic and peoples' rights but also for civil and political rights. With regard to the challenges affecting the implementation of civil and political rights, it was posited that, while proposing economic measures that would increase human and financial resources may be outside the purview of the book, the other challenges like culture and ignorance may be reasonably countered through effective promotion by all of the relevant actors. Such step requires a concerted effort by these actors to meet the huge need for knowledge of these rights and how to protect them through a viable Plan of Action. It is important to recall at this stage that promotion of human rights is also one of the key duties of the Commission which will be further examined in the next chapter.

With regard to socio-economic rights, the case was made for the justiciability of these rights. Even though resource constraints constitute a major impediment, it was argued that states should subject themselves to that minimum level of accountability provided by the courts. The case was further made for the Commission, exploiting the non-justiciability of these rights in many states, to adjudicate on issues arising therefrom thereby developing the jurisprudence in that area. In any event, it was pointed out that justiciability should not be viewed as an end in itself but only a means to such end. Even though it may not necessarily guarantee the implementation of these rights in some countries, justiciability is a necessary first step.

The chapter further dealt with the issues of political will and cooperation from member states. Here it was established that African states are generally not fully committed to the regional system especially in the area of judicial accountability. Even commitment to the regional normative standards is questionable for some states. While the African regional system has adopted a gradual initiation process to introduce otherwise dictatorial regimes to a functional regional human rights system, it appears that some states by their positive systemic violations of rights are not quite ready to commit to these standards. Thus, after acceding to these standards, these few states have accorded priority to other political considerations in their dealings with their respective citizenry. The implication of this is that, to the extent that the lack of political will constitutes a problem to the implementation of the Charter, policy reforms offer little hope for improvement. This is because sincere political commitment is necessary for the application of these reforms. For human rights to thrive, African governments must be willing to enforce the Charter and also subject themselves to accountability under the regional system. Since human rights are owed to the individual, it makes little sense that these same individuals are not, for instance, allowed access to the Court by over 86% of member states. While they do have access to the Commission, the latter has been plagued with concerns about the status of its decisions or 'recommendations', which explains the subsequent creation of a Court. Theoretically, the Court should ideally be best placed to play the role of arbiter, but with just over a dozen decisions on the merit since its inception, having been largely constrained by jurisdictional limitations, the Commission necessarily occupies this position, at least in the interim. What this entails is that member states have to develop a culture of implementing decisions of the Commission and this requires a higher level of commitment than being currently displayed. It has already been demonstrated, through the example of the ECCJ, that African governments can indeed make some of these concessions and commitments. This would likely require constant prodding from external actors like NGOs, a subject briefly examined in the next chapter.

## Notes

1. Human Rights Watch, "World Report 2014: Nigeria", accessed April 12, 2016, http://www.hrw.org/world-report/2014/country-chapters/nigeria.
2. Michelle Faul, "Nigeria's Military Killing Thousands of Detainees" (Lagos: Associated Press, October 18, 2013).
3. Republic of Malawi, "Report to the African Commission on Human and Peoples' Rights: Implementation of the African Charter on Human and Peoples Rights 1995–2013 and the Protocol to the African Charter on Human and Peoples Rights on the Rights of Women 2005–2013" (2014) para 44.
4. Abdullahi An-Na'im, *Human Rights Under African Constitutions* (University of Pennsylvania Press 2003) 23.
5. Republic of Nigeria, "4th Periodic Country Report on the Implementation of the African Charter on Human and Peoples' Rights in Nigeria" (2011) 36, http://www.achpr.org/files/sessions/50th/state-reports/4th-2008-2010/staterep4_nigeria_2011_eng.pdf.
6. Republic of Uganda, "Periodic Report by the Government of Uganda to the African Commission on Human and Peoples' Rights" (2011) 27.
7. Michelo Hansungule, "The African Charter on Human and Peoples' Rights: A Critical Review" (2000) 8 *African Yearbook of International Law* 265, 325.
8. Hansungule, "African Charter," 325.
9. An-Na'im, *Human Rights.*

10. John Mubangizi, "A South African Perspective on the Clash Between Culture and Human Rights, with Particular Reference to Gender-Related Cultural Practices and Traditions" (2012) 13(3) *Journal of International Women's Studies* 33.
11. Nina Lakhani, "Victory in Sight for Revolution Over Female Genital Mutilation" (2012) cited in John Mubangizi (n 31).
12. Bonny Ibhawoh, "Between Culture and Constitution: Evaluating the Cultural Legitimacy of Human Rights in the African State" (2000) 22(3) *Human Rights Quarterly* 838, 859.
13. Ibhawoh, "Culture".
14. Ibid., 857–858.
15. Mackie and others, 'Social Dynamics of Abandonment of Harmful Practices: A New Look at the Theory' (2009) cited in Mubangizi, "South African."
16. Mubangizi, "South African," 45.
17. Sonia Cardenas, "Constructing rights? Human Rights Education and the State" (2005) 26(4) *International Political Science Review* 363, 368.
18. One such measure is the African Human Rights Education which is a four-year programme developed by Amnesty International to promote human rights through education in 10 African nations: Benin, Burkina Faso, Cote d'Ivoire, Ghana, Kenya, Mali, Senegal, Sierra Leone, Togo and Uganda. See "The East and Horn of Africa HRDs Project", accessed July 21, 2016, https://www.defenddefenders.org/african-human-rights-education-project/.
19. Section 16 of Amendment 17 of the Constitution of Zimbabwe 2005.
20. Communication Nos. 140/94, 141/94, 145/95 (1999).
21. Precious Ndlovu, 'Campbell v Republic of Zimbabwe: A Moment of Truth for the SADC Tribunal' (2011) 1 *Southern Africa Development Community Journal* 63, 72.
22. Bill Kinsey, "Zimbabwe's Land Reform Program: Underinvestment in Post-conflict Transformation" (2004) 32(10) *World Development* 1669.
23. See David Blaire, *Degrees in Violence: Robert Mugabe and the Struggle for Power in Zimbabwe* (New York: Continuum) 2002; D. Lessing, "The Jewel of Africa" (2003) 50 *New York review of Books*, 6–10.
24. Rhoda Howard-Hassmann, "Mugabe's Zimbabwe, 2000–2009: Massive Human Rights Violations and the Failure to Protect" (2010) 32(4) *Human Rights Quarterly*, 900.
25. Communication No. 245/2002.
26. Laurie Nathan, "The Disbanding of the SADC Tribunal: A Cautionary Tale" (2013) 35 *Human Rights Quarterly* 870; W. Sandholtz, Y. Bei, and K. Caldwell, "Backlash and International Human Rights Courts" in *Contracting Human Rights: Crisis, Accountability, and Opportunity* (2018) 159.

27. Amnesty International, "Sudan: Entrenched repression—Freedom of Expression and Association under Unprecedented Attack" (2015), accessed August 15, 2017, https://www.amnesty.ch/de/laender/afrika/sudan/dok/2015/sudan-zunahme-der-repression-vor-den-wahlen/amnesty-bericht-entrenched-repression-freedom-of-expression-association-under-unprecedented-attack.
28. For instance, in 2006 the Sudan Organisation against Torture drew attention to instances of censorship of the media. See Sunday Tribune, "Human Rights Alert" (2006) http://www.sudantribune.com/spip.php?article17559, accessed February 6, 2016.
29. Lutz Oette, "In Bad Company: South Sudan's Proposed New Security" (Sudan: Sudan Tribune, October 6, 2014), http://www.sudantribune.com/spip.php?article52644.
30. Amnesty International, *Agents of Fear: The National Security Service in Sudan* (Amnesty International, London 2010).
31. *Commission Nationale des Droits de l'Homme et des libertes v. Chad*, Communication No. 74/92.
32. Amnesty International, "Agents," 12.
33. L. Helfer and A. Showalter, "Opposing International Justice: Kenya's Integrated Backlash Strategy Against the ICC" (2017) iCourts Working Paper Series.
34. African Charter Preamble.
35. Republic of Kenya, "Combined 8th–11th Periodic Report on the African Charter on Human & Peoples' Rights" (2014) para 179, accessed January 22, 2019, http://www.achpr.org/files/sessions/57th/state-reports/8th-11th-2008-2014/kenya_state_report_eng.pdf.
36. Ngozi Okonjo-Iweala, *Fighting Corruption Is Dangerous: The Story Behind the Headlines* (MIT Press, London 2018) 37–39.
37. Ibid.
38. Office of the Accountant General of the Federation, May 2015, Record of Transactions in the Bank for International Settlements account obtained through the Central Bank of Nigeria; cited in Ngozi Okonjo-Iweala, *Fighting Corruption Is Dangerous* 69.
39. QZ, "Nigeria Has Issued an Arrest Warrant for Its Former Oil Minister", accessed July 4, 2019, https://qz.com/africa/1484980/diezani-alison-madueke-nigeria-issues-arrest-warrant/.
40. Transparency International, "Index 2018", accessed July 4, 2019, https://www.transparency.org/cpi2018.
41. Rhoda Howard-Hassmann, *In Defense of Universal Human Rights* (Polity Press 2018) 132.
42. Christopher Mbazira, "Enforcing the Economic, Social and Cultural Rights in the African Charter on Human and Peoples' Rights: Twenty

Years of Redundancy, Progression and Significant Strides" (2006) 6 *AHRLJ* 333, 334.

43. The World Bank, accessed October 8, 2018, http://datatopics.worldbank.org/sdgatlas/archive/2017/SDG-01-no-poverty.html.
44. Frans Viljoen, *International Human Rights Law in Africa* (Oxford University Press 2012) 481.
45. Republic of Kenya, "Combined 8th–11th Periodic Report on the African Charter on Human & Peoples' Rights" (2014), http://www.achpr.org/files/sessions/57th/state-reports/8th-11th-2008-2014/kenya_state_report_eng.pdf, accessed January 12, 2016.
46. Republic of Ethiopia, "The Fifth and Sixth Periodic Country Report 2009–2013 on the Implementation of the African Charter On Human and Peoples' Rights in Ethiopia" (2014), http://www.achpr.org/files/sessions/56th/state-reports/5-2009-2013/ethiopia_state_rport_eng.pdf.
47. Cameroon, "Report," para 304.
48. The Women's Protocol and the African Charter on the Right and Welfare of the Child.
49. Manisuli Ssenyonjo, "Analysing the Economic, Social and Cultural Rights Jurisprudence of the African Commission: 30 Years Since the Adoption of the African Charter" (2011) 29(3) *Netherlands Quarterly of Human Rights* 358.
50. Takele Soboka Bulto, "The Utility of Cross-Cutting Rights in Enhancing Justiciability of Socio-Economic Rights in the African Charter on Human and Peoples' Rights" (2010) 29(2) *The University of Tasmania Law Review* 142, 162.
51. See Chapter 4. The Commission has regularly raised the issue of prison congestion in its Concluding Observations.
52. Kenneth Asamoa Acheampong, "Reforming the Substance of the African Charter on Human and Peoples' Rights: Civil and Political Rights and Socio-Economic Rights" (2001) 2 *AHRLJ* 185.
53. Chidi Odinkalu, "The Role of Case and Complaints Procedures in the Reform of the African Regional Human Rights System" (2001) 2 *AHRLJ* 225, 244.
54. See, for instance, C. M. Wotipka and K. Tsutsui, "Global Human Rights and State Sovereignty: State Ratification of International Human Rights Treaties, 1965–2001" (2008) 23(4) *Sociological Forum* 724.
55. Michelo Hansungule, 'The African Charter on Human and Peoples Rights: A Critical Review" (2000) 8 *African Yearbook of International Law* 265.
56. Ibid.
57. See Chapter 2. Also, Shivji, *The Concept*, 94.
58. Michelo Hansungule, "The African Charter on Human and Peoples Rights: A Critical Review" (2000) 8 *AYBIL*.

59. Christof Heyns, "Some Thoughts on Challenges Facing the International Protection of Human Rights in Africa" (2009) 27 *Netherlands Quarterly of Human Rights* 447, 448
60. See Hansungule, "African Charter," 268; Mbazira, "Enforcing," 333.
61. A proposed coalition of the African Court of Human and Peoples' Rights and the African Court of Justice.
62. Monica Mark, *The Guardian*, "African Leaders Vote Themselves immunity from New Human Rights Court" (2015), accessed September 26, 2016, http://www.theguardian.com/global-development/2014/jul/03/african-leaders-vote-immunity-human-rights-court.
63. Kealeboga Maphunye, "Weaning African Leaders Off Their Addiction to Power Is an Ongoing Struggle" (Quartz Africa, April 2018), https://qz.com/africa/1255609/africas-longest-serving-presidents-in-uganda-cameroon-equatorial-guinea-others-are-addicted-to-power/.
64. See Chapter 7.
65. Mbazira, "Enforcing," 333.
66. ECW/CCJ/JUD/01/04.
67. Laurence R. Helfer and others, "A New International Human Rights Court for West Africa: The ECOWAS Community Court of Justice" (2013) 107(4) *African Journal of International Law* 737.
68. Premium Times, "ECOWAS Frowns at Non-enforcement of Decisions by Member States", accessed April 22, 2014, https://www.premiumtimesng.com/news/159166-ecowas-court-frowns-non-enforcement-decisions-member-states.html.
69. Viljoen, *International*, 215.
70. UN Committee on Economic, Social and Cultural Rights, *General Comment No. 3, The nature of States parties obligations* (art 2, para 1 of the Covenant), UN Doc E/1991/23 (1990) para 9, cited in Dennis M Davis, "Socioeconomic Rights: Do They Deliver the Goods?" (2008) 6(3&4) *International Journal of Constitutional Law* 687, 699.
71. Athew C. Raven, *The International Covenant of Economic, Social and Cultural Rights* (Clarendon Press 1995) 138.
72. Raylene Keightley, "The Challenges of Litigating Socio-Economic Rights in South Africa" (2011) *New Zealand Law Review* 296, 305.
73. Christopher Mbazira, "Appropriate, Just and Equitable Relief' in Socio-Economic Rights Litigation: The Tension between Corrective and Distributive Forms of Justice" (2008) 125 *South African Law Journal* 71 at 86 cited in Keightley, "Supra," 305.
74. See *Mazibuko v City of Johannesburg* [2009] ZACC 28, 2010 (4) SA 1 at 61; Government of the Republic of South Africa & Ors v Grootboom & Ors 2000 (11) BCLR 1169. (CC) where the court held that the applicants were entitled to be provided with basic shelter as Article 28 of the South African Constitution was not subject to available resources.

75. Davis, "Socioeconomic."
76. Ibid.
77. Communication No. 241/01.
78. Para 84.
79. Mbazira, "Enforcing," 353.
80. Agbakwa, "Reclaiming," 177.
81. Bulto, "Utility," 152.
82. Nana K. A. Busia, Jr and Bibiane G. Mbaye, "Filing Communications on Economic and Social Rights Under the African Human and Peoples' Charter (The Banjul Charter)" (1996) 3(2) *East African Journal of Peace and Human Rights* 188, 197 cited in Bulto, "Utility," 149.
83. Chidi Anselm Odinkalu, "Analysis of Paralysis or Paralysis by Analysis? Implementing Economic, Social, and Cultural Rights under the African Charter on Human and Peoples' Rights" (2001) 23 *Human Rights Quarterly* 327, 366.

CHAPTER 6

# Institutional Enforcement of the Charter: Challenges Faced by the African Court and Commission

## 6.1 Introduction

The previous chapters have so far examined the principles of the Charter and states' implementation of those principles. This chapter begins the third part of the book by examining the effectiveness of institutional framework for enforcing the Charter.

Two distinct bodies were created to oversee the implementation of the Charter and its Protocol. They are the African Commission and the African Court. While the African Commission is charged with the promotion and protection of human rights, the Court is to complement the protective mandate of the Commission. The creation of a Court to complement the protective mandate of the Commission can already be viewed as an admission, by the relevant parties, of the inadequacy of the former in that respect. These perceived inadequacies are introduced in this chapter and further examined in the next. The chapter also briefly examines the promotional mandate of the Commission and identifies some of the challenges that arise in the fulfilment of this mandate.


A. Uwazuruike, *Human Rights under the African Charter*,
https://doi.org/10.1007/978-3-030-41739-0_6

## 6.2 Regime for the Enforcement of Human Rights in Africa: The Commission and Court

In order to ensure compliance and protect guaranteed rights, the African Charter established the African Commission which was to play both promotional and protective roles. However, given what was a less than satisfactory result, a court was created in 2004 to complement the Commission's work and mandate. The following sections are brief introductions to these bodies and their intended roles.

## 6.3 The Commission

Article 30 of the Charter provides for the creation of an African Commission 'to promote human and peoples' rights and ensure their protection in Africa'. Chapter 2 of the Charter further classifies the mandate of the Commission into four categories:

a. Promotion of human and peoples' rights,
b. Protection of human and peoples' rights,
c. Interpretation of the provisions of the Charter,
d. Performance of any other tasks entrusted to it by the Assembly of Heads of State and Government.

### *6.3.1 Promotional Role*

While not strictly defining the term 'promotion', Article 45 of the Charter sets out three categories of activities that fall under it. They are:

a. To collect documents, undertake studies and researches on African problems in the field of human and peoples' rights, organise seminars, symposia and conferences, disseminate information, encourage national and local institutions concerned with human and peoples' rights, and give views or make recommendations to governments.
b. To formulate and lay down principles and rules aimed at solving legal problems relating to human and peoples' rights and fundamental freedoms upon which African governments may base their legislations.

c. Cooperate with other African and international institutions concerned with the promotion and protection of human and peoples' rights.

Article 30 of the Charter provides for the establishment of a Commission to 'promote human and people's rights and ensure their protection in Africa'. The Commission's duty of promotion is further explained, in Article 45, to include: collecting documents, undertaking studies and researches on African problems in the field of human rights, organising seminars, symposia and conferences, disseminating information, encouraging national and local human rights institutions, and making human rights recommendations to governments.

The Commission has, accordingly, carried out its promotional role through publications, resolutions and press releases, missions, lectures and conferences, research and state reports. The Commission had also previously set up a 'fairly respectable' documentation centre, for human rights studies and research, at its secretariat.[1] It has also organised several seminars, symposia and conferences aimed at promoting human and peoples' rights on the continent.[2] As part of its sensitisation programme, the Commission passed a 'Resolution on the celebration of an African Day of Human Rights'.[3] Governments and Commissioners were expected to engage in activities on 21 October, the day on which the Charter entered into force, with the aim of raising awareness of human rights and the Charter. The Commission has also collaborated with other institutions to hold conferences. One result of such conferences was the development of a draft of the Women's Protocol and the appointment of the Special Rapporteur on the Rights of Women.

Commissioners, together with legal officers from the Secretariat, undertake promotional visits to a few countries each year. Article 46 of the Charter, which requires the Commission to use 'any appropriate method of investigation', is the legal basis for missions. The aim of such missions is to promote the rights in the African Charter and other regional instruments by engaging governments and civil society as well as gathering information, in particular in relation to the thematic mandates of the commissioners participating in the visit.[4]

Another key means of promotion is through the examination of State Reports which has been described as the core of the Commission's promotional mandate.[5] Through this process, the Commission examines reports of various states on the practice and implementation of human rights in those states and then makes recommendations for reform. These recommendations, as shown in Chapter 4, are often in the form of suggested policy and legislative reforms and ratification and implementation of treaties.

#### *6.3.1.1 Challenges to Promotion*

The Commission's exercise of its promotional mandate has met with a number of criticisms and challenges. One of these criticisms concerns the Commission's failure to use the media and other outlets in creating the necessary publicity and awareness. Commentators have, over the years, highlighted the importance of creating awareness and publicity of the Commission's activities. For instance, while pointing out the Commission's failure in its promotional mandate, Kiwinda has stated the need to publicise the regional system through 'publications, promotional missions, hosting more sessions in all states and through the mass media'.[6] Former Chairman of the Commission, Oji Umozurike, also noted the need for the Commission to improve in the areas of advertising its work and disseminating its publications. He lamented the lack of publicity of the Commission's decisions many of which were not known even in the states where the complaints originated. Publicity, he argued, must be sought through enhanced cooperation with the media, NGOs and institutions of higher learning.[7] Similarly, Isanga has identified the need to educate Africans about the regional mechanism. He argues that unless mechanisms like the Court are 'popularised in the African consciousness [they] will remain at the periphery of peoples' lives'.[8]

Another challenge to the Commission's exercise of its promotional mandate is its lack of adequate funding.[9] Lack of funding means that the Commission cannot undertake promotional visits in many countries with its few visits being made possible mainly by donations from outside the continent.[10] In one instance, the Special Rapporteur on Prisons reported that, while he received numerous requests to conduct prison inspections in some countries, none materialised due to a lack of resources.[11] This situation also means that the overwhelmed commissioners cannot appoint enough staff to oversee the day-to-day activities of the Commission. This problem of funding has remained persistent and unresolved with the call for financial and other support to the Commission being the most consistently recurring theme in the resolutions and decisions of both the OAU and the AU Assembly.[12]

Following the AU's seeming failure to come it its aid, the Commission has had to largely rely on external donations. Such donations have come from the European Union and United Nations Commission on Human Rights as well as foreign institutions like the Danish Agency for International Development, Swedish International Development Agency and Raoul Wallenberg Institute for Human Rights and Humanitarian Law. With the support of these bodies, the Commission has been able to hire a few staff, organise conferences and engage in other promotional ventures.

A third challenge is the lack of adequate support from member states. For instance, in one of its recent Activity Reports,[13] the Commission stated that it was unable to undertake any promotional mission during the reporting period partly because the designated member states had not responded or authorised the requested promotional missions. Also, as highlighted in Chapter 4, the Commission's promotional duty has been severely affected by the failure of states to submit their reports when due, if at all. As of early 2019, 19 states were late by one or two reports while 18 others were late by three or more reports. Six states had not yet made any submissions to the Commission. Such failure by states invariably results in an inability on the part of the Commission to perform its promotional mandate.

### 6.3.2 *Protective Mandate*

On the Commission's protective role, the Charter provides that it is to ensure the protection of rights under conditions laid down in the Charter. These conditions are basically outlined in the communications procedure through which the Commission addresses complaints of violations of rights protected under the Charter. By Article 47, a state may institute a complaint against another state where it believes that that state has violated the provisions of the Charter. By Article 50, the Commission can only deal with a matter submitted to it after making sure that all local remedies, if they exist, have been exhausted, unless it is obvious to the Commission that the procedure of achieving these remedies would be unduly prolonged. This provision prevents forum shopping and duplication of actions.

It is interesting to note that, unlike for state communications, the Charter does not expressly provide for individual and NGO complaints.

The existence of this group of complaints can only be deduced from Article 55 which provides for the Secretary of the Commission to transmit to other members a list of communications 'other than those of state parties' for the purpose of deciding which communications would be considered. Article 56 goes on to provide the criteria such communications must meet in order to be eligible for consideration. These include an indication of the authors, compatibility with the Charter, exhaustion of domestic remedies and the use of non-disparaging language.

The Charter does not expressly grant the Commission any clear judicial authority to make binding decisions or impose sanctions on states. Rather Article 52 provides that the Commission, in the case of state communications, shall prepare a report to the states concerned and transmit same to the Assembly of Heads of State and Government. While transmitting the report to the Assembly, the Commission may make 'such recommendations as it deems useful'.[14] The Commission is again required to draw the attention of the Assembly to special cases involving serious or massive violations of human rights and undertake in-depth studies of these cases accompanied by its findings and recommendations upon the request of the Assembly.

The Commission's protective mandate was recently called into question by no less a body than the AU Executive Council. At its 33rd Ordinary Session, in June 2018, the Executive Council called on state parties to 'conduct an analytical review' of the Commission's 'interpretative mandate' citing the Court's similar mandate and the need to avoid a potential jurisprudential conflict. It also called on the Commission to 'address the ambiguity of its status' within the framework of ongoing revision of its Rules of Procedure.

### 6.3.3 *Individual and NGO Communications*

Communications from individuals and NGOs need to pass admissibility tests based on the decision of a simple majority of members of the Commission. Some conditions that need to be met include compatibility with the African Charter and exhaustion of public remedies. With regard to the latter, the Commission has developed principles for when a complainant would not need to exhaust public remedies. They include the following:

- Where the victim is indigent
- Where the complaint involves serious or massive violations of rights

- Where domestic legislation ousts the jurisdiction of national courts
- Where the rights claimed are not guaranteed by domestic laws
- Where it is physically dangerous for the complainant to return to the erring state in order to exhaust domestic remedies
- Where the complaint involves an impractical number of potential plaintiffs
- Where the procedure for obtaining domestic remedy will be unduly prolonged
- Where it is simply illogical to require exhaustion of domestic remedy.

Other admissibility requirements are that the communications indicate their authors, are not written in disparaging language and not based exclusively on news disseminated by the media. The Charter is largely silent on what happens after individual communications have been considered. Cues can, however, be taken from the provisions relating to state communications as well as Article 58 relating to special cases of serious or massive violations. With regard to the latter, the Charter provides that the Assembly of Heads of State and Government ('the Assembly') may request the Commission to undertake an in-depth study of such cases and make a factual report accompanied by its findings and recommendations. Similarly, on state communications, the Charter provides that the Commission may, while transmitting its report to the Assembly, make 'such recommendations as it deems useful'. As previously stated in Chapter 3, both of these provisions appear to limit the Commission's role in the communications process to writing reports and making recommendations to the Assembly. Furthermore, all measures taken under the Charter are to remain confidential until the Assembly decides otherwise.[15]

The Commission appears to operate on these principles of confidentiality for individual and NGO complaints with its Rules of Procedure setting out more detailed provisions on the procedure and steps to be followed in the communications process. Thus, hearings on communications are held in camera with a final decision on the merit remaining confidential until its publication is authorised by the Assembly. Such decision would then be transmitted to the parties and posted on the Commission's website.

### 6.3.4 *The Nature of Recommendations*

It has already been pointed out that the Charter does not grant the Commission any express judicial authority under the communications procedure. By requiring the Commission to make 'recommendations' to the Assembly, it appears that the final say on the steps to be taken in the aftermath of a communication largely rests with the Assembly. Unfortunately, the Charter does not state what the Assembly should do after recommendations have been made and how effect, if any, would be given to these recommendations.

Taking advantage of this loophole the Commission has argued that its decisions become binding after they have been adopted by the Assembly after the latter's consideration of the Commission's annual Activity Reports.[16] Given that its decisions are routinely adopted by the Assembly, the practical implication is that they are binding on the states against whom they have been made. This position is, however, contentious—the reason being that the Charter did not make any clear provision in that regard. Also, what the AU adopts, through the Assembly or Executive Council, is the Activity Report of the Commission which contains several matters aside from communications. To impute to the Assembly the intention of adopting the particular decisions in each communication based on the mere adoption of the Activity Report appears to be a step too far. Such adoption, it is argued, is merely to make way for the publication of the report as envisaged under Article 59(3) of the Charter which provides for the Commission to publish a report on its activities after the same has been considered by the Assembly. This position is more compelling given that one of the chief reasons for the creation of an African Court was the general perception of the non-binding nature of the Commission's decisions.

The Commission's position is tenable to the extent that the Charter intended for the Assembly to bestow binding character on the Commission's decisions. The Charter does not, however, state how this is to be done. Rather, it merely provides that reports on the activities of the Commission would be published only after they have been 'considered' by the Assembly. There is nothing to show that such publication or consideration would amount to bestowing binding force.

The Commission's position on the binding nature of its decisions is reflected in its 2010 Rules of Procedure which makes provisions for following-up states' implementation of those decisions. Rule 112 mandates parties to, within 180 days after a decision has been made against a state party, inform the Commission in writing of any steps taken to implement the decision. A specially designated rapporteur is also to monitor the implementation of each communication.

The provisions for follow-up of the Commission's decisions were, in part, influenced by a number of earlier studies on the effectiveness of such procedure in improving state compliance with decisions of the Commission. In one of such studies, Viljoen and Louw[17] found that in four out of six cases of full compliance with the Commission's decisions, there had been some attempt by the latter to follow up on the steps taken by parties to implement its recommendations. They concluded that as the Commission did not undertake any similar actions in the majority of 'noncompliant' cases, the issue of following-up cases played a role in compliance. In other research,[18] Wachira and Ayinla proposed the establishment of an institutionalised follow-up mechanism by the African Commission for the purpose of monitoring the implementation of its decisions.[19]

It would not be far-fetched to state that these studies are based on the assumption that the Commission's decisions are, or should be, binding—an assumption that appears to be, at least by implication, increasing adopted by experts.[20] This would be at variance with earlier views that the Charter did not allow the Commission to issue binding decisions. Thus, Mutua described the available remedy under the Charter as largely ineffectual,[21] with Nmehielle remarking that there was 'in fact, no remedy within the Charter'.[22]

The advantages of the later view notwithstanding, it is difficult to reconcile the development of the Charter's institutional machinery with the view that the Commission's decisions are binding. Were this to be the case, then there would have been very little basis for the subsequent creation of an African Court to 'complement' the Commission's protective mandate. Unlike in other regional systems—the Inter-American and former European human rights systems—the African Commission performs both promotional and protective mandates without any appellate or clear system of referral to the Court. These two bodies operate distinctly from each other with different Rules of Procedure. Were its decisions to be binding upon the mere consideration of its Activity Reports, the Commission would not have any need for the Court whose only clear distinctive characteristic is its judicial nature demonstrated by its authority to pass binding judgements. It is also worth noting that, unlike its predecessor, the Court's authority to issue binding decisions is backed by unequivocal provisions in its enabling instruments.

It has also been further argued that some provisions of the Commission's Rules of Procedure are inconsistent with the position that the body's decisions are binding.[23] One such provision is Rule 118 which provides for the Commission to submit a communication to the African Court where the former considers that the respondent state has not complied or is unwilling to comply with its recommendations in respect of the communication. Such submission to the Court, it is argued, would be unnecessary were the Commission's recommendation to be binding as a decision of the AU Assembly as the appropriate body to take action in such an event would be the Assembly itself through warnings and sanctions. The provision for further referral to the Court arguably amounts to a concession on the binding nature of those recommendations.

### *6.3.5 States' Response to Decisions of the Commission on Communications*

It would come as no surprise that states do not generally share the Commission's view on the binding nature of its decisions. Firstly, it should be noted that implementation of the Commission's decisions has generally been low. One study put the rate of full compliance at 12% with cases of partial compliance at 34%.[24] A previous study of the period 1994–2004 found only 6 cases of full compliance as against 13 cases of non-compliance and 14 instances of partial compliance. The general attitude of states, it has been pointed out, has generally been to ignore these recommendations, with no attendant consequences. In the Commission's own assessment, 'member states generally do not comply with the decisions of the Commission or implement its recommendations'.[25]

Statistics of states' implementation of the Charter are, however, not conclusive or, one may argue, even indicative, of states' perception of their binding power. Indeed, states, not least in Africa, are known to routinely ignore 'binding' decisions of local and regional courts.[26] However, it must be stated that some states have challenged the competence of the Commission to issue binding decisions. The classic example is Botswana's reaction to the Commission's decision in the case of *Good v. Botswana*[27] which involved the deportation of an Australian Professor in 2005 after he had co-authored an article concerning presidential succession in Botswana. Botswana, in its response to a complaint brought before the Commission, challenged the latter's authority to issue binding decisions. Even after the Commission's finding in favour of Mr. Good, including an award of compensation, Botswana refused to comply. Botswana's Foreign Affairs Minister was quoted as saying:

> We are not going to follow the recommendation made by the Commission. It does not give orders, and it is not a court. We are not going to listen to them. We will not compensate Mr Good.[28]

States have also been known not to comply with provisional measures. In the 1998 case of *International Pen and Others (on behalf of Saro-Wiwa) v Nigeria*,[29] the Commission called on Nigeria not to execute Ken Saro-Wiwa pending the final outcome of the communication before it. Ken Saro-Wiwa, an environmental rights activist, was the leader of the Movement for the Survival of the Ogoni People (MOSOP), a group canvassing for the rights of the Ogoni people. The Ogoni, an indigenous group in Nigeria, were often victims of environmental pollution and degradation occasioned by the activities of foreign oil extraction companies particularly the British-Dutch conglomerate, Royal Dutch Shell. In addition to protesting the degradation of Ogoni land, MOSOP also demanded greater autonomy and control of the resources of the Ogoni people. This drew the ire of the then military government of General Sani Abacha and Saro-Wiwa was arrested and detained without charge on a couple of occasions. Events however took a different turn when, in May 1994, four Ogoni chiefs were murdered. Even though he had not been in Ogoni land on the day of the murders, Saro-Wiwa was arrested on charges of inciting the murders. The Sani Abacha led government then constituted a special tribunal that found Saro-Wiwa guilty and sentenced him to death. The Nigerian government carried out the execution despite the provisional measure by the Commission. The Commission subsequently found that the death penalty imposed violated the African Charter.[30]

Granted that it may very well be the case that other factors contribute to states' non-implementation of the Commission's decisions on communications, the apparent lack of binding authority certainly plays a central role in this state of affairs. It has even been noted that the Commission's lack of binding authority is the most cited reason for states' non-compliance with the Commission's decisions on communications.[31] In any event, it has to be pointed out that, in practice, several other factors contribute to the poor implementation of the Commission's decisions. It must also be noted that the non-binding status of these recommendations would not detract from their intended role of drawing attention to infringements of the Charter and facilitating the necessary reforms. Given that states are obligated under the Charter to give effect to its provisions, they are therefore expected to implement these recommendations to the best of their abilities. It is important here to clear up any seeming contradiction with the earlier position that the Commission's decisions are not ordinarily binding on states. In the first instance, it was argued that the Charter intended for the Commission to make recommendations to the Assembly which would, should it deem necessary, see to their enforcement. However, in the latter case, it is argued that states, being ordinarily obligated to implement the Charter, should ideally view recommendations on communications as guides to such implementation. In this sense, such recommendations would be no different from recommendations in the Commission's Concluding Observations after having examined a state's periodic report. It is clear in such cases that those recommendations are only persuasive and lack general binding force. However, states are still expected to implement them and report on implementation in subsequent periodic reports.[32] The fact that states choose to ignore most of the Commission's recommendations issued in fulfilment of its protective mandate signals the absence of goodwill and the existence of other underlying factors aside the non-binding nature of these recommendations. The following sections will briefly examine two such factors, namely the lack of political will and the failure by the Commission to specify clear remedies after finding a violation.

### *6.3.6 Lack of Political Will*

The lack of political will is probably at the forefront of non-implementation of decisions arising from communications. Granted that recommendations may not be viewed as binding, states have often failed to implement them simply because they lack the will to do so. The lack of binding force of these decisions, it can be argued, is therefore only a smokescreen behind which these states avoid performing their duties under the Charter. It has correctly been argued that the respect for and compliance by states with any decision by a supranational human rights body do not necessarily derive from the judicial or quasi-judicial nature of the decision-making body and the consequent nature of its decision, but depend on the presence of the requisite political will to honour their international treaty obligations.[33] In furtherance of this argument, Murray and Long point out that the rate of compliance where there is a 'binding' ruling is not significantly higher than non-binding decisions of quasi-judicial bodies. Thus, the nature of rulings in itself is a 'useful but unwelcome distraction'.[34]

This absence of political will is not restricted to the level of member states but may also be noticed at the top level of the Assembly which consists of Heads of States of the respective member states. It should be recalled that the Assembly is indeed the 'chief enforcer' of the Charter and of recommendations issued under the communications procedure. Articles 52, 53 and 58 of the African Charter make it clear that the Commission's role is merely that of passing on findings and recommendations, and 'drawing the attention' of the Assembly to special cases of massive violations. It is, therefore, the Assembly's prerogative to take whatever step it deems fit to ensure the implementation of these recommendations, a position it has evidently not been too keen to utilise. When one takes into consideration that the Assembly 'considers' final decisions of the Commission (as contained in the latter's Activity Reports) and is, given its composition, in the best position to take a strong stance against defaulting states, it becomes difficult to defend blatant non-implementation of these recommendations by the same states that approved their publication.

This lack of political will is even more concerning in cases of serious and massive violations of human rights. It would be recalled that the Charter mandates the Commission to draw the attention of the Assembly to such special cases. However, it was found that the Assembly took no steps in five such special cases after clear non-compliance by states.[35] Accordingly, the Commission has stopped referring such cases to the Assembly such that its practice has now gone into abeyance.[36] The Peace and Security Council, formed in 2003, has since become the de facto first port of call in such instances.

The PSC is a decision-making organ within the AU charged with the prevention, management and resolution of conflicts and crisis situations in African states. By Article 7(e) of the Protocol relating to the Establishment of the PSC, the PSC is empowered to recommend military intervention in a member state in very serious cases bordering on war crimes, genocide and crimes against humanity. Thus, under Rule 80 of the Commission's Rules of Procedure, the Commission is required to draw the attention of the PSC to such cases of emergency.

The Commission itself has identified, as one of its major challenges to implementing its duties under the Charter, a general trend indicating the lack of political will by member states to support and cooperate with the Commission and its subsidiary mechanism. This is evidenced, *inter alia*, by failure to implement the Commission's decisions.[37] Such a declaration by the Commission highlights the central role that member states play in not only fulfilling their duties under the Charter but also ensuring that the Commission fulfils its.

### *6.3.7 Commission's Failure to Provide Remedies*

Another impediment to states' implementation of the Commission's recommendation is the latter's failure to provide for specific remedies after reaching its decisions. It has been observed that the Commission has in some cases, after finding that a state is in breach of a Charter right, failed to recommend a clear remedy. This failure to provide a clear remedy has been noticed in cases where the Commission awards compensation without determining what such compensation should be thereby leaving such determination to the defaulting state. Thus, even in the rare case of a state willing to comply with the recommendation, it has occasionally been found that such compliance is not easy to determine or even implement. This challenge has mostly arisen in cases of financial compensation or the award of damages. For instance, in *Embga Mekongo Louis v Cameroon*[38] the victim claimed $150 million as damages for false imprisonment and miscarriage of justice. The Commission found that the victim's rights had been breached and that he had in fact suffered damages. Acknowledging that it was unable to evaluate the amount of damages to be awarded, the Commission recommended that this be determined under the law of Cameroon—leaving room for uncertainty and, consequently, non-implementation. The lack of a policy to determine the quantum of damages in awarding compensation has accordingly been identified as a definite factor influencing state compliance. In their research, Viljoen and Louw found that in the six cases where the Commission had recommended the payment of compensation to victims without stipulating the amount, no compensation had been paid.[39]

A second, and even more serious, situation is where the Commission makes a finding of violation without providing for any remedy. Mbazira observes that, rather than make simple declarations of violation of rights, the African Commission had often not made any substantive recommendations to remedy the violations.[40] For instance, in *Huri-Laws v Nigeria*,[41] the Commission found Nigeria to be in violation of seven articles of the Charter including freedom from torture, right to a fair trial, right to property and right to liberty. However, the Commission went no further than these findings as it failed to make provisions for remedies to the identified violations.

It is easy to see how the failure to provide remedies could affect the implementation of the Commission's decisions as such failure allows for ambiguity and uncertainty over what particular steps are to be taken. Also, states and victims alike are less likely to take the Commission seriously where it acknowledges a serious breach of individual rights without accompanying remedies.

### 6.3.8 The Commission's Follow-Up on Recommendations

In establishing the Commission's position on the nature of its recommendations, it was stated above that the Commission introduced follow-up measures to monitor and improve states' compliance with its decisions on communication. Having now briefly examined the response of states, as well as the hindrances to the implementation of these decisions, it is important to assess the impact, if any, of the Commission's 2010 Rules of Procedure on follow-ups. Before this can be done, it is important to appreciate the content of this procedure.

By Rule 112, the parties to the communication are to inform the Commission in writing, within 180 days of being informed of the decision, of all measures of implementation taken by the state. The Commission may require further information from the state to which the latter is to respond within 90 days. A reminder is to be sent in the event of the state's failure to respond on time. This process is monitored by a rapporteur who eventually submits a final report to the Commission.

On the establishment of the follow-up procedure, there were concerns that reporting activities would not be well organised or consistently documented. To this end, it was suggested that a registry be established within the Commission's Secretariat to track compliance with the Procedure. One possibility would be for the Commission to commit to reporting on implementation in its Activity Reports. This suggestion obviously distinguishes Rule 112(9) by which the Commission is mandated to include information on any follow-up activities in its Activity Reports. While the latter appears to focus on providing information on the follow-up actions of the rapporteur, the former focusses on reporting on compliance by states with their responsibilities under the follow-up procedure. However, beyond asking parties to inform it of the steps taken to implement recommendations, the Commission's Activity Reports do not report positive steps on follow-up, nor do they detail steps taken by states towards compliance. It is important to note that the Commission has only recently committed in its 36th Activity Report (para 27) to include in later reports a section detailing the implementation of its decisions by member states. Again, it is important to note that cooperation from the parties is necessary for a proper execution of this role and this appears to be lacking based on recent information from the Commission. For instance, the Commission has stated that despite an Executive Council Decision requesting parties to communications to provide the Commission with information on the implementation of recommendations, the latter have generally failed to do so notwithstanding letters and notes from the Commission to that effect.[42] This, in effect, means that there is a break in the chain of communication and the Commission is, therefore, unable to properly monitor implementation as envisaged under its Rules.

While the Commission generally appears to struggle for information on the state of implementation of its decisions, it has nonetheless provided such information in a few cases. Two of such instances are the already discussed case of *Good v. Botswana* and the *Endorois* case. In the former, the Commission reported Botswana's unequivocal response through a diplomatic note thus: 'the government has made its position clear; that it is not bound by the decision of the Commission'.[43] In another case,[44] the Commission reported that Ethiopia had not complied with provisional measures to prevent irreparable harm to the victim.[45] The case concerned the indigenous people of the lower Omo in Ethiopia whose population has been threatened by government projects in the Omo river especially the construction of a dam to support commercial plantations. The Ethiopian government failed to comply with provisional measures relating to the constructions.[46]

Reports on compliance have however not always been negative. For instance, the Commission has reported Cameroon's compliance with one decision including the payment of compensation to victims. In another case, the complainant informed the Commission that the recommendation had been 'partially implemented'.[47]

In summary, it would not be far-fetched to conclude that the Commission's adopted follow-up process has not quite achieved the intended objectives. This lack of success, as pointed out in the Commission's Activity Reports, owes largely to the lack of cooperation by states in playing their role as envisaged by the 2010 Rules.

## 6.4 The African Court

The African Court on Human and Peoples' Rights was the AU's response to complaints about the weak protective mandate of the Commission. Ironically, the decision to create a court in the future may have been taken as far back as the drafting of the African Charter which created the Commission as the enforcement body. The non-provision for a court in the African Charter may have merely represented a concession to the prevailing political climate at the time.[48] Even though the widely published reason may have been that the Commission standing alone reflected African traditions of conciliation rather than confrontation, the real reason may have had more to do with the widespread reluctance among member states to subordinate themselves to a supranational judicial organ. Thus, it was anticipated that muted suggestions for the creation of a court would arise again in the future.

The Protocol to the African Charter on Human and Peoples' Rights on the Establishment of an African Court on Human and Peoples' Rights (African Court Protocol) came into force in 2004, and the Court was officially installed in 2006. The function of the Court as stated in the Protocol was to complement the protective mandate of the African Commission.[49] By Article 5 of the Protocol, the following may submit cases to the Court: the Commission, state party, state party whose citizen is a victim of human rights violation, and African intergovernmental organisations. Thus, unlike as is the case with the Commission, individuals and NGOs cannot institute cases in the Court as of right. However, the Court may entitle individuals and NGOs with observer status before the Commission to directly institute cases before it. However, this can only be done if, at the time of the ratification of the Protocol or any time thereafter, the state concerned has made a declaration accepting the competence of the Court to receive such cases.[50] As of 2019, only ten States have made this declaration. They are Benin, Burkina Faso, Côte d'Ivoire, Ghana, the Gambia, Malawi, Mali, Rwanda, Tanzania and Tunisia. However, Rwanda withdrew its declaration in 2016 citing its exploitation by 'convicted genocide fugitives' who used it as a 'platform for reinvention and sanitisation'.[51] It has however been noted that this withdrawal conveniently came just one week before the scheduled hearing of the case of Ms. Victoire Umuhoza,[52] an incarcerated opposition leader.

### *6.4.1 Impact of the Court's Binding Power*

Article 27 of the Court's Protocol authorises the Court to make appropriate orders to remedy violations of human and peoples' rights, including the payment of fair compensation or reparation. Article 30 mandates state parties to the Protocol to undertake to comply with the judgement in any case to which they are parties within the time stipulated by the Court and to guarantee its execution.

Despite this new laudable dimension to the African human rights system in the form of the African Court, it is still evident that states play a huge role in making the system work by complying with judgements against them. The change that the Court brings is the finality of its judgements and their binding force on states unlike 'recommendations' of the Commission. The Court's Protocol also provides for the transmission of the Court's judgements to other member states of the AU as well as the Council of Ministers which is to monitor their execution on behalf of the Assembly.[53] It further provides for the Court to submit its reports to the Assembly, specifying cases in which a state has failed to comply with the Court's judgement.

In 2005, the AU decided to merge the African Court with the African Court of Justice created by the Constitutive Act of the AU. The latter, which never came into existence owing to the subsequent merger, was largely modelled on the International Court of Justice, to adjudicate on matters of international law between member states. By virtue of the supervening merger, the two courts would form the African Court of Justice and Human Rights. This merger which proposed the creation of two chambers—the Human Rights Section and the General Affairs Section—would not affect the modalities and powers of the Court already described above. Developments on the proposed merger are further discussed in the next chapter.[54]

### 6.4.2 The Court's Protective Role

As explained above, the creation of a human rights court became imperative owing to the Commission's weak protective mandate under the Charter. Many critics saw the Commission as largely 'ineffectual'[55] with its recommendations merely urging states to comply with its directives.[56] This common position among writers led to clamours for the creation of a court with judicial and binding authority. In canvassing for a court, some commentators appeared to question the significance of the Commission. It was believed that the Court would fill the huge void left by the Commission. For instance, Mutua opined thus:

> The African Human Rights Court is a potentially significant development in the protection of rights on a continent that has been plagued with serious human rights violations since colonial rule. The problems of the African human rights system, including the normative weaknesses in the African Charter and the general impotence of its implementing body, the African Commission, may now be addressed effectively and resolved by the establishment of this new adjudicatory body.[57]

Viljoen was of the view that the mere existence of a Court would generate greater media interest and exposure and a much clearer identity in the minds of Africans.[58] Also, the 'psychological effect' of an international court's judgement on a state would be 'critical'.[59]

Following such wide support for a Court, it came as little surprise when, in 1998, members adopted the Protocol to the African Charter on Human and Peoples' on the Establishment of an African Court on Human and Peoples' Rights (African Court Protocol). The Protocol came into force in 2004, and the Court was officially installed in 2006.[60]

### 6.4.3 The Court's Contribution to the Protection of Rights

It will be recalled that the Court was only created to complement the protective mandate of the Commission and, as such, does not share a promotional mandate. It however regularly undertakes promotional activities aimed at raising awareness about its existence as provided under its Rules. These activities are mainly in the form of sensitisation visits, regional and continental seminars, retreats and networking. The Court has accordingly conducted sensitisation visits to the Gambia, Cameroon, Côte d'Ivoire,

Kenya, Burundi, Mauritius and Senegal, among others. It has also established formal relations with similar institutions like the Inter-American Court of Human Rights and the United Nations International Criminal Tribunal for Rwanda.

A proper assessment of the Court's protective role is marred by the dearth of decided cases, a situation which could nonetheless provide a basis for evaluating such mandate. Even though the Court had been installed in 2006 with judges appointed, by 2010 the Court had received only one application, *Michelot Yogogombaye v. Republic of Senegal*,[61] which was struck out for lack of jurisdiction.[62] The application was brought by a Chadian national, Michelot Yogogombaye, challenging the proceedings instituted by the Senegalese government against the then exiled former Chadian leader, Hissène Habré. Habré who had been accused of torture, war crimes and crimes against humanity had been indicted by the ICC and taken repose in Senegal. However, rather than hand him over to the ICC, Senegal, supported by an AU resolution, amended its constitution to pave way for Habré's trial in Senegal. Yogogombaye's application challenged this amendment arguing that it was politically motivated and that it violated the principle of non-retroactivity of criminal law. However, as Senegal had not accepted the right of individuals to bring complaints, the Court could not consider the substantive issues.

Aside from challenges relating to jurisdiction, the lack of a registry, offices, budget and even rules of Court meant that the judges could not begin receiving applications. The first two years were, therefore, spent negotiating a host agreement for the seat of the Court in Tanzania, devising a registry structure, recruiting registry staff, submitting budget proposals and adopting an Interim Rules of Procedure. By September 2012, the Court had received 21 applications in contentious matters and three requests for advisory opinions and conducted two public hearings on contentious issues of public interest. By December 2015, the Court had received about 60 applications on contentious cases of which less than half had been finalised and nine requests for advisory opinions. The obviously low numbers were compounded by the fact that all but two of the Court's finalised cases were struck out for lack of jurisdiction. The Court has since seen a higher increase in the number of applications owing mainly to dozens of new suits instituted against its host country, Tanzania, since the start of 2016. Thus, by March 2019, the Court had received 202 applications, 146 of which were pending.

This recent rise should not, however, mask the challenge of the court's dearth of cases especially as a majority of the applications have been against one state—Tanzania—due to its position as the Court's host state. As will be discussed in the section below, the court is hampered by a range of factors top of which is the limited access available to individual complainants.

### 6.4.4 *Factors Impeding the Court's Discharge of Its Duties*

This section will examine the impact of the following factors on the Court's discharge of its duties: Ratification of the Court's Protocol, failure to make the declaration under Article 34(6), non-compliance by member states, restrictions on the Court's reporting, limited use of the Court's resources and the lack of human and material resources.

#### *6.4.4.1 Ratification and Art 34(6) Declaration*

While there may be a debate on the level of acceptance of the Commission's authority over states, the lack of acceptance of the Court is even more glaring. Unlike the Charter which has a near total acceptance in the form of ratifications, the African Court Protocol, as of 2019, had been ratified by only 30 African countries—just a little over half of AU member states. As a direct consequence of this, complaints cannot be initiated against non-ratifying countries as they have not accepted the jurisdiction of the Court. While this in itself is a huge limitation, it is compounded by the reluctance of states to make the declaration under Article 34(6) of the Protocol. By this provision, a state may make a declaration accepting the competence of the Court to hear cases from individuals and NGOs (i.e. those having observer status with the Commission) against the state. Where the respondent state has not made such a declaration, the Court would only be able to receive complaints from the Commission, other states and intergovernmental organisations. In fifteen years of the Court's coming into force, only ten states have made this declaration meaning that individuals and approved NGOs can only bring applications against those states (excluding Rwanda which withdrew its declaration) out of the total 30 states that have ratified the Protocol. This is all the more significant when one considers that of the 202 applications in contentious matters since the Court's inception, 199 have been initiated by individuals and NGOs. The practical implication of this would be that those states that have not made the declaration are effectively outside the reach of the

Court. While there may be no clear pattern in terms of how states choose to ratify the Protocol, it has been noted that the most repressive regimes generally avoided the Court. However, states that had recently undergone democratic transitions as well those that had experienced the most serious human rights violations were more likely to ratify in an apparent attempt to bind future governments. Ironically, the more established democracies were also less willing to submit to the Court's jurisdiction, and one such country, Mauritius, was even noted to have been one of the most vocal opponents to the optional declaration allowing individual and NGO access.[63]

Unsurprisingly, the Court has consistently identified the low level of ratification and lower number of declarations as significant challenges to the effective discharge of its judicial mandate. Apart from hindering the initiation of applications, this limitation saw the dismissal of most of the early applications brought before the Court. The Court adjudicated on questions of admissibility and merits for the first time in 2013 because all previous applications had not been within its jurisdiction either because the matter was against a state that had not ratified the Court's Protocol or had not made the Article 34(6) declaration. Accordingly, the Court has stated that this impediment seriously compromises the effective discharge of its mandate and, if allowed to continue, would adversely affect the entire system of judicial protection of human rights at the continental level.[64]

It can be argued that by failing to ratify the Protocol, the defaulting states do not want to be held accountable for infractions of the Charter and other human rights treaties that they have signed up to. Equally questionable are the other half that have ratified but failed to make the Art 34(6) declaration—a failure that effectively waters down their initial ratification. The Protocol's Preamble declares a firm conviction on the need for a Court to complement the Commission on the attainment of the Charter's objectives. However, the failure of 22 member states, out of 30 ratifications, to make the Article 34(6) declaration appears to conflict with this affirmation. As individuals and groups are the sole beneficiaries of rights under the Charter, denying them direct access to the Court is arguably a clear sign of double standards.

Rather than allow individual access, the Court's Protocol only permits access to the Commission, state parties and 'African Intergovernmental Organisations'. Such a restriction is arguably an indirect way of hindering applications as the aforementioned bodies have, thus far, not shown much zeal in bringing complaints forward. No state or African Intergovernmental Organisation has initiated a case at the Court. On its part, the Commission has only made three applications in contentious matters. The first was for massive violation of the rights of protesters by the Libyan government during protests held in 2011. Government forces had reportedly opened fire on protesters prompting a series of interventions that ultimately led to a civil war and the overthrow of the government.

The second application, African Commission v Kenya,[65] challenged the Kenyan government's eviction of the Ogiek people, an indigenous group, from the East Mau forest. The third application was also against Libya with the Commission calling the Court's attention to the incommunicado detention without trial of Saif Al-Islam Gaddafi in the immediate aftermath of the Libyan Civil War. Needless to say, the Commission's statistic of three applications is significantly dwarfed by the 199 applications from individuals and NGOs, a number that would have been significantly higher had every African state allowed individual access.

#### 6.4.4.2 *Lack of Cooperation and Non-compliance by Member States*

It will be recalled that part of the reasons for the support of the Court's creation was the perceived unenforceability of the Commission's recommendations. Unlike the case with the Commission, the Court's Protocol is unambiguous in its assertion of its binding authority. Article 28 of the Protocol states that the judgement of the Court decided by a majority shall be final and not subject to appeal although there is the possibility of reviewing such decision in the light of new evidence. By Article 30, state parties undertake to comply with the judgement in any case to which they are parties and to guarantee its execution. These provisions are also reiterated in Rule 61 of the Court's Rules of Procedure. However, while these provisions clarify the Court's binding power, they would not necessarily guarantee compliance by member states as the cooperation of the latter remains crucial. And despite the small sample of roughly a dozen decisions on the merits against a handful of states, the initial signs are not very positive. Perhaps, a glimpse into the future pattern of states' response to the Court's decisions was seen in the response to two provisional measures against Kenya and Libya. While the former complied with the Court's orders, the latter blatantly refused to comply.[66] The latter order concerned the detention and possible ill-treatment of Saif Al-Islam

Gaddafi, son of the deposed Libyan leader, Muammar Gaddafi. Libya neither responded to the order nor the reminder sent after the deadline for response prompting the Court to file an Interim Report with the Secretariat of the African Union Commission (AUC) with a view to drawing the attention of the Executive Council to the non-compliance, and for the Council to bring the matter to the attention of the Assembly. Libya's non-compliance led the Court to cite the lack of cooperation from state parties as one of the serious challenges in the implementation of its judicial mandate. The Court summarised this challenge as follows:

> The failure of Libya to comply with the Order of the Court threatens the very foundation of the existence of the Court as a judicial arm of the African Union. It erodes public confidence in our judicial system and mobilises negative public perception about the ability of the Court to protect human rights on the continent. Furthermore, such non-compliance by any member state has a tendency to put into question the credible utility of the judicial system created by the African Union for the enforcement of the African Charter on Human and Peoples' Rights.[67]

Incidentally, the situation does not seem to have changed very much when one considers the response of Tanzania—the respondent state in half of the Court's dozen decisions on the merit. Despite engaging actively with the Court's proceedings, the host state appears reluctant in implementing the Court's final decisions. For instance, after the decision in the *Mtikila case*—which was briefly discussed in Chapter 3—Tanzania refused to implement the Court's judgement by allowing independent candidates to run for election. The government's response to other judgements of the Court has been described as suggesting 'a broader stance of noncompliance'.[68] Daly and Wiebusch give broader details of this stance thus:

> While implementation of the Thomas and Abubakari judgments has been delayed by the State's requests for interpretations of the judgments (provided in late 2017), the State has provided no report to the Court on implementation of the Court's decision in the Onyango... Beyond the claims that the African Court's judgments are wrong, it is hard to find any more detailed position on the Court articulated by government actors. The pattern of resistance, if there is one, is of stubborn refusal by the government to abide by the Court's judgments or engage with its orders.[69]

In each of the three cases mentioned above, the Court had found Tanzania in violation of the right to a fair trial. For instance, in the 2013 case of *Onyango v Tanzania*,[70] it was held that the undue delay in hearing criminal charges pending since 2006 was an infringement of the right to a fair trial. The Court ordered the state to provide legal aid to the applicants and to expedite the hearing in the domestic courts.

Interestingly, Tanzania hosts the Court and has recently been the subject of a majority of applications brought before it. One would therefore be forgiven for doubting the future effectiveness of the Court's rulings where the host state itself, which should arguably show more goodwill than the other states, clearly refuses to implement the Court's decisions. Indeed, as the host state, Tanzania did not easily have at its behest the choice exercised by Rwanda—which was simply to withdraw its commitment—after an application was brought against it. It would be recalled that having been faced with a number of individual applications, Rwanda, which had previously made the declaration allowing individual and NGO applications, simply withdrew its commitment. Such purported withdrawal was done one week before the scheduled hearing of the case of Ms Victoire Umuhoza, an incarcerated opposition leader. Rwanda hinged its withdrawal on the claim that 'convicted genocide fugitives' were exploiting the individual complaints system as a 'platform for reinvention and sanitisation'.[71]

Of course, as would be the case with almost any judicial institution, not every case has ended on a negative note. For instance, Burkina Faso is reported to have complied with the Court's order in the case of *Zongo v Burkinafaso*[72] by paying compensation to the victim's family and reopening an investigation into the death of a Burkinabé journalist in 1998. This case notwithstanding, it is not difficult especially in the context of the other cases highlighted above, to see the Court facing the same challenge of non-compliance as the Commission despite the accepted binding nature of its decisions. To that end, the issue of getting states to comply with these judicial and quasi-judicial decisions must be a matter of priority for the African regional human rights system. This issue is looked at in more depth in the next chapter.

#### 6.4.4.3 *Restriction on the Court's Reporting*

Another challenge cited by the Court is the newly imposed reporting procedure. By Article 31 of the Court's Protocol, it is required to report to each regular session of the Assembly. The Court has carried out this function accordingly. However, in 2012, the AUC directed that organs of the Union, including the Court, were henceforth required to report only once a year, that is, in any of the two annual summits of the Union. The Court contends that this requirement limits it from reporting incidences of non-compliance as well as situations of serious human rights violations that may arise. For instance, this directive made it 'difficult' to bring the attention, in May 2013, of the Executive Council to Libya's non-compliance as, when the matter was to be brought up, the Court was not scheduled to present any report having already presented one in January. As such, the report was only noted under 'any other business' and was not transmitted to the Executive Council.

#### 6.4.4.4 *Lack of Human and Financial Resources*

The Court has cited other impediments such as the part-time nature of the judges' work and the inadequacy of resources. On the former, the Court has stated that as judicial work can only be done when the judges meet during quarterly sessions, this inevitably results in delays in finalising some matters.[73] With regard to the latter, the Court has noted that it suffers from a shortage of resources. One of such complaints noted staff shortages in every department of the registry compelling staff to perform functions for which they had little competence. The Court also reported a lack of basic furniture and working equipment for judges and staff members alike.

## 6.5 The Relationship Between the Commission and Court

At the risk of repetition, it is worth reiterating, in the briefest fashion, the standard of relationship as already explained in Chapter 3. The first is that the Court complements the Commission's protective mandate. This it does by passing binding judicial decisions. Additionally, the Commission is entitled to submit cases to the Court[74] and the latter may transfer inadmissible cases to the Commission.[75]

Rule 118 of the Commission's Rules of Procedure make provisions for when the Commission is to submit a communication to the Court pursuant to Article 5(1) of the Court's Protocol. The first instance is where a state is unwilling to comply with the Commission's recommendations with regard to a communication. The Rules provide that the Commission may, in this instance, submit the communication to the Court. The Court may make similar submissions where provisional measures have not been complied with or in situations of serious or massive violations of human rights. Finally, it is provided that the Commission may seize the Court at any stage of the examination of a communication 'if it deems necessary'.

However, the records show that the African Commission has not been performing optimally in this regard as it has submitted only three cases against two countries: Libya and Kenya. In the first Libyan case, the Commission submitted the communication to the Court on the ground of serious and massive violations of human rights.[76] In the second case,[77] the Commission submitted the communication on the ground that Libya had not complied with its provisional measures while the case against Kenya was submitted on the ground of serious and massive violations of the rights of the indigenous people of Ogiek.[78]

It is obvious that the Commission has not taken full advantage of submitting cases to the Court. This is clear not only from the few cases submitted but also the failure to submit finalised communications where the Commission has reached a decision and the respondent state has failed to implement or comply with such decision. It is important here to note that, given the already discussed challenges of individual/NGO access to the Court, the Commission is a very important source of cases reaching the Court. It is no surprise therefore that the Commission's lack of initiative in presenting cases to the Court has been identified as the principal problem in getting the African Court to hear meritorious cases.[79]

Two reasons can be proffered for this situation. The first is that the Commission has succeeded in finalising few communications in recent years and most of the respondent states in those cases are not parties to the Court Protocol. Another even more important concern is that the Rules appear to put the issue of referral at the discretion of the Commission, a discretion which appears not to have been optimally exercised. Both of these challenges are addressed in the next chapter which seeks to address some of the highlighted deficiencies of the continent's regional human rights system.

## 6.6 The Extent of Utilisation of the Court and Commission

This final section seeks to evaluate the practical reality of the institutions' protective mandates based on the statistics of their use and finalised decisions. Thus, do the statistics on the use of the Commission or in the number of findings against states measure up to reports of human rights violations as illustrated in Chapter 4?

A brief outline of the Court's statistics has already been set out above where it was pointed out that the Court had been seized of relatively few cases. As at the end of 2015, the Court had recorded only 60 contentious cases although this number has drastically increased since the turn of 2016 owing largely to dozens of new suits filed against Tanzania. On the other hand, an examination of the Commission's Activity Reports and list of cases reveals that, in its 28 years of existence, the Commission has presided over roughly 500 cases, delivering decisions in less than half of these. While these numbers show low levels of utilisation (especially given the findings of violations in the previous chapter), more concerns are raised over the fact that the Commission is yet to deliver a decision for or against nearly half of AU member states. What this means is that the Commission's protective mandate has not been of practical consequence in those states. The Court's situation is even direr given that it can only extend its protective mandate to 30 countries, a number that drastically reduces to eight when individual access is considered. However, while the Court is hindered by these jurisdictional limitations, the Commission is not. Given that the Charter envisaged protection for the entire continent, the Commission's failure to find any violation against nearly half of its members is a cause for concern.

Finally, it is important to assess what the low numbers on usage mean for human rights practice. For more viability, there is the need to illustrate this from the relative perspective of other regional human rights systems and from the particular situation of Africa given the analysis of the previous chapter. For instance, by way of comparison, the much older European system is saddled with cases and faces recurrent backlog challenges. At the start of 2010, there were nearly 120,000 applications pending before a decision body of the European Court of Human Rights.[80] The court's caseload has multiplied tremendously such that more than 90% of its judgements have been delivered between 1998 and 2008 alone.[81]

Considering that the African Charter has more signatories with corresponding higher reports of violations, one would expect a similar or even higher number of complaints and caseload. This, unfortunately, has not been the case. A number of reasons have been adduced for this anomaly. Probably the most common of these is the failure by the institutions to undertake adequate promotional measures and effective advertisement. For instance, Viljoen has argued that the Commission has been 'ineffective in disseminating information about its existence and its case law and has failed to exploit media exposure possibilities'.[82] Similarly, Heyns has pointed out that failure in educational and other initiatives has led to a 'minute number of cases per year' and even no cases in respect of some countries with the worst human rights records.[83] Also, in accessing the Commission's record of 241 communications after its first 14 years of existence, Odinkalu stated thus: 'The conclusion from this has to be that the Commission is very much unknown and underutilised'.[84] More recently, Isanga has opined that part of the reasons for few cases reaching the Court 'may be due to the fact that very few Africans or organisations even know of the existence of the African Court or of their rights'.[85] Another possible factor could be the potential risk to life and property that complainants from repressive regimes face both for themselves, their families and even witnesses.

Another contributing factor, at least in the case of the Commission, is the low level of participation of NGOs in the communications process. A 2011 study found that, out of 44 decided cases on the merit between the year 2000 and 2009, 30 had the direct involvement of NGOs either as representatives, applicants or amicus.[86] Consistent with these findings, a previous review of the Commission's Activity Reports found that a majority of applications—28 out of 48—that led to decisions on the merits from 1997 to 2003 had been filed by one or more NGOs.[87] Given their crucial contribution, it is, therefore, reasonable to assume that an increased participation of these bodies in the communications process would invariably translate to more communications been filed. Accordingly, a section of Chapter 7 is dedicated to examining the relationship between NGOs and the Commission/Court and how this relationship could be further developed to improve human rights protection.

## 6.7 Conclusion

This chapter set out to examine and evaluate the impact of the African Commission and Court. Overall, it was concluded that the Commission and Court had failed to adequately perform their stated duties of promotion and protection. While the former was evident in the poor utilisation of both bodies, the latter could be seen in the poor records of compliance, ratification and Article 34(6) declarations. In the case of the Commission it was explained that, in order to make up for its weak mandate under the Charter, the Commission had adopted a rather positive stance on the nature of its recommendations after the consideration of its Activity Reports by the Assembly. It was argued that this stance acutely exposed the weakness in the Charter and demonstrated a clear instance of discrepancy from the set standard. In furtherance of its stance, the Commission adopted follow-up measures in its Rules of Procedure to monitor and improve the rate of compliance with its recommendations. However, it was shown that these new rules have largely failed to meet their aims as states have mostly failed to report on the steps taken to implement decisions even after several reminders from the Commission.

It was also considered that, their non-binding nature notwithstanding, states still had a duty under the Charter, or at least were free, to implement the decisions of the Commission. Failure to do so, therefore, meant that there were other factors aside from the non-binding nature of recommendations that contributed to poor compliance. One major factor was the lack of political will on the part of member states to implement these recommendations. It was also pointed out that the Commission had occasionally compounded this challenge by failing to provide or specify remedies after having found a state to be in violation of the Charter.

The impact of the lack of political will was more noticeable in the case of the Court where only ten states had made the Article 34(6) declaration allowing individual and NGO applications—with one of those states (Rwanda) later withdrawing—and only 53% had ratified the Protocol. It was also noted that at least one state had not complied with a provisional measure issued by the Court.

Another major challenge was the lack of human and financial resources to carry out the assigned tasks of both institutions. This was a major restraint for the Commission especially in the area of promotion. Thus, such tasks as embarking on promotional missions and advertising the protective role of the Commission were often hindered by the lack of funds.

This was also a challenge for the Court which reported staff shortages and lack of office furniture as impediments to its operation.

On the relationship between the Court and Commission, it was shown that the latter had not developed a viable system or practice of submitting communications to the Court. Such failure further compounded the Court's dearth of cases. On the actual practice of the institutions, it was shown that there was very low general usage of both the Court and Commission. This limited use could be attributed mainly to such challenges as non-enforceability in the case of the Commission, and the lack of ratifications and Article 34(6) declarations in the Court's case. However, there have also been questions concerning the institutions' efforts to create more awareness and sensitisation.

At the end of this assessment, it may be concluded that the institutions have not been able to meet their mandates under the Charter. However, the major causes of this have been the weak and compromising nature of Charter provisions as well as the sheer lack of political will by member states.

## Notes

1. Victor Dankwa, "The Promotional Role of the African Commission on Human and People's Rights" (2002) in Malcolm Evans and Rachel Murray (eds.) *The African Charter on Human and People's Rights: The System in Practice, 1986–2000* (Cambridge University Press 2002) 352.
2. Treva Braun and Lucy Mulvagh, The African Human Rights System: A Guide for Indigenous Peoples (Forest Peoples Programme, 2008) 25, accessed July 4, 2014, http://www.rightsandresources.org/documents/files/doc_1178.pdf.
3. See African Commission, "Resolution on the celebration of an African Day of Human Rights" (1989), http://www.achpr.org/sessions/5th/resolutions/1/.
4. Magnus Killander and Bright Nkrumah, "Human Rights Developments in the African Union During 2012 and 2013" (2014) 14(1) *African Human Rights Law Journal* 275, 281.
5. Frans Viljoen, *International Human rights Law in Africa* (Oxford University Press 2012) 349.
6. Morris Mbondenyi, *International Human rights and their Enforcement in Africa* (LawAfrica Publishing, 2014) 419.
7. Oji Umozuruike, "The African Charter on Human and Peoples' Rights: Suggestions for More Effectiveness" (2007) 13 *Annual Survey of International and Comparative Law* 179, 189.

8. Joseph Isanga, "The Constitutive Act of the African Union, African Courts and the Protection of Human Rights: New Dispensation?" (2013) 11 *Santa Clara Journal of International Law* 267, 301.
9. This issue is examined at depth in Chapter 7.
10. Michelo Hansungule, "The African Charter on Human and Peoples' Rights: A Critical Review" (2000) 8 *African Yearbook of International Law* 265, 298.
11. African Commission, *23rd Activity Report* (2008), EX.CL/446(XIII).
12. Viljoen, *International*, 179.
13. African Commission, *37th Activity Report* (2015), accessed June 13, 2018, http://www.achpr.org/files/activity-reports/37/actrep37_2015_eng.pdf.
14. Article 53.
15. Article 59.
16. African Commission, *Information Sheet No.3: Communication Procedure*, http://www.achpr.org/files/pages/communications/procedure/achpr_communication_procedure_eng.pdf.
17. Frans Viljoen and Lirette Louw, "State compliance with the recommendations of the African Commission on Human and Peoples' Rights, 1994–2004" (2007) *African Journal of International Law* 1.
18. George Wachira and Abiola Ayinla, "Twenty years of elusive enforcement of the recommendations of the African Commission on Human and Peoples' Rights: A possible remedy" (2006) 6(2) *African Human Rights Law Journal*, 465.
19. George Wachira and Abiola Ayinla, "Twenty years," 465
20. See for instance, F Viljoen, "Impact in the African and Inter-American Human Rights Systems: A Perspective on the Possibilities and Challenges of Cross-Regional Comparison" In P. Engstrom (ed.) *The Inter-American Human Rights System* (Springer 2018) 303–326; F. Viljoen and L. Louw, "The Status of the findings of the African Commission: from moral persuasion to legal obligation" (2004) 48(1) *Journal of African Law* 1–22.
21. Makau wa Mutua, "The African Human Rights Court: A Two-legged Stool?" (1999) 29 *Human Rights Quarterly* 342, 351
22. Vincent Nmehielle, "Toward an African Court of Human Rights: Structuring and the Court" (2000) 6 *ASICL* 27, 39.
23. Allwell Uwazuruike, "A Proposal for the Effective Implementation of the Protective Mandate of the African Commission on Human and Peoples' Rights ref" (2019) *African Journal of Legal Studies*.
24. The Open Justice Initiative, From Judgment to Justice: Implementing International and Regional Human Rights Decisions, accessed February 17, 2017, http://www.opensocietyfoundations.org/sites/default/files/from-judgment-to-justice-20101122.pdf.

25. African Commission, "Combined 32nd and 33rd Activity Report" (2013) para 28, http://www.achpr.org/files/activity-reports/32-and-33/achpr5152_actrep32and33_eng.pdf EX.CL/782(XXII) Rev.2.
26. Allwell Uwazuruike, "An Analysis of Nigeria's Soft Non-Compliant Approach to Domestic and Regional Court Orders and its Implication for Human Rights and the Rule of Law".
27. Communication No. 313/05.
28. Simisani Chilisa, "Botswana Will Not Honour African Union Ruling on Prof Good", *Sunday Standard News* (Botswana, August 2, 2010).
29. Communication Nos. 137/94, 139/94, 154/96 and 161/97 (1998).
30. See *The Guardian*, Shell pays out $15.5 over Saro-Wiwa killing, accessed June 29, 2019, https://www.theguardian.com/world/2009/jun/08/nigeria-usa.
31. Wachira and Ayinla, "Twenty Years," 471.
32. Rules of Procedure of the African Commission on Human and Peoples' Rights 2010, r 78.
33. Wachira and Ayinla, "Twenty Years," 491.
34. R. Murray and D. Long, *The Implementation of the Findings of the African Commission on Human and Peoples' Rights* (Cambridge University Press, 2015)
35. Viljoen and Louw, "State Compliance," 20–21.
36. Ibid. See also Rachel Murray, "Massive or serious violations under ACHPR: A comparison with the Inter-American and European Mechanism" (1999) *Netherlands Quarterly of Human Rights* 109, 128.
37. African Commission, "Combined 32nd and 33rd Activity Report".
38. Communication No. 59/91 (2000).
39. Frans Viljoen and Lirette Louw, "State compliance," 22.
40. Christopher Mbazira, "Enforcing the economic, social and cultural rights in the African Charter on Human and Peoples' Rights: Twenty years of redundancy, progression and significant strides" (2006) 6. *African Human Rights Law Journal* 333, 347.
41. Communication No. 225/98 (2000).
42. African Commission, "37th Activity Report" para 50, http://www.achpr.org/files/activity-reports/37/actrep37_2015_eng.pdf.
43. African Commission, "37th Activity Report".
44. *The Indigenous Peoples of the Lower Omo (Represented by Survival International Charitable Trust) v Ethiopia*, Communication No. 419/12.
45. African Commission, "35th Activity Report" para 27, http://www.achpr.org/files/activity-reports/35/achpr54eos14_actrep35_2014_eng.pdf.
46. See Survival International, https://www.survivalinternational.org/tribes/omovalley.
47. African Commission, "36th Activity Report" para 25, http://www.achpr.org/files/activity-reports/36/achpr54eos15_actrep36_2014_eng.pdf.

48. Julia Harrington, "The African Court on Human and Peoples' Rights" (2002) in Malcolm Evans and Rachel Murray (eds.) *The African Charter on Human and People's Rights: The System in Practice, 1986–2000* (Cambridge University Press 2002) 306.
49. African Court Protocol, Article 2.
50. Articles 5(3) and 34(6).
51. Office of Public Relations and Communications, Clarification, (2016), accessed 12 August, 2017, http://www.minijust.gov.rw/fileadmin/Documents/Photo_News_2016/Clarification2.pdf.
52. Application No. 003/2014.
53. Article 29.
54. See Chapter 7.
55. Makau wa Mutua, "The African Human Rights Court: A Two-legged Stool?" (1999) 29 *Human Rights Quarterly* 342, 351.
56. Christof Heyns, "African Regional Human Rights System: The African Charter" (2003) 108 *Pennsylvania State Law Review* 679, 698.
57. Mutua, "African," 353.
58. Frans Viljoen, "A Human Rights Court for Africa, and Africans" (2004) 30 *BJIL* 1, 22.
59. Nmehielle, "Toward."
60. African Court, accessed June 16, 2018, en.african-court.org.
61. Application No. 001/2008.
62. African Court, "Report of the African Court on Human and Peoples" Rights on the Relevant Aspects Regarding the Judiciary in the Protection of Human Rights in Africa by Justice Sophia A. B. Akuffo, President of the Court', http://en.african-court.org/images/Other%20Reports/Report_of_the_African_Court_on_Human_and_Peoples_Rights_in_the_Protection_of_Human_Rights_in_Africa_final.pdf.
63. Simon Zschirnt, "Locking In Human Rights in Africa: Analyzing State Accession to the African Court on Human and Peoples' Rights." (2018) 19(1) *Harvard Rights Review* (2018) 97.
64. African Court, "Activity Report 2012" EX.CL/718(XX).
65. Application No. 006/2012.
66. African Court, "Activity Report 2013".
67. Ibid.
68. Tom G. Daly and Micha Wiebusch, "The African Court on Human and Peoples' Rights: Mapping Resistance Against a Young Court" (2018) 14(2) *International Journal of Law in Context* 294.
69. Ibid.
70. ACHPR, Application No. 006/2013.
71. Office of Public Relations and Communications, Clarification, (2016), accessed 12 August 2017, http://www.minijust.gov.rw/fileadmin/Documents/Photo_News_2016/Clarification2.pdf.

72. Application No. 013/2011.
73. African Court, "Activity Report 2013" (n 85), para 115.
74. African Court Protocol, Article 5(1)(a).
75. Ibid., Article 6(3).
76. *African Commission v Great Socialist People's Libyan Arab Jamahiriya*, Application No. 004/2011.
77. *African Commission v. The Republic of Libya*, Application No. 002/2013.
78. *African Commission v Republic of Kenya*, Application No. 006/2012.
79. See The Open Justice Initiative (n 33) 96.
80. The Open Justice Initiative (n 34).
81. Ibid. The role of new member states, like Russia and Turkey, should be taken into account.
82. Viljoen, "A Human Rights Court for Africa" (n 70) 21.
83. Christof Heyns, "Some thoughts on Challenges facing the International Protection of Human Rights in Africa" (2009) 27 *Netherlands Quarterly of Human Rights* 447.
84. Chidi Odinkalu, "The Role of Case and Complaints Procedures in the Reform of the African Regional Human Rights System" (2001) 2 *African Human Rights Law Journal*, 225, 244.
85. Isanga supra at 285.
86. Lloyd Hitoshi Mayer, "Collection of Data from the Decisions Rendered by the African Commission, European Court and Inter-American Commission and Court from 2000 to 2009" (May 22, 2011) (unpublished collection, Notre Dame University) 934.
87. Annakaun Lindblom, "Non-Governmental Organisations in International Law" cited in Mayer, "Collection."

CHAPTER 7

# Institutional Enforcement of the Charter: Resolving the Challenges Faced by the African Court and Commission

## 7.1 Introduction

The preceding chapter highlighted some of the key challenges to the promotional and protective mandates of both the African Court and Commission. This chapter consolidates the work done in that section by examining proposals for addressing some of the key challenges faced by both institutions. It, therefore, touches on important issues such as funding, ratification and states' implementation of decisions. In relation to the latter, it explores the idea of introducing sanctions for member states that fail to comply with the decisions of the African Court. It concludes by examining the role of NGOs in improving and monitoring compliance with the decisions of both bodies.

## 7.2 The African Commission

The Commission has so far proven to be the continent's main body for human rights promotion, and protection based on years of operation as well as statistics of general usage. Given the jurisdictional limitations of the Court, the Commission stands as the only regional body before which individuals can bring human rights complaints against any AU member state. With such wide coverage, it is, therefore, a cause for concern that the Commission has received just over 700 complaints in its 32 years of operation with less than 500 of these being finalised, and just over a hundred findings on the merit. By way of comparison, its European



A. Uwazuruike, *Human Rights under the African Charter*,
https://doi.org/10.1007/978-3-030-41739-0_7

counterpart (the European Court of Human Rights) had 56,350 at the start of 2019.[1] When one considers that just five states namely Russia, Turkey, Romania, Ukraine and Italy—given their relatively poor human rights reputation—accounted for more than 68% of those applications, it is logical to expect that a similar translation in Africa, where quite a few countries have a penchant for human rights violation (not to talk of the frequent occurrences of sectarian crises including cases of genocide), would ideally run into millions of applications. That this is not the case, even remotely so, is a testament to the gross inefficiency and underutilisation of the system.

A number of reasons have been adduced for the Commission's low numbers ranging from lack of enforcement of its decisions to a general lack of awareness of the workings of the system. Having already identified some of these challenges in the previous chapter, the following sections examine propositions for addressing them. The starting point is the Commission's duty of promotion which is followed by discussions of the protective mandates of both the Court and Commission.

### 7.2.1 The Commission's Duty of Promotion

Previous chapters have already touched on the subject of promotion and its importance in tackling some of the challenges to the implementation of the Charter. It was demonstrated that the level of promotion in the continent had to be improved to address not only the huge gap in knowledge but also pockets of harmful cultural practices. This chapter addresses some of the particular challenges of promotion as it relates to the Commission's duty under the Charter. The following sections will examine the challenges to promotion under the following headings: challenges faced under the state reporting system and the lack of general awareness and publicity on the use and activities of the Commission.

#### 7.2.1.1 The Challenges of the State Reporting System

The examination of state reports has been described as the 'core' of the Commission's promotional mandate.[2] In Chapter 4, which examined the content of state reports, it was explained that this promotional duty of monitoring compliance was severely affected by the failure of states to submit their reports as and when due. Records from recent years show that the practice has worsened rather than improve.

The extent of non-compliance with the submission of state reports is better grasped when one realises that no state has met the prescription of Article 62 of the Charter requiring that reports be submitted every two years.[3] Thus, even the handful of states that have submitted all of their reports have only managed to do so after having being encouraged by the Commission, via a *note verbale* (a formal note used in diplomatic communication), to consolidate outstanding reports into a single report, thus catching up on any backlog in one go. The next section examines some of the factors that affect states' timely submission of reports including suggestions for addressing or ameliorating the situation.

#### *7.2.1.2 Factors Affecting the Timely Submission of Reports*

Two main factors can be identified here; they are the ambitious time period imposed by the Charter and the lack of resources demonstrated by inadequate national structures and inefficient governmental processes.

**Ambitious Time Period**

Much has been said in the previous chapter of the arguably ambitious normative standards set by the Charter. Another area where this ambitiousness is noticeable is in the time period set for submission of state reports. Article 62 mandates state parties to submit such a report every two years. While this may appear reasonable, it has been argued that 'when compared with other human rights treaties, the period of two years is unrealistically short'.[4] This position has been canvassed in some state reports with Kenya stating in its report that the two-year rule was 'too short' and had 'the potential of undermining the quality of expected reports'.[5] The Commission's encouragement of consolidated reports could be interpreted as a tacit acknowledgement of the impracticality of this provision. Going even further, it has been recommended at a brainstorming meeting between the Commission and Court, for the AU to consider reviewing the Charter to render the submission and presentation of state reports from two to four years.[6]

**Lack of Adequate Resources**

Just as is the case with the enforcement of rights, the lack of resources and structures at the national levels affect administrative functions like the preparation of state reports. In its report, Kenya alluded to a lack of 'requisite resources' to undertake the close-spaced reporting process.[7] Also, the African Peer Review Mechanism (APRM) Country Review Team, while reporting on Ghana, identified 'a major weakness in the internal systems of the Ministries of Foreign Affairs and Justice' and suggested that the government strengthen those departments and institute a mechanism for 'automatic compliance' with reporting obligations.[8] The APRM is an agency of the AU through which member states undertake self-monitoring in areas relating to governance and socio-economic development. It is clear that the APRM's automatic compliance suggestion should apply to those states facing similar challenges which conceivably will be quite a few going by the number of defaulting states.

While the creation/strengthening of national structures to respond to basic duties like state reporting is a necessary first step, it is reasonable to suggest that such efforts do not end there. Efforts should also be made towards developing national systems and bodies tasked with overseeing the implementation of decisions of the Commission and Court. Even though some states have set up specific units within their Justice or Foreign Affair Ministries for this role and even gone further to create national human rights institutions, it is clear that such steps are not universal. To buttress the importance of this approach, the ECOWAS Court (ECCJ), which was briefly examined in the previous chapter, has continually urged countries to appoint competent national authorities for the enforcement of that court's decisions.[9] This is because, despite its earlier highlighted jurisdictional successes, the ECCJ faces similar challenges as the Commission with regard to the implementation of its decisions. Also, in one study of states' compliance with decisions of the European Court of Human Rights,[10] it was found that variation in state implementation performance was closely linked to the overall legal infrastructure capacity and government effectiveness of a state. Where capacity and effectiveness were high and diffused, there was less likelihood that adverse judgements would be obstructed or ignored, even when the government, political elites or other actors were reluctant and not in favour of substantive remedies.

Even though based on the European system, it is easy to see how the results of that study apply to the African situation even beyond the enforcement of decisions to the performance of such basic duties as submitting state reports. It makes sense to assume that the required administrative functions will very likely not to be performed where there are no institutions or administrative bodies to ensure their implementation. Thus, Viljoen asserts that inadequate internal governmental processes and bureaucratic bungling, among others, account more for failure to submit reports rather than a concerted lack of political will.[11]

It is important to note the recurrence of this theme of lack of adequate structures and resources which has already been identified in the previous chapter. Its role in such areas as the preparation of state reports highlights the interconnectedness of the three identified core hindrances (states' cooperation, economic and other practical challenges, and institutional effectiveness) to the effective implementation of the Charter. The impact of corruption on the availability of funds but also be taken into consideration.

**Political Will**

Granted that poor or inadequate structures affect the preparation of State Reports, it would be naïve to rule out, at least in some cases, the lack of seriousness or political will that accompanies non-submission of State Reports. When one considers the number of countries, even relatively economically stable ones, that have not submitted any reports or that are late by more than three reports, the case for a lack of interest or seriousness in compiling these reports becomes even stronger. Having already examined at length the subject of political will in previous chapters, this chapter will, in later sections, address the question of how the institutions can play a role in improving compliance and propelling states to fulfil their duties under the Charter. Much of this is done in later sections.

*7.2.1.3 Publicity and Awareness*

Crucial to the Commission's promotional duty is the need to educate and create awareness on human rights in the continent. Some of the steps specified in the Charter include organising seminars, symposia and conferences, disseminating information, and 'encouraging' national and local institutions concerned with human rights. While the Commission has undoubtedly taken bold initiatives to promote human rights in target countries, it must be acknowledged, as pointed out in previous chapters, that such steps are minuscule relative to the size of the continent and number of countries involved. It would be harsh, however, to solely criticise the Commission for this failure as the task of promoting human rights across the continent cannot reasonably be foisted on the shoulders of a lowly manned and underfunded body. That being said, the Commission, as previously shown, has not quite demonstrated the required competence in the area of promotion. Given that the Commission is no doubt aware of the need for publicity and promotion, the question that arises is why it has not taken the necessary steps to increase publicity. To answer this question, it is necessary to study the composition of the Commission and the resources allocated to it.

#### *7.2.1.4 Structure of the Commission*

Having so far made a case for the poor state of human rights in Africa and the magnitude of work needed to rectify the various lapses, one would expect that the body primarily tasked with this role would be adequately empowered and capacitated to do so. The reverse is, however, the case as the Commission is grossly understaffed being composed of only eleven members who act on a part-time basis. Umozurike, himself a Former Chairman of the Commission, has argued for an increase in the number of Commissioners as dividing eleven part-time Commissioners among 52 states only made the task of promotion harder.[12] By way of comparison, he points out that the European Commission had a member from each member state and even though the Inter-American Commission had just seven members, promotion was not included in their functions. Considering, on the other hand, the amount of promotional work left to the Commission, one wonders why all the Commissioners work part-time. Given that some of them are full-time law teachers, members of NGOs and even ambassadors of their respective countries, they cannot reasonably be expected to devote full attention to the Commission's promotional work.[13] This challenge is also shared with the Court, as it would be recalled from Chapter 6 that the Court has consistently cited the part-time nature of the judges' work as a constraint to the effective performance of its duties under the Charter.

Despite calls to increase the number of commissioners, the status quo remains unchanged. Even calls to have the Chairperson of the Commission serve on a full-time basis have generally gone unheeded. Viljoen opines that this situation, coupled with the fact that the Commission meets only twice annually for less than 15 days, shows that the Commission was designed to accomplish very little. This situation has also been linked to the small number of annual decisions by the Commission.[14] One would expect that an important body like the Commission would have full-time members dedicated to the promotion of human rights. The current situation, it is argued, is clearly at odds with the level of work required.

It would be recalled that the Commission was created with a weak mandate, at least in the area of protection. The existence of a fully manned body would have at least compensated in some measure for this defective mandate. It, however, appears to be the case that the Commission is weak both in mandate and operation, and worse still is the fact that such weakness appears to be intentional, or at the very least the product of indifference. The outcome is more so surprising given the high expectations required of states by the Charter. That a weak body was created both in mandate and operation to oversee the Charter's implementation only goes to support previously analysed arguments that the Charter was largely a charade with no real intent of implementation, an argument that has surfaced a few times over the course of this book.

While the structuring of the Commission no doubt affects the fulfilment of its promotional duties, there is yet another equally debilitating constraint which is the lack of adequate funding.

#### *7.2.1.5 Inadequate Resources and Funding*

The inadequacy of resources available to the Commission has been described as the most important challenge to its operation.[15] Lack of funding means that the Commission cannot undertake promotional visits to many countries with its few visits being made possible mainly by donations from outside the continent.[16] This situation also means that the overwhelmed commissioners cannot appoint enough staff to oversee the day-to-day activities of the Commission. This problem of funding has been persistent and unresolved with the call for financial and other support to the Commission being the most consistently recurring theme in the resolutions and decisions of both the OAU and the AU Assembly.[17]

These calls notwithstanding, the Commission is yet to see a significant change in the resources allocated to it. Following the AU's failure to come to its aid, the Commission has had to largely rely on external donations. With these donations, the Commission has been able to hire a few staff, organise conferences and engage in other promotional ventures. Like the shortage of manpower, lack of resources is not peculiar to the Commission as this challenge is also experienced by the African Court. It would be recalled from Chapter 6 that the Court reported a 'lack of resources' to include the lack of basic furniture and working equipment.

#### 7.2.1.6 *Potential Way Forward*

The underfunding of the Commission and Court does not bode well for the regional system. In the case of the Commission, its initial neglect had partly been attributed to the fact that its budget was subsumed under that of the Political Affairs Department of the AUC, a situation which changed in 2008.[18] With this change came an increase of 400% in the Commission's budget from $1,199,557 in 2007 to $6,003,856 in 2008.[19] The Commission's budget has remained within this range with the AU approving a budget of $6,319,680 in 2018.[20] The initial increase notwithstanding, the Commission remains seriously impaired in its operation. An indication of this is seen in the Commission's 37th Activity Report where, in discussing its financial situation, the Commission gives a glimpse into its poor state:

> Communication with the Commission and its Secretariat remains a huge challenge... Telephone landlines do not work and the Office has to rely on a form of cordless phone system...which is not as efficient...the fax is not working; internet connectivity continues to be a major problem for the Commission; even the Microsoft Outlook installed by the AU Commission Headquarters to link all AU organs and offices is erratic at best... both member states and stakeholders have expressed frustration regarding the difficulties of transmitting documents to the Commission.

Such recent state of affairs, as shown above, is no doubt unfortunate and only goes to highlight the near indifference to such an important institution. The Commission's budget has averaged less than 2% of the AU's general budget and has, on at least three occasions from 2005 to 2007, accounted for less than 1% of the Union's total budget.[21] What these figures show is a lack of commitment towards empowering the Commission and by extension the African regional human rights system. While the Commission has struggled to make gains despite its lean resources, the AU has not responded with appropriately increased funding. It has accordingly been contended that the AU's 'schizophrenic' pattern of praising the Commission's accomplishments while starving it of resources suggests that it does not intend for it to become more effective and forceful. Failure by the AU to meet the Commission's needs, it has been argued, 'displays a cynical satisfaction with the Commission's minimal success'.[22] Given some of the aforementioned facts above, it is difficult to argue with this position. Such a systematic short-changing of the Commission is in line with the clear restriction of its protective mandate under the Charter. One would have thought that, with its protective mandate effectively curtailed, the Commission would be given maximum support in fulfilling its promotional mandate. The contrary, however, appears to be the case. Furthermore, no programme budget is allocated to the Commission from the member states meaning that the Commission effectively relies on partner funds to implement its promotional mandate.[23] While international assistance of the Commission is a welcome development, it goes to show the failure and reluctance of African states to grow their own regional human rights institution.

The challenge of funding has prompted suggestions and moves towards ensuring the independence of the Commission with regard to resource and budgetary matters. One such proposal has been for the establishment of a Fund to be financed by voluntary contributions from member states, international and regional institutions, and even private sources. In 2006, the Commission passed a Resolution which called upon the AU Commission to present to the Executive Council a draft decision for the establishment of a Fund, for the Commission, to be financed by voluntary contributions.[24] In line with the call, the Executive Council made the necessary request to the AU Commission to put such a system in place. It is not clear what steps, if any, have been taken towards this end. Rather, the Commission has recently taken to revealing the contribution of 'partners' in its approved final budgets. Such contributions average less than 30% of the budget with the remainder being member states' assessed contributions.

In terms of money approved for its operation, not much has changed for the Commission as it continues to voice complaints about the inadequacy of the approved budget for the wide range of activities it is required to perform. It is obvious that proactive steps ought to be taken by both the AU, individual states, and the Commission towards augmenting the resources available to the Commission.

On the part of the AU, it must augment the resources currently assigned to the Commission to reflect the human right needs of the continent. A starting point would be allocating a programmes budget to the Commission, a step the AU has failed to take so far. Given the importance of promotional activities, it is surprising that the AU does not allocate programme budgets to either the Commission or Court. In the case of the Court, it must be recalled that even though it does not have a promotional mandate, it still undertakes promotional activities aimed at raising awareness about its existence and operation. Also, aside their assessed contributions, states could initiate a policy of funding promotional activities in their respective states.

It should be noted that the Court is also funded by the AU and is usually allocated more resources than the Commission.[25] It would also be recalled that the Court's mandate is to 'complement' the protective mandate of the Commission.[26] It is, therefore, difficult to appreciate why the Commission receives lesser resources when it is mandated to fulfil the twin duties of promotion and protection as opposed to the Court which has only a 'complementary' protective mandate. The disparity becomes even more questionable when one considers that the Commission, due to the jurisdictional restraints of the Court, is expected to perform even more protective duties than the latter. The fact that the Court which according to its Protocol was created to 'complement and reinforce the functions of the [Commission]' receives far more in budgetary allocations is evidence of the latter's poor funding.

A path forward would be the implementation of initiatives to create a Fund for the Commission. More important, however, is an increment in the allocation of funds to the Commission especially for its duties of promotion. In addition, states may initiate a policy of funding specific promotional programmes in their respective territories. This may entail the Commission publishing a list of promotional programmes it intends to undertake in each country pointing out the most important and those for which it may need sponsorship or support from the said state with the states invited to support such programmes. Such request may even be extended to private entities such as institutions which may be willing to host seminars and conferences, corporations, and even individuals. By encouraging public sponsorship of its promotional events the Commission would not only gain in popularity but could also fuel human rights awareness as sponsors would relish the tag of 'human rights supporters'.

It is instructive to note that even though this chapter is dedicated to what may be termed 'the third major challenge' to the implementation of the Charter namely institutional ineffectiveness, so far the emphasis has been on how the first two main hindrances (state commitment and practical challenges) have affected and constrained institutional effectiveness. This highlights the interconnectedness of the various challenges to the full implementation of the African Charter. In order to ensure better promotion and protection of rights, adequate steps have to be taken to address each group of challenges.

### 7.2.2 *Commission's Duty of Protection*

Much has already been said of the Commission's protective mandate. In summary, the OAU, the AU's predecessor, set out to create a weak body that would only pass on recommendations and findings to the Assembly of Heads of States and Government. Thus, even though the Commission had a mandate to 'protect' human rights, its ability to do this was effectively watered down by the provisions of the Charter. Previous chapters have already identified how the Commission has set about ameliorating this situation and strengthening its weak protective mandate under the Charter. Firstly, it has gone on to fill in gaps in the Charter through favourable proactive interpretations. Such gaps include hearing individual communications and reviewing state reports. In the case of the former, the Charter does not specifically refer to individual communications only making references to 'communications other than those of state parties'. In the latter case, the Charter does not state the recipient of state reports or what should be done after their submission.

This proactive approach was further extended to the interpretation of Charter provisions. The Commission expanded provisions on civil and political rights, socio-economic rights and peoples' rights, and even interpreted the absence of a derogation clause from the Charter to mean that no derogation was allowed under the Charter. The Commission has gone further to adopt Rules of Procedure that strengthen its enforcement mechanism through the creation of a follow-up procedure that provides for the appointment of a rapporteur for each communication and the provision for transfer of unimplemented cases to the African Court. These steps have obviously been in response to the low rate of compliance with the Commission's decisions with some states unequivocally challenging their enforceability. The creation of a Court seemingly put the question of enforceable decisions at the regional level to rest. However, given its jurisdictional constraints, this appears to be mainly a solution on paper, with the practical implication that the Commission remains the sole avenue for many victims of human rights violations to lay their complaints. It follows that in order to guarantee the availability of recourse at the regional level, the Commission—given the jurisdictional limitations of the Court—has to be made more effective. To this end, the following section examines the argument for imbuing the Commission's decisions with binding authority through the machineries of the AU Assembly and Executive Council. Other sections will examine the cooperation between the African Court and Commission and the viability of treaty reform.

#### *7.2.2.1 The AU's 'Executive' Role in Implementation*

The AU Assembly has an important role to play in the effective discharge of the Commission's protective mandate. This is largely due to the fact that the Commission is under the overall supervision of the Assembly throughout the exercise of its protective mandate. It should be noted here that the Assembly has since delegated its task of considering the Commission's reports to the Executive Council.

Aside from submitting reports on state complaints and drawing the attention of the Assembly to the existence of massive violations of rights, the Commission is also mandated by the Charter to keep all measures taken under its protective mandate confidential unless otherwise decided by the Assembly. This incidentally is a point many commentators often overlook or do not pay sufficient attention to. Curiously, this point has not been paid deserved attention by authors who have examined the Commission's protective mandate. While bemoaning the absence of real enforcement or binding power of the Commission, some of these authors have ended up concluding that there is no remedy under the Charter.[27] This, however, cannot be entirely correct as, from the language of the Charter, there is provision for the 'possibility' of an effective remedy albeit through the Assembly enforcing the reports and submissions of the Commission.

It is important to note that the situation would not be very different were the Commission to be given explicit powers to make binding decisions as the Assembly would still be final recourse in the event of states' failure to implement the decisions. This is the case with the Court which, even though its decisions are binding, is required to submit reports to the Assembly specifying the cases in which a state has not complied with its judgement. Thus, just as enforcement and other institutions of the executive arm of government (such as state sheriffs) play a key role in the enforcement of domestic judgements, the AU Assembly and other relevant institutions of the AU's executive arm are responsible for seeing to the enforcement of judgements of its regional court.

The situation is however slightly tricky in the case of the Commission as the Assembly cannot be seen to demand the implementation of a non-binding decision. This would however not be the case were a literal reading and interpretation of the Charter to be adopted. By Article 53 of the Charter, the Commission is to submit its reports along with 'such recommendations as it deems useful'. The Charter does not state what happens thereafter leaving the option open to the Assembly to act on the finding as a decision of the Assembly which in turn would be binding on member states. This is arguably how the OAU, the AU's predecessor, intended for it to be. The Union would decide which decisions to adopt and which to ignore, not necessarily having to dance to the tune of the Commission on every single occasion.

The provisions that the Commission only forward reports and recommendations to the Assembly, rather than take decisions itself, and not publish any of its findings until authorised by the Assembly, clearly demonstrate the intention of the latter to be in control of the entire process. This also informs the Commission's stance, as seen in the previous chapter, that its decisions become binding after its annual report containing them is adopted by the Assembly.[28] This, of course, is based on the position that decisions of the AU in the form of regulations or directives (under which these should fall) are expressly binding.[29] This being the case therefore, it stands to reason that the Assembly can, unambiguously, give effect to the findings and decisions of the Commission. The requirement for clarity on the status of recommendations from communications is important because of the uncertainty that trails the mere adoption of Activity Reports which may be interpreted as only playing the Assembly's part in the Commission's duty of 'transmitting its report' to it. As the intent is mainly to inform the Assembly of the Commission's activities, it becomes slightly presumptuous to expect that recommendations become binding by the mere adoption of the Activity Reports by the Executive Council. On this note, it becomes necessary for the AU, through the Assembly, to take extra steps to ensure clarity in its adopted position on the status of recommendations forwarded to it by the Commission. The Assembly, it is suggested, should take the extra step of adopting the Commission's findings, not merely as part of the latter's Activity Reports, but as distinct decisions of the Assembly thereby making them legally binding. This could take the form of normal regulations and directives of the Assembly which would ordinarily be published in the official journal of the African Union.[30] By Rule 34 of the Assembly's Rules of Procedure, these regulations and directives become automatically enforceable 30 days after the date of their publication in the official journal of the African

Union or as specified in the decision. The added effect of this, apart from bestowing binding force, is that the Assembly will then be in a position to impose sanctions on defaulting states which would not have been possible for mere recommendations.

It is also important to point out the possible effect of this proposed practice on the actual content of recommendations. It was stated in Chapter 5 that one of the possible challenges to states' implementation of the Commission's recommendations has been the failure of the latter to provide clear and specific remedies in some cases. While this is a challenge that can be, and indeed has been, progressively addressed by the Commission, it is reasonable to surmise that the adoption of the above procedure will further spur the Commissioners to carry out this role effectively. This would be done in the knowledge that such decisions would be formally tabled before the Assembly for adoption as decisions of the Assembly.

#### *7.2.2.2 Imposition of Sanctions*

The imposition of sanctions is certainly one way that the Assembly can improve the effectiveness of the Commission's decisions. And, as has been shown above, this can be done if the Assembly takes the initiative of specially adopting them as AU decisions. States would no doubt fail to implement decisions whether binding or not if they do not see any benefits of doing so or any repercussions by the way of sanctions or negative publicity. Arguing along this line, Viljoen states that the binding authority of the Commission's decisions is largely a red herring because compliance would ultimately depend on political factors such as the possible application of sanctions for non-compliance.[31]

The power of imposing sanctions of a 'political and economic nature' for non-compliance with decisions and policies of the AU is provided for in Article 23(2) AU Constitutive Act with Rule 36 of its Rules of Procedure specifying the denial of transport and communication links as possible forms of sanctions. However, the AU has hardly imposed any sanctions under the authority of this Article.[32] This, of course, raises concerns as member states have, at least during the era of the OAU, the AU's predecessor, been in the habit of 'blatantly ignoring' the decisions adopted by OAU organs and rather adopting national policies which directly violated them.

The failure to apply sanctions, however, appears to be limited to this class of breach, that is, failure to comply with AU (and previously OAU) decisions as opposed to the other two classes of breach for which sanctions are also applied namely non-payment of budgetary contributions under Article 23(1) and unconstitutional change of government Article 30. While the OAU expectedly did very little in the latter case owing to the sacrosanct principles of non-intervention and interference on which it was built, it was 'forced' to respond with sanctions to address the challenge of member states' contributions in arrears. A new Rule was inserted in the OAU Financial Rules and Regulations to the effect that member states in arrears of contributions would not participate in OAU decisions and votes. Furthermore, in 1990, the Council of Ministers decided that such states would also be deprived of the right to speak at OAU meetings and to present candidates for OAU positions. A 'Credentials Committee' was even set up for the purpose of applying these sanctions.[33] A number of states have accordingly been sanctioned with countries such as Liberia, Somalia, Central African Republic, Seychelles, Democratic Republic of Congo and Guinea-Bissau remaining under long periods of sanctions despite prolonged internal crises in some of these countries.

With regard to unconstitutional change of government, following the shift in the ideology of the AU which included the creation of a framework for a regional response to unconstitutional changes of government, the Peace and Security Council (PSC) has 'been actively exercising its mandate'.[34] For instance, the PSC has suspended Togolese authorities from participating in the AU following an unconstitutional change of government. The PSC has also called for the enforcement of a travel ban on Mauritania after the country's military government was banned from attending the AU summit in Ethiopia. The AU has also imposed travel bans and frozen the assets of Guinean officials. Similar travel restrictions were also imposed on Madagascar following that country's failure to set up a unity government. Furthermore, the PSC suspended Togolese authorities from participating in the AU following an unconstitutional change of government. The AU has also threatened similar measures in the aftermath of the military overthrow of Omar al-Bashir of Sudan should the country's Transitional Military Council fail to hand over power to civilians.[35]

The idea of the above expositions is to make the case for similar assertive steps to be taken in respect of recommendations of the Commission subsequently adopted as decisions of the Assembly. By ascribing the same level of importance to these decisions as to the above-discussed classes, the Assembly would be passing a strong positive message on the importance of human rights observance. Such a message would be stronger were the Assembly to adopt similar non-discretionary procedures as in the two classes discussed. For instance, Art 23(1) of the AU Assembly Constitutive Act mandates the Assembly to impose sanctions on defaulting member states. Similarly, there is no political discretion in cases of unconstitutional takeovers of government. This would mean that non-compliance with the Commission's decisions would be met by, at least, preliminary measures like warnings by the Assembly and subsequent measures if need be, as opposed to the present regime of silence. As done in the two classes above, a special body or committee should be assigned the role of imposing these sanctions.

It is important to note that this proposal is also applicable in the case of decisions by the African Court. It would be recalled that the Court's Protocol provides for the Court to report a failure to comply with its decisions to the Assembly without further details on what the Assembly would do in such cases. Therefore, concerns have already been voiced as to how the Court would enforce its decisions in the case of states who adopt to simply wait out the process.[36] It is argued here that the Assembly can adopt similar steps as proposed for the Commission above.

#### 7.2.2.3 *The Alternative of Using the Court's Binding Power*

Another proposal for sidestepping the challenge of the binding power of the Commission's decisions is for the latter to refer finalised cases or those that have not been complied with to the Court with the idea that the Court would give binding force to these decisions. While similar to the first proposal above, this is different to the extent that it is a legal solution as opposed to the former which could be hampered by the political reticence of AU member states.

Already, the Commission's Rules of Procedure provide for such a relationship between the Court and Commission. By Rule 118, the Commission 'may' submit a communication to the Court where a state has not complied with, or is unwilling to comply with, its recommendations or provisional measures. Unfortunately, the Commission has not cultivated a culture of submitting finalised cases to the Court. One reason for this is that the Commission has succeeded in finalising few communications in recent years and most of the respondent states in those cases are not parties to the Court Protocol.[37] Another even more important concern is that the Rules appear to put the issue of referral at the discretion of the Commission, a discretion which is often not exercised in favour of the

Court. Hence, the argument has been made for a mandatory requirement to 'automatically' refer a case to the Court after a stipulated time period of non-compliance.[38] Such a practice would guarantee certainty and better highlight the complementarity of the two institutions. It would also bestow a 'binding' authority on the decisions.

The Commission itself is not unaware of the possible impact of the Court's pronouncements. In the early stages of the Libyan crisis of 2011, an application was brought before the Commission regarding the serious and widespread violations of human rights in Libya. In a sense of urgency, the Commission, rather than grant provisional measures, immediately referred the matter to the Court. The Commission appears to have considered the grave situation in Libya and whether its intervention would elicit any response from the government and adopted the above approach because the chances of a provisional measure eliciting a response from the government were 'very slim taking into consideration the situation in Libya'.[39] While such referrals are no doubt a positive step in the development of the relationship between the two bodies, the Commission's self-assessment is evidence of its diminished status as occasioned by its weak protective mandate. Future discussions on the Court will further address this issue of referral of cases from the Commission.

#### *7.2.2.4 The Alternative of Treaty Reform*

A third possible way of overcoming the shortcomings of the Commission is by reforming, through the means of an amending protocol, those parts of the Charter deemed to be inimical to the proper functioning of the Commission. There have accordingly been some arguments down the years for a reform of the Charter both as to its normative contents and institutional framework. While such a process would appear logical, at least with regard to the Commission's protective mandate, its practicability and even necessity are in doubt. Firstly, the Commission's perceived defects have already been addressed, albeit with minimal success, in the form of the Court's Protocol. The challenges currently faced by the Court namely low numbers of ratification and declarations allowing individual access are likely to be encountered by the creations of any future Protocols. Secondly, as suggested in the sections above, there are already viable options for improving the force of the Commission's decisions through the instruments of the Assembly and Court. What may be needed are clarifications and possibly additions to the Rules of Procedure to adopt the Commission's decisions in the case of the Assembly and, in the case of the Commission, to make clearer and more mandatory provisions for referrals to the Court both of which are presumably less onerous than an outright revision of the Charter.

#### *7.2.2.5 Publication of Findings*

Despite most of the analysis above focussing mainly on the binding nature of the Commission's recommendations and follow-up processes as factors inhibiting enforcement, there are other steps that the Commission can take to improve compliance. One area that has been identified is the publication of the Commission's findings. Originally, the Commission gave a strict interpretation to Article 59 of the African Charter which preserves the confidentiality of all measures taken within the Charter until otherwise decided by the Assembly of Heads of State and Government. However, the Commission now issues its findings as an annexe to its Annual Activity Reports which are published semi-annually after their adoption by the AU Assembly.[40] While this is a positive development, it is noted still that the Commission has not made the best use of the media to publish its findings on decisions, to publicise instances of governmental compliance and non-compliance. Rather, press involvements in the past can largely be attributed to the efforts of NGOs. The Commission's efforts at disseminating information through the Internet must, however, be commended. The Commission's website is rich in information ranging from its recent activities, minutes of sessions, decisions on communications, Mission Reports, and state reports. It is recommended that the Commission put in more effort to publicise instances of compliance and non-compliance by states in their human rights responsibilities. The possible impacts of such media publicity are further examined in subsequent sections.

#### *7.2.2.6 Amicable Processes*

Also identified as impeding, the implementation of findings is the perception that the decisions, the decision process, and the follow-up system of the Commission are purely adversarial. From the reaction of the government of Botswana in *Good v Botswana*,[41] the interpretation could be made that it viewed the Commission's actions as adversarial and a threat to its sovereignty. This fear and protection of sovereignty has long characterised Africa's dealings with supranational bodies and is arguably responsible for the many restrictions on the Commission as well as the initial reluctance to create a court. Thus, it has been suggested that there be a shift away from confrontation towards a more integrated approach of constructive dialogue, decision making and follow-up.[42] It has also been suggested that, as a follow-up to the above approach, the African Commission, perceiving of itself as only one key player in the development of human rights, must also further engage with other key political organs by finding alternative fora outside the summit in which to discuss its findings. For instance, by Article 19 of its Protocol, the PSC is required to seek close cooperation with the African Commission on all matters relevant to its objectives and mandate. It would be recalled from the previous chapter that the PSC is responsible for preventing, managing and resolving conflicts within the continent. They may also recommend military intervention in cases of genocide, war crimes and crimes against humanity. Murray and Mottershaw[43] believe that the PSC could arguably in this context examine decisions of the African Commission as indicators under their early warning system.

## 7.3 The African Court

Created to provide a judicial human rights body for the continent and make up for some of the shortcomings of the Commission, the African Court has failed to reach its full potential. This failure, it has been shown, is largely due to a lack of support by states in the form of ratifications and declarations allowing individual and NGO access to the Court. Given that only ten states have made the latter declaration, it means that individuals cannot bring complaints against 46 states of the Union. Again, it must be noted that Rwanda has withdrawn its declaration—a move which the Court has ruled is within the country's rights. Also, no cases, whether by the Commission or state, can be brought against nearly half of African states who have not ratified the Court's Protocol. This outcome is quite detrimental to human rights development given that the Court was ideally poised to make an impact based on its structural and judicial capacity.

It appears from the above that the obvious solution would be to encourage states to ratify the Protocol as well as make the Article 34(6) declaration. Herein, however, lies the challenge. Previous chapters have demonstrated a strong attachment to state sovereignty and general distrust of regional judicial mechanisms by African states. It has also been opined that the ECOWAS approach, which was successful in getting states to endorse similar powers for its Court, be considered for the African

Court. Such efforts, it is conceded, would involve a much greater number of actors and diplomacy on an even grander scale. Such rigours and machinations are obviously beyond the scope of this book. However, this step appears to be the most realistic for the development of the Court. And, while the Court may acquire more ratifications in the future, it has to be accepted that this process will be very slow and gradual. In the meantime, however, it has been readily pointed out that the Commission can act as a conduit for transferring cases to the Court due to the latter's restrictions on individual access. The following sections will analyse the extent of this means.

### *7.3.1 Indirect Access Through the Commission*

The Commission's Rules of Procedure allow it to refer a matter to the Court 'at any stage of the examination of a communication'.[44] This provision allows matters that ordinarily would not come before the Court, due to restrictions under Article 34(6) to be so brought. Given the very limited ability of individuals and NGOs to institute cases and the general disinterest of states in this regard, the Commission appears to be the likeliest source of cases for the Court. It has even been suggested that the Commission has a 'paramount' role or duty to supply the Court with cases.[45] However, the Commission has obviously not played its part in this regard. A review of the Court's case list shows that the Commission has initiated only three cases before the Court. It, of course, does not help that the Commission's Rules are silent as to when exactly a complaint may be referred or submitted to the Court. That this is left entirely to the Commission's discretion would necessarily result in a small number of cases being referred as the Commission, it is expected, would ordinarily want to hear and decide every case brought before it.

It has been pointed out that such a difficulty was experienced with the Inter-American Court where it took six and four years, respectively, for the Inter-American Court to receive cases from its counterpart Commission.[46] Viljoen[47] identifies another possible restraint to referrals as being a possible apprehension on the part of the Commission that a referred case would undergo a 'de novo consideration' including reconsideration of the facts, law, admissibility, merits and remedial orders. It is such situations as these that have led to some calls for the Commission to be practically dissolved and merged with the Court.[48]

In contesting this position, it must be clarified that referring cases to the Court is not among the Commission's chief duties, nor is ensuring a full docket for the Court. While it may help to have some guidance on when to refer cases, the Commission, as every party that can bring a case before the Court, should have a level of discretion. The case could, however, be different for complaints involving a serious breach of human rights or where the Commission's decisions have not been implemented—both of which are provided under different sections of the Rule in question, and in which circumstances the Commission has referred a couple of cases. It will arguably, therefore, be a step in the right direction for the Commission to amend its Rules to mandatorily refer to the Court cases that fall under the latter two categories. However, all other instances should ideally be left to the discretion of the Commission.

It should be pointed out that matters referred by the Commission lose their 'individual flavour' in the sense that the Commission, being the initiating party, makes all the important decisions rather than the affected individual who is not a party to the case. In other words, the individual has no control of the proceedings and cannot decide which matters are brought before the Court. Thus, while it may be ideal to have the Commission keep the Court afloat with a regular referral of cases, this cannot substitute for individual/NGO initiation of complaints. This is more so the case as the Commission can only refer cases against parties to the Protocol. It cannot therefore refer cases against some states like Angola, Ethiopia, Sudan and Zimbabwe, against whom it has found violations but which have not ratified the Court's Protocol. States must, therefore, be strongly persuaded to ratify the Charter and make the Article 34(6) declaration. Of course, this is easier said than done and would involve intense lobbying and political machinations. It is, however, the most viable way forward for the African Court.

### *7.3.2 The Future of the Court*

As already highlighted in the previous chapter, there is a Protocol proposing the merger of the African Court with the African Court of Justice to create an African Court of Justice and Human Rights (ACJHR). Thus, the African Court would operate as a chamber in this projected merged court. Unfortunately, not much has changed between the current system and that proposed under the ACJHR in terms of individual complaints as similar provisions exist in the latter's Protocol. Just as in the present system, Art 8(3) of the Protocol on the Statute of the ACJHR allows states to make a declaration accepting the competence of the Court to receive cases from individuals and accredited NGOs.

It is also important to note the recent steps towards the creation of a criminal chamber in the proposed ACJHR. Such a chamber would have the competence to hear and determine matters of genocide, crimes against humanity, war crimes, corruption and money laundering among others. However, in a move that has been described as an 'own goal',[49] African Heads of State, in 2014, voted to grant serving Heads of State and 'senior state officials' immunity from prosecution.[50] The provision of immunity for serving leaders in the yet to be implemented Protocol sets the criminal court apart from other international criminal tribunals where the absence of immunity has become 'axiomatic'. This proposal for immunity can be linked to the AU's continued disagreements with the International Criminal Court especially in the latter's efforts to prosecute two serving Heads of State in Kenya and Sudan. The alleged targeting of sitting African leaders by the ICC has remained one of the central themes of the AU's strained relationship with the ICC. This has subsequently induced the AU to take 'retaliatory' measures by conferring international criminal jurisdiction on its proposed Court.[51]

The move to grant immunity to serving Heads of States and senior state officials has been roundly criticised by both local and international NGOs. One major criticism is that it contradicts the spirit of the AU's Constitutive Act which contains 'broad and inspiring language' obliging the Union, among other responsibilities, 'to intervene in a member state…in respect of grave circumstances, namely: war crimes, genocide and crimes against humanity'.[52] Another criticism is that it could further encourage leaders to seize office for life, a problem the continent already grapples with.

So far, however, the ACJHR exists only on paper with a rather long route to operationalisation given the many changes and proposals. These changes ordinarily require the ratification of legal instruments, an outcome which does not seem likely in the near future given that more than ten years after adoption of the merging Protocol, less than half of the required 15 states needed to bring the Protocol into force, have ratified it, and even here it is argued that the Protocol is already defunct given the subsequent amendments to it. States that have ratified the Protocol include Benin, Burkina Faso, Congo (Brazzaville), Libya and Mali.

The question that arises, after a glimpse into the possible future of the regional system, is whether such a future solves some of the challenges, or at least the institutional ones, that have so far been identified. Quite clearly, the answer is no. As it appears, the regional judicial system would be starting afresh—what is a rather uncertain and likely bleak future. Firstly, the merger of institutions and the addition of a criminal chamber do not address the key issue of whether states would cooperate with the institution through funding, ratifications and compliance with decisions. As pointed out above, even the ACJHR Protocol has not been able to garner near substantive ratifications. In over a decade of its existence, the African Court has been able to garner just a little over half of ratifications by all AU states with only a handful of individual and NGO declarations under Article 34(6). There is no reason to expect that the situation would be any different in a new tripartite court. If anything, one would expect fewer ratifications and more reservations given the increased requirements as is currently the case with the African Court. It is interesting to note how easily African states adopt Protocols and create institutions and subsequently become reluctant to ratify and cooperate with them. As amply stated by one commentator: 'African states are notoriously quick to adopt treaties but excruciatingly slow to ratify them'.[53]

Furthermore, the issue of funding has not been sufficiently thrashed out especially given that the proposed merged court would require much more funding and resources both to carry out and promote its activities. Additionally, the proposed criminal chamber, being a novel concept, would come with its own new challenges of operation and implementation. Overall, the region runs the risk of losing the gains of the present system for a future with uncertain and minimal chances of success. The various analyses in this book show that the continent is generally not ready for such a complex system especially as the relatively less complex institutions have been largely ineffective and yet to find their feet. To prepare itself for possible future developments, the current challenges of the system must first be addressed and resolved. Thus, a comprehensive and viable financial plan must be developed along with the firm commitment of a significant number of member states to completely support the new body. This support, as has been seen in the case of the Court, must go beyond mere adoption of Protocols and extend further into ratification, domestication, declarations allowing individual and NGO access, and compliance with decisions. Any institutional changes that do not take these issues into consideration can be likened to changing into dry clothes while still in the rain.

## 7.4 Improving Compliance—The Role of NGOs

NGOs and civil society have long been considered beneficial for the promotion of human rights. International NGOs, like Amnesty International and Human Rights Watch, have grown a reputation for drawing attention to human rights violations and calling on states to abide by their human rights obligations. In the African case, NGOs have also been noted to contribute significantly to the enforcement of rights. The contribution of NGOs comes in different forms including the promotion of human rights through sensitisation, education and investigation of cases of abuse or violations. NGO impact also comes in the form of applying pressure on key actors to perform their functions. It has, for instance, been noted that Commission has been held accountable in practice more consistently by NGOs than by the AU.[54]

There is also no denying the important role that NGOs have to play in the protective mandate of the institutions. This is demonstrated through, for instance, bringing complaints before the relevant body and monitoring compliance with final decisions. NGOs have often been known to follow up on decisions of the Commission, ensuring through mass campaigns and media sensitisation, that state parties comply.[55]

Aside lobbying states to enforce decisions, NGOs have also played institutional roles in volatile areas with limited statehood. Studies have revealed the far-reaching effect of NGOs in the Democratic Republic of Congo, a conflict-ridden state with dilapidated institutions. Despite its raging conflict and failing institutions, local courts in the Eastern Democratic Republic of Congo remained active and, since 2006, produced an extraordinary number of judicial decisions convicting perpetrators of sexual and gender-based violence owing largely to the influence of NGOs.[56]

The next sections will highlight previous achievements of NGOs with the aim of demonstrating the need for policies that would promote their growth and development in the continent and, by implication, improve their engagement and contribution towards solving some of the challenges facing the African human rights system. These previously identified problems include lack of cooperation and political will by member states, economic and cultural challenges, and institutional ineffectiveness.

### *7.4.1 NGOs and States*

The ability of NGOs to persuade or even induce cooperation from states cannot be overemphasised. Given the indifference that often greets the required performance of their duties, states need that extra push to fulfil those responsibilities. One ready tool of the NGOs in achieving this aim is media publicity.

History has shown that African states are generally averse to negative publicity against their regimes especially in the area of human rights. It would be recalled, for instance, that the Charter provides for secrecy of 'all measures' taken by the Commission until otherwise decided by the Assembly. Even the report on the activities of the Commission is not to be published until it has been 'considered' by the Assembly. These provisions were no doubt inserted in order to exercise a measure of control over what gets into the public sphere about findings of violations against member states. This is because negative human rights reports diminish the reputation of states internationally—as well as the individuals running the states—and could often disqualify them from receiving financial aid as well as impact international trade and investment.

It is through publicising human rights violations and even perceived lack of cooperation from certain states, that pressure may be mounted on those states to comply. As the Commission cannot adequately perform this role, owing to political and financial constraints, the baton is necessarily passed on to NGOs. Such an important task as this should however not be left to randomness. NGOs with observer status should devise a comprehensive policy for coordinated publicity of both the activities of the Commission and violations by states.

NGOs' ability to influence state compliance is not limited to cases of violations. As demonstrated in the process of the adoption and ratification of the Supplementary Protocol to the ECCJ discussed in a previous chapter, NGOs can also play a crucial role in influencing states to embark on initiatives that they may otherwise not have done. As already pointed out, this Supplementary Protocol of the ECCJ introduced novel features such as direct access by individuals, open-ended legal norms and non-exhaustion of domestic remedies. One of the main reasons for states' acceptance of these features was attributed to intense lobbying by NGOs.[57] While not discounting efforts already made in that regard, it could yield positive fruits—given the EECJ example—for NGOs in conjunction with the African Court, to launch a concerted massive programme aimed towards encouraging ratification of the Court's Protocol and Article 34(6) declarations. In any event, the main idea that should be gleaned from the above is that the regional institutions need to form more purposive partnerships with the NGOs aimed at achieving set goals. These partnerships could even extend into more robust promotional activities given the financial constraints faced by the institutions.

Another area that NGOs can play a crucial role is in situations of 'serious or massive violations' of human rights. According to the Charter, the Commission is to draw the attention of the Assembly to special cases involving a series of serious violations of rights and make factual reports on them accompanied by findings and recommendations. Of course, one would expect the Assembly to act quickly on these reports of serious violations. Unfortunately, this has not always been the case as the Assembly has often met these reports with inaction such that the practice has now reportedly gone into abeyance.[58] The role of an effective NGO network would be to bring these situations into focus and mount pressure on the AU to act on them. Fortunately, however, there have been positive developments in the area of interventions and peacekeeping through the creation of the peace and security architecture with the PSC fast becoming the first port of call in such instances.

### *7.4.2 NGOs and the Logistics Challenge*

Practical challenges like the lack of resources and cultural impediments have been identified as some of the main obstacles to the implementation of the Charter. Naturally, NGOs should step in, and have occasionally done so, to cushion the effect on both the states and institutions. In tackling the challenge of obnoxious cultural practices, NGOs have tirelessly sought to create awareness on such harmful practices as female genital cutting, child marriages and forced labour. Here, reference may be made to the example of the NGO 'Tostan' which was discussed in Chapter 5.

The importance of NGOs is more pronounced in societies where there is a near total failure of governance and the rule of law as NGOs have been known to step 'into the void left by weak or dysfunctional states'.[59] A good example is that of the Democratic Republic of Congo which, despite sectarian crises and derelict institutions, was able to maintain local courts and the judicial process owing largely to the efforts of NGOs. A brief narration of the events is necessary to grasp the important role played by NGOs in the conflict.

On New Year's Day 2011, violence escalated in the Congolese eastern town of Fizi. A group of civilians had attacked and killed the bodyguard of one Lieutenant Kifaru Alexis for firing a shot at a store-tender who had refused his lieutenant access to a female customer in his shop. Enraged by violence and death of one of his soldiers, Lieutenant Colonel Mutuare Kibibi drafted officers to round up those responsible. Following instructions, hundreds of soldiers descended on the town wreaking havoc, looting houses, assaulting locals and raping women and children. At least seventy local women and children were confirmed to have been violently raped and tortured by Congolese soldiers in a matter of hours. Even though atrocities like this were not unusual in conflict-ridden Congo, the ensuing response was surprising. Despite a domestic court system in disrepair and an overwhelming lack of judicial resources allocated by the central government, in just six weeks a full investigation had been carried out and Lieutenant Colonel Kibibi and ten of his officers were arrested, tried, and convicted for sexual assaults carried out against nearly 100 civilian women. They were found guilty of civil, criminal and international crimes of terrorism, rape, forced imprisonment, sexual brutality, sexual torture and inhumane sexual acts among others—a judgement that combined elements of Congolese civil, criminal and military law with the most up-to-date international human rights protections regarding SGBV. This outcome was largely attributed to the role of external actors, mainly NGOs, in the domestic structures of Congo. Given the fragile state of the country, NGOs filled the void in the judicial systems and exerted considerable influence over judicial processes.[60]

The distinctive attribute of the above case was the speed and effectiveness of the judicial process in such a failed and volatile state. Since the start of the Second Congo War in 1998, the death toll has been estimated to be between three to five million people, representing the single greatest loss of life in any conflict since the Second World War. Armed militias had killed and wreaked havoc in a battle for supremacy and there was no single central authority over the entire Congo region. It was thus surprising that such a swift and effective process could be launched to remedy the abuse occasioned by the invasion of Fizi by Lieutenant Colonel Kibibi's men. Lake attributes this effectiveness to the rise of local and international NGOs and transnational actors who exploited the gaps in authority by assuming some of the basic functions of governance in order to create a society where human rights are respected and enforced.[61]

Even in states with functioning governments and institutions, NGOs can help in curbing practices that militate against human rights by collaborating with local authorities and getting them to combat obnoxious practices. The importance of developing allies among customary legal officials has been identified in the area of women's rights where there are many entrenched traditional attitudes towards women. The application of customary legal rules has been identified as the most significant barrier to altering practices that do not conform with the rights of women.[62]

By identifying with local authorities, NGOs can initiate a process of adaptation. Such adaptation could take the same route as FGM in some Kenyan communities as highlighted in Chapter 5, where alternative circumcision rites were introduced to replace old traditions. Under the new procedure arrived at through communal dialogue and consensus, the people within these communities agreed to do away with the physical mutilation of the woman's body during the traditional female circumcision rites while retaining other harmless aspects of the circumcision rites. Such concessions as this can hardly be achieved solely through legal processes such as the passing of statutes. This is proven by comparing results in other countries that passed FGM legislation without the accompanying interactions at the local level. These experiences, it is argued, show that formal legislative enactments alone cannot change pervasive cultural attitudes. There usually is a need for collaboration and sensitisation—a role which is effectively played by NGOs.

### *7.4.3 NGOs and the Regional Institutions*

The Commission continues to work with a network of NGOs many of whom have observer status with it. Some of the basic roles of the NGOs include drawing the attention of the Commission to violations of the Charter, bringing communications on behalf of individuals, monitoring compliance with the Charter and raising awareness of the Commission's activities. However, collaboration between the two goes even further. NGOs participate in the Commission's public sessions and submit shadow reports. These reports which would often be on a particular state are read alongside that state's own report and aid the Commission in having a constructive dialogue with that state. In a 2019 Activity Report, the Special Rapporteur on Rights of Women identified the submission of state and shadow reports as "one of the areas where we need to see more progress".[63] NGOs with observer status are required to submit a report of their activities every two years.

The participation of NGOs increased significantly in recent years with more than a hundred NGOs represented at each of the Commission's session. However, this 'sizable representation' does not always translate into effective engagement such as submitting communications and shadow reports to the Commission.[64] While NGOs may need to improve in this aspect there is no denying that they have played a huge role in the few successes of the Commission. For instance, of the 44 decisions on the merit delivered by the Commission between 2000 and 2009, 30 had direct NGO involvement either as representatives, applicants and amicus.[65] A similar review from 2003 to 2007 had also found that 28 out of 48 communications had been filed by NGOs.[66]

With regard to the Court, NGOs need to have observer status in order to bring a matter before it. Observer status is granted by the African Commission to NGOs that meet the requirement, and as of April 2019, there are 517 NGOs with such status. It is worthy to note that this status is not bestowed solely on local NGOs. Currently, there are NGOs with observer status from 14 countries outside Africa consisting of 12 European countries, the United States and Brazil. Switzerland, the UK and the United States alone account for 67 NGOs.[67] The significance of this is that these NGOs can potentially bring cases before the Court for those countries that have made the Articles 5(3) and 34(6) declaration. This, however, has not materialised with only 12 applications being made to the Court by NGOs as of 2019. While their efforts at assisting and representing individual applicants cannot be overlooked, it is argued that NGOs can do more to bring cases before the Court and Commission.

Questions were asked about the independence of the Commission when, in August 2018, it withdrew the observer status of an NGO, the Coalition of Lesbians (CAL) citing two AU Executive Council decisions as the reason for the withdrawal. The first decision which came in 2015 directed the Commission to award observer status in accordance with 'fundamental African values, identity, and good traditions'.[68] It went on to expressly direct the withdrawal of CAL's status. In June 2018, the Executive Council again directed the withdrawal of CAL's observer status this time within a deadline of December 31, 2018.[69] The Commission ultimately succumbed to this pressure. This development is quite worrying as it demonstrates an undue influence on what should be an otherwise independent human rights body. The withdrawal of CAL's observer status also calls into question the Commission's protection of LGBT rights.

While NGOs have certainly helped in propping up the regional system, it is clear that much more can be done to improve their contribution. Often, just a few NGOs are responsible for most of the positive impact while the majority make little or no contributions. For instance, a greater proportion of the cases brought in the past before the Commission was attributable to the role of two NGOs: the Institute for Human Rights Development in Africa and the International Centre for the Legal Protection of Human Rights headquartered in the Gambia and the UK, respectively.[70] A stronger and more meaningful organisation of the NGOs aimed directly at aiding the improvement of the regional system will go a long way in ensuring its improvement and success.

## 7.5 Conclusion

This chapter set out to analyse the major challenges impeding the functioning of the regional human rights institutions under the Charter and its Protocol as well as proposals to overcome or mitigate them. It was shown that the previously identified challenges, namely the lack of political will and financial/logistical factors, had a significant impact on the proper functioning of the institutions especially with regard to the Commission's promotional mandate. These were often in the form of lack of funding, undermanned institutions, non-implementation of decisions, and failure to ratify and support the full implementation of treaties.

In analysing these challenges, a number of ways for overcoming them were examined. First, it was contended that the weak protective mandate of the Commission could be remedied by the Assembly adopting its decisions and ensuring their implementation through a system of sanctions as applied in cases of default in budgetary contributions. Such a step would necessitate the creation of a body or committee tasked with ensuring such adoptions and removing any room for discretion or bias that would naturally arise in an Assembly session. An alternative that has been highlighted by some writers is for the Commission to routinely refer cases to the Court for the latter to make binding pronouncements in their favour. However, this option has the drawback that many states have not ratified the Court's Protocol and are therefore not amenable to its jurisdiction. Furthermore, the individual may not have all the benefits that accrue from being a party to the case and is wholly reliant on the discretion of the referring body. A number of ways were also highlighted by which the Commission could improve compliance notwithstanding the perceived status of its decisions. Some of the important tools that were identified include media publicity and the creation of a follow-up database which would be publicly accessible.

In the case of the Court, the clearest path forward was for states to ratify the Court's Protocol and make the declaration under Articles 5(3) and 34(6) allowing individual and NGO access. Obviously, the states have indicated that this is not a step that they are prepared to take. Borrowing from the unique example of the ECCJ's Supplementary Protocol, the case was made for a concerted effort by NGOs, working in unison with the Court, to canvass and lobby state support. In any event, the inability of individuals and NGOs to bring cases before the Court would mean that the onus falls on the Commission and other African Intergovernmental Organisations. However, no matter the degree of zeal exercised by these bodies, it is clear that they cannot adequately substitute for direct representation nor replicate the proactivity of NGOs.

In the area of promotion, the case was made for increased funding for the Commission's promotional activities, and the allocation of a programme budget as canvassed by the Commission. It was also reasoned that, given its limited resources, the Commission could improve partnerships with states, the Court and NGOs to work together on some of its promotional programmes. These steps could also be attempted by the Court which faces similar challenges.

Finally, the chapter examined the role of NGOs in tackling some of the challenges faced by the institutions. It was argued that an improved partnership with NGOs would result in the amelioration of some the challenges of the institutions especially with regard to promotion. While the regional system already works with over 500 NGOs with observer status, there is a need for more NGOs to aid in promoting and monitoring compliance. Also, the current members could improve their output given the weak resources of the institutions. The poor financial state of the institutions demands that all the players pool their resources to ensure effective implementation of the Charter. It is mostly here that NGOs are important as they can take over/fund some of the promotional programmes of the institutions which would otherwise not be carried out for lack of funds. In simpler terms, the current challenges show the need for better team spirit and cooperation. In the meantime, political will and other practical (mainly financial) challenges continue to be the main obstructions. The continent must rise up to these challenges and address them first before embarking on any further proliferation of regional judicial bodies. Failure to do this would mean that any future court, whether criminal or not, would suffer from lack of acceptance and political rejection.

## Notes

1. ECHR (2019), https://www.echr.coe.int/Documents/Stats_pending_2019_BIL.pdf.
2. Frans Viljoen, *International Human Rights Law in Africa* (Oxford University Press 2012) 349.
3. Viljoen, *International*, 355.
4. Ibid.
5. Republic of Kenya, *Combined 8th–11th Periodic Report on the African Charter on Human & Peoples' Rights* (2014) para 182, http://www.achpr.org/files/sessions/57th/state-reports/8th-11th-2008-2014/kenya_state_report_eng.pdf.
6. Viljoen, *International*.
7. Kenya, "Report".
8. APRM, "Country Review Report of the Republic of Ghana" (June 2005) paras 12–13 cited in Viljoen (n 6) 355.
9. Premium Times, "ECOWAS Frowns at Non-Enforcement of Decisions by Member States" April 22, 2014, https://www.premiumtimesng.com/news/159166-ecowas-court-frowns-non-enforcement-decisions-member-states.html.
10. Dia Anagnostou and Alina Mungiu-Pippidi, "Domestic Implementation of Human Rights Judgments in Europe: Legal Infrastructure and Government Effectiveness Matter" (2014) 25(1) *European Journal of International Law* 205, 224.
11. Viljoen, *International*, 355.
12. Oji Umozurike, "The African Charter on Human and Peoples' Rights: Suggestions for More Effectiveness" (2007) 13 *Annual Survey of International and Comparative Law* 179, 185.
13. Michelo Hansungule, "The African Charter on Human and Peoples Rights: A Critical Review" (2000) 8 *African Yearbook of International Law* 265, 298.
14. Jeremy Sarkin, "The Role of Regional Systems in Enforcing State Human Rights Compliance: Evaluating the African Commission on Human and Peoples' Rights with Comparative Lessons from the Council of Europe and the Organisation of American States" (2008) 1(2) *Inter-American and European Human Rights Journal* 199, 221.

15. Frans Viljoen, "A Human Rights Court for Africa, and Africans" (2004) 20 *BJIL* 1, 55.
16. Hansungule, "African Charter," 298.
17. Viljoen, *International*, 179.
18. Ibid., at 294.
19. African Commission, "Combined 32nd and 33rd Activity Report of the African Commission on Human and Peoples' Rights" (2013) EX.CL/782(XXII) Rev 2, 26.
20. African Union, Assembly/AU/Dec.642(XXIX), https://au.int/sites/default/files/decisions/33559-assembly_au_dec_642_-_664_xxix_e_1.pdf.
21. African Commission, "Combined 32nd and 33rd Activity Report".
22. Viljoen, *International*, 297.
23. African Commission, "37th Activity Report' supra".
24. See Paragraph 23 of the Kigali Declaration of the AU Ministerial Conference on Human Rights in Africa 2003; also Umozurike (21) 188.
25. In 2016, the Court's budget stood at over $10 million, nearly twice the Commission's. See Decision on the Budget of the African Union for the 2016 Financial Year, Doc Assembly/AU/3(XXV), Decision no: Assembly/AU/Dec. 577(XXV).
26. Article 2 of the Court's Protocol.
27. See, for instance, Vincent Nmehielle, "Toward an African Court of Human Rights: Structuring and the Court" (2000) 6 *Annual Survey of International and Comparative Law* 27, 39.
28. Murray and Mottershaw supra at 353.
29. Rules of Procedure of the Assembly of the Union 2002, r 33. See Viljoen, International Human Rights Law in Africa supra at 339.
30. By r 34 of the Assembly's Rules of Procedure, regulations and directives become automatically enforceable 30 days after the date of their publication in the official journal of the African Union or as specified in the decision.
31. Viljoen, *International Human Rights Law in Africa* supra at 340.
32. In his 2011 paper, Magliveras notes that: It would appear that the Assembly has never imposed any sanctions on the authority of Article 23(2). See Konstantinos D. Magliveras, "The Sanctioning System of the African Union: Part Success, Part Failure?" (Institute of Security Studies Expert Roundtable on "The African Union: The First Ten Years", Addis Ababa, October 2011) 8.
33. Council of Ministers, Resolution on Arrears of Contributions, OAU Doc CM/Res 1279 (LII) 1990. See Magliveras (n 62) 2.
34. Viljoen, *International*, 197.
35. Reuters, "African Summit Gives Sudan Three Months for Reforms", https://www.reuters.com/article/us-egypt-africa-sudan/african-summit-gives-sudan-military-three-months-for-reforms-idUSKCN1RZ16M.

36. See Carolyn S. Martorana, "The New African Union: Will It Promote Enforcement of the Decisions of the African Court of Human and Peoples' Rights?" (2008) 40 *George Washington International Law Review* 583, 603.
37. Viljoen, *International*, 460.
38. Joseph Isanga, "The Constitutive Act of the African Union, African Courts and the Protection of Human Rights: New Dispensation?" (2013) 11 *Santa Clara Journal of International Law* 267, 282. This practice would be similar to the Inter-American system where the Commission is required to refer a case to the Court where a party had not complied with its recommendations.
39. Judy Oder, "The African Court on Human and Peoples' Rights' Order in Respect of the Situation in Libya: A Watershed in the Regional Protection of Human Rights?" (2011) 11 *AHRLJ* 495, 498.
40. Frans Viljoen and Lirette Louw, "State Compliance with the Recommendations of the African Commission on Human and Peoples' Rights, 1994–2004" (2007) *African Journal of International Law* 1, 30.
41. Communication No. 313/05.
42. Murray and Mottershaw supra at 356.
43. Ibid., at 372.
44. R 118(4).
45. Oder supra at 510.
46. Viljoen, *International*, 427.
47. Frans Viljoen, "Understanding and Overcoming Challenges in Accessing the African Court on Human and Peoples' Rights" (2018) (1) *International and Comparative Law Quarterly* 63.
48. Isanga supra at 301.
49. Monica Mark, "African Leaders Vote Themselves Immunity from New Human Rights Court" (2014), http://www.theguardian.com/global-development/2014/jul/03/african-leaders-vote-immunity-human-rights-court.
50. Beth Van Schaack, "Immunity Before the African Court of Justice & Human & Peoples Rights—The Potential Outlier," accessed May 9, 2017, https://www.justsecurity.org/12732/immunity-african-court-justice-human-peoples-rights-the-potential-outlier/.
51. Ademola Abass, "The Proposed International Criminal Jurisdiction for the African Court: Some Problematic Aspects" (2013) *Netherlands International Law Review* 28, cited in Mbori H. Etieno, "The Merged African Court of Justice and Human Rights (ACJ&HR) as a Better Criminal Justice System than the ICC: Are We Finding African Solution to African problems or Creating African Problems Without Solutions?" (2014) http://ssrn.com/abstract=2445344.
52. Article 4. See Van Schaak, "Immunity."

53. Mbori H. Etieno, "The Merged African Court of Justice and Human Rights as a Better Criminal Justice System than the ICC: Are We Finding African Solution to African Problems or Creating African Problems Without Solutions?" (2014) Electronic copy Available at, http://ssrn.com/abstract=2445344.
54. Viljoen, *International Human Rights Law in Africa* supra at 383.
55. See, for instance, the case of *John Modise v Botswana*, Communication No. 97/93_14AR.
56. Milli Lake, "Organizing Hypocrisy: Providing Legal Accountability for Human Rights Violations in Areas of Limited Statehood" (2014) 58(2) *International Studies Quarterly* 515.
57. Lake, "Hypocrisy".
58. Rachel Murray, "Massive or Serious Violations Under ACHPR: A Comparison with the Inter-American and European Mechanism" (1999) *Netherlands Quarterly of Human Rights* 109, 128.
59. Viljoen, *International*, 571.
60. See Lake, "Hypocrisy," 2.
61. Ibid.
62. Angela Banks, "CEDAW, Compliance, and Custom: Human Rights Enforcements in Sub-Saharan Africa" (2008) 32 *Fordham International Law Journal* 781, 795.
63. Inter-Session Activity Report (November 2018–May 2019), http://www.achpr.org/files/sessions/64th_os/inter-act-reps/333/intersession_activity_report_comm_asuagbor_64os_srrwa_eng.pdf.
64. Viljoen, *International Human Rights Law in Africa*, 298.
65. NGOs acted as representatives in 30 cases, applicants in 3, and amicus in 1. See Lloyd Hitoshi Mayer, "NGO Standing and Influence in Regional Human Rights Courts and Commissions" (2011) 36(3) *Brooklyn Journal of International Law* 911, 934.
66. Annakaun Lindblom, "Non-Governmental Organisations in International Law" (2005) at 283 cited in Lloyd Hitoshi Mayer, "NGO Standing and Influence in Regional Human Rights Courts and Commissions" (2011) 36(3) *Brooklyn Journal of International Law* 911, 935.
67. ACHPR, NGOs with observer status, accessed July 27, 2016, http://www.achpr.org/network/ngo/.
68. Decision on the Thirty-Eighth Activity Report of the African Commission on Human and Peoples' Rights Doc.EX.CL/921(XXVII), at EX.CL/Dec.887(XXVII) para 7.
69. Decision on the Report on the Joint Retreat of the Permanent Representatives' Committee (PRC) and the African Commission on Human and Peoples' Rights (ACHPR) DOC.EX.CL/1089(XXXIII) I.
70. See Mayer, "NGO," 394.

CHAPTER 8

# Conclusion

This book set out to critique the African human rights system based on its own internal standards as represented by the African Charter on Human and Peoples' Rights. This required an evaluation of the rights and duties under the African Charter as well as the institutional framework for protecting those rights. It has already been explained that such an analysis was necessitated by the dearth of texts that examine the unique jurisprudential, institutional and other developments within the African regional human rights system. It was also important to point out that the region had a viable system that, if supported, could effectively promote and protect human rights in the continent. The presence of such an efficient and effective regional system could potentially eliminate any basis for the allegations of Western imperialism and interventionism that occasionally trail Western states and NGOs criticism of human rights violations in Africa. However, for the African regional human right system to make meaningful progress, some core challenges to implementation would need to be addressed. The preceding chapters identified two main obstacles to non-implementation namely low-level commitment by member states, such as the reluctance to promote judicial accountability at the regional level, and other practical challenges such as poverty, lack of resources, ingrained cultures and illiteracy. It was also shown that corruption contributed to this lack of resources.

These obstacles, it was shown, were not exclusive of the other but rather had the cumulative effect of impeding the full implementation of Charter rights. Thus, even if it were the case that every member state

 
A. Uwazuruike, *Human Rights under the African Charter*,
https://doi.org/10.1007/978-3-030-41739-0_8

had the political will to optimally implement the rights guaranteed under the Charter, they would generally fall short of the required standards. This is especially the case as, despite its laudable intentions, the Charter's goals and standards could be described as ambitious in the context of the political and economic histories of a majority of African states.

Firstly, even though generally commendable, the Charter's position on the justiciability and non-distinctive nature of socio-economic rights made implementation generally difficult and near impossible for a majority of African states mired in economic difficulties. Even the more economically stable countries like South Africa had found the implementation of these rights challenging. Accordingly, the African Commission has had to read the notions of 'progressive realisation' and 'availability of resources' into the Charter. In reaching this decision, the Commission noted that African countries were generally faced with the problem of poverty which rendered them incapable of providing the necessary amenities, infrastructure and resources that facilitate the full enjoyment of these rights. This challenge is worsened by the high rate of corruption in many countries that sees leaders siphoning and diverting funds for personal use.

It has further been shown that this economic challenge is not limited to the protection of socio-economic and peoples' rights but also extend to civil and political rights. Thus, states often lack the necessary resources to set up adequate and well-manned structures like courts and prisons for the effective protection of basic civil and political rights. Other identified practical challenges include cases of repugnant cultural practices, illiteracy and general ignorance of human rights by the populace as well as ignorance of the remedial resources available under the regional system. Some of these challenges could be adequately countered through improved promotional methods and allocation of resources. The case was made for a comprehensive Plan of Action on promotion and human rights education involving the key human rights actors namely the states, regional human rights institutions and civil society. Such unified Plan of Action is necessary to meet the huge deficit in knowledge or awareness of human rights and the remedies offered at both the national and regional levels. With particular reference to the Commission it was suggested that, in addition to increased allocation of funds, steps be taken to implement initiatives on creating a Fund for the Commission to enable it carry out promotional missions. In addition, states may initiate a policy of funding specific promotional programmes in their respective territories. The Commission on its part may publish a list of its intended promotional programmes inviting states to support such programmes. Such a request could be extended to NGOs, and corporate and private entities which may be willing to host seminars and conferences and even sponsor entire promotional programmes as acts of goodwill.

Despite the conclusion that the complete implementation of the Charter, especially positive socio-economic rights, was well above the reach of most African countries, it is suggested that there still be clear and concerted efforts towards protecting these rights according to the available resources of each state as provided by the Commission in the *Purohit* case. Also, governments should, by making these rights justiciable, subject themselves to a minimum level of judicial accountability for certain economic decisions or failure to protect these rights especially in extreme cases of violation where it can be shown that there are resources (or should have been through proper management) to tackle such infringements.

The findings on the inhibiting extent of these practical challenges do not in any way diminish strong evidence of lack of cooperation and political will by member states. These are evidenced mainly by the failure of these states to implement the decisions of the Commission/Court and to ratify the Court Protocol—including allowing individual and NGO access to Court. With regard to the decisions of the Commission, it has been shown that the Charter did not intend them to be binding on states. This notwithstanding, it still behoves on member states to implement them as acts of goodwill and in keeping with their commitment to protect rights under the Charter. The failure to implement a majority of these decisions is a clear testament to the lack of cooperation and political will on the part of these states. States' lack of political will is further demonstrated in their overall attitude to the enforcement of positive socio-economic rights. Many African constitutions still deem these rights to be non-justiciable against the spirit and clear intent of the Charter even though some of those constitutions were drafted after the adoption of the Charter.

Case studies examined showed that states often placed domestic political considerations over their human rights responsibilities. This called to question their commitment to the Charter. Here, it was considered, from the arguments of some commentators, whether the theoretical standards of the Charter, including references to the judicial/quasi-judicial nature of the institutions, were mere products of lip service such that states had created and adopted these systems with no real intention of making them work. While this position does have its merits, it may however appear weak in the light of other recent occurrences that point to the contrary. One of these was the transformation of the Organisation of African Unity (OAU) into the African Union (AU). While the former was built on the principles of non-interference and state sovereignty, the latter initiated a shift in ideology towards the principles of responsibility to protect and intolerance of undemocratic change of governments. Chapter 7 highlights instances of the AU sanctioning government officials in the aftermath of such undemocratic upheavals. The AU has also authorised interventionist missions in several states including Burundi, Sudan, Somalia and the Central African Republic. If anything, these developments show that African states are willing to cede some level of state sovereignty to the regional system.

A more compelling example is that of the ECOWAS Community Court of Justice (ECCJ) which was given a human rights mandate even though the court was originally created to adjudicate economic and cross-border disputes. Even more important is that individuals and NGOs are able to directly institute matters before the court without the need to exhaust local remedies—elements clearly lacking in the African Court. Furthermore, ECOWAS member states resisted efforts by the Gambia to revisit and restrict the wide jurisdictions of the court. The interesting and ironic twist is that some of these same West African states have not made the equivalent declaration under the African Court Protocol allowing individual access. Ironically the Gambia, which sought to restrict the ECCJ's jurisdiction, has become the latest state, in 2018, to make the declaration allowing individual access to the African Court. This commitment can, of course, be attributed to the recent political developments in that country which saw a change in government in 2017. While it is impressive that six of the nine declarations allowing individual access to the African Court are from ECOWAS member states (comprising only 15 states), there are still questions as to why the other member states have not made this declaration. Of course, this book has examined some of the factors behind the emergence of the ECCJ's Protocol. One of the reasons adduced was that human rights NGOs lobbied hard for these features especially the omission of an exhaustion of local remedies requirement. Their arguments and propositions were in turn accepted by ECOWAS officials who recognised, inter alia, that it was difficult for individuals to access national courts in human rights cases. It is not clear how much of a similar effort has been put into the African Court and if this would pay similar dividends as in the ECCJ. Such a project should be the task of future research on the subject. The conclusions that may be gleaned from this and other examples are that there are strong arguments against general categorisations of African states as clinging to absolute models of state sovereignty.

In addition to lack of cooperation from states and other economic and cultural challenges, the ineffectiveness of the Charter's institutional framework has been identified as an inhibitor to the effective implementation of the Charter. It was found that the Commission and Court had generally failed to adequately perform their duties of promotion and protection under the Charter. To a large extent, the already identified obstacles—states' lack of cooperation and financial limitations—had a huge role to play in the ineffectiveness of the institutional systems. For instance, the failure of states to comply with decisions on communications or make the declaration allowing individual access to the Court severely undermined the protective mandate of the institutions. Furthermore, that the Commission had not adequately carried out its promotional mandate was also largely down to its paucity of funds and failure of some states to play their part in promotion. Allocations from the AU to the Commission were relatively meagre such that the Commission had to rely substantially on foreign donations to carry out some of its basic functions. These notwithstanding, it was demonstrated that there were some foundational flaws in the institutional framework leading to two institutions with overlapping protective mandates. There is little indication of an end to these institutional tensions given the proposed changes to the Court. The proposed addition of a Criminal Chamber, while laudable in itself, could amount to overstretching member states' already thin and feeble levels of commitment and cooperation. For these proposed institutional changes to be meaningful, the continent has to first address and resolve the major challenges highlighted above.

With particular regard to the Commission, it is opined that there is little need for treaty reform as a similar step in the form of the Court's Protocol had failed to attain the desired results. Rather, the system could still be made effective without departing from the original intention of the Charter which was to give the Assembly of Heads of State and Government the mandate to oversee the enforcement of the Commission's decisions. This would entail that the Assembly, or the Executive Council acting in its stead, takes the extra step of specially and routinely adopting the Commission's recommendations as its own decisions.

This improved status would mean that their implementation would be directly overseen by the Assembly and backed by possible sanctions.

Such a step would necessitate the creation of a body or committee, similar to the Credentials Committee, tasked with ensuring such adoptions and removing any room for discretion or bias that would naturally arise in an Assembly session. It was established that the AU has consistently imposed sanctions in two areas of infringement namely: failure of states to make their periodic payments to the Union and the unconstitutional overthrow of government. It may therefore be argued that extending this sanction regime to instances of failure to comply with the AU's decisions, which in this case would include recommendations of the Commission, would better ensure their enforcement.

A number of ways were also highlighted by which the Commission could improve compliance notwithstanding the perceived status of its decisions. Some of the important tools that were identified include media publicity and the creation of a publicly accessible follow-up database. This was based on the finding that states generally abhor negative publicity especially those relating to violations of human rights.

In the case of the Court, it is clear that the surest way to effectiveness was in the general ratification by member states and subsequent declarations allowing individual and NGO access to the Court. In the absence of these, stringent steps have to be taken to improve the 'case flow' to the Court through the Commission and other African Intergovernmental Organisations. With regard to the former, it is suggested that steps be taken to clarify and strengthen the provisions on the referral of cases to the Court in the Commission's Rules of Procedure. It is specifically recommended that the Rules be amended, or at least interpreted, to make mandatory the referral of complaints involving a serious breach of human rights or where the Commission's decisions had not been implemented.

## 8.1 Implications for Future Research and Development

This book raises a number of implications and possible roadmaps for future research on the subject. Firstly, it has shown how an appreciation of the challenges currently facing the system is necessary for any future reforms. Unfortunately, current proposals for reform in the form of the African Court of Justice and Human Rights do not appear to take these challenges into consideration. Should such proposals proceed into fruition, then it is expected that the regional human rights system would continue to be mired in difficulties. For such a proposed system to work, the challenges of the current system must first be addressed and resolved. This would entail the development of a comprehensive financial plan along with the firm commitment of a significant number of states to completely support the new body. Such support should ideally go before mere adoption and extend into ratification, domestication and declarations allowing individual and NGO access.

One possible area for future research would be on how to get states to ratify the Court's Protocol and accept individual and NGO access to the Court. Such research would necessarily deal with issues of international politics and diplomacy. As a guide, such research may take into consideration the processes adopted in persuading ECOWAS states to accept similar propositions for the ECCJ. A different approach may be to carry out further research into the reasons for states' failure to ratify the Court's Protocol and make the declaration allowing individual access. Such research may investigate individual stances of states on such declarations and the reasons behind their reluctance to ratify or make the declaration.

Finally, this book has hopefully revealed the need for further discussions and research into the economic and social factors inhibiting the practice and implementation of human rights. While global efforts have no doubt been made towards curbing menaces like poverty and civil wars, it is clear that there is still room for improvement and research into just how much these occurrences and situations affect the individual's (and even group's) rights protected not only in the African Charter but also other regional and global human rights instruments.

# Index




A. Uwazuruike, *Human Rights under the African Charter*,
https://doi.org/10.1007/978-3-030-41739-0

The manufacturer's authorised representative in the EU is Springer Nature Customer Service Centre GmbH, Europaplatz 3, 69115 Heidelberg, Germany. If you have any concerns regarding our products, please contact ProductSafety@springernature.com

Printed and bound by CPI Group (UK) Ltd, Croydon, CR0 4YY
23/09/2026
02221520-0003